PUBL
COMMUNICATION

Tom Reisner
V.O. 112
949-0553

PUBLIC COMMUNICATION

Second Edition

RODERICK P. HART
University of Texas

GUSTAV W. FRIEDRICH
University of Oklahoma

BARRY BRUMMETT
Purdue University

1817

HARPER & ROW, PUBLISHERS, New York
Cambridge, Philadelphia, San Francisco,
London, Mexico City, São Paulo, Sydney

ACKNOWLEDGMENTS

Chapter 1: Page 7, Forsyth, Monkmeyer; page 11, Bellerose, Stock, Boston; page 17, Chester, Leo de Wys Inc. Chapter 2: Page 26, Vine, Leo de Wys Inc. Chapter 3: Page 62, Michel Craig; page 69, Wolinsky, Stock, Boston. Chapter 4: Page 81, Karalies (c) Peter Arnold; page 82, Brinzac, (c) Peter Arnold; page 82, (c) Hankin, Stock, Boston; page 99, Conklin, Monkmeyer; page 100, Diakopoulous, Stock, Boston. Chapter 5: Page 113, Hall, Stock, Boston; page 114, Leo de Wys Inc.; page 138, Bellerose, Stock, Boston. Chapter 6: Page 148, Leo de Wys Inc.; page 158, Conklin, Monkmeyer. Chapter 7: Page 176, Burnett, Leo de Wys Inc.; page 181, Leo de Wys Inc. Chapter 8: Page 203, (c) Gscheidle, Peter Arnold (Graham); UPI (JFK and King). Chapter 9: Page 244, Patterson, Stock, Boston. Chapter 10: Page 259, (both photos), Leo de Wys Inc. Chapter 11: Page 292, Culver; page 308, Bellerose, Stock, Boston. Chapter 12: Page 318, Bellerose, Stock, Boston; page 319, Miller, Monkmeyer.

Sponsoring Editor: Neale Sweet
Project Editor: Pamela Landau
Production: Delia Tedoff
Photo Researcher: Mira Schachne
Compositor: Com-Com, a division of Haddon Craftsman Inc.
Printer and Binder: R. R. Donnelley & Sons Company
Art Studio: Fine Line Inc.

PUBLIC COMMUNICATION, Second Edition

Copyright © 1983 by Roderick P. Hart, Gustav W. Friedrich, and Barry Brummett

Library of Congress Cataloging in Publication Data

Hart, Roderick P.
  Public communication.

  Includes index.
  1. Public speaking. I. Friedrich, Gustav W.
II. Brummett, Barry, 1951-   . III. Title.
PN4121.H264 1983   808.5'1   82-23382
ISBN 0-06-042687-X

CONTENTS

PREFACE

In revising *Public Communication,* we have tried to retain many of the features that characterized its predecessor. The book is written for the student of public speaking, not for his or her instructor. The book presents a *way of thinking* about public speaking, not a list of gratuitous rules and regulations for reaching health, wealth, and unthinking happiness. The book attempts to avoid the moralisms found in public speaking books of a bygone era. Finally, the book continues to assume that: (1) the enterprise of public speaking is something that must be examined with care, (2) research and theory in communication can provide practical help for speaking effectively, and (3) contemporary students will forgive almost anything in a textbook except poorly reasoned suggestions or scholarly discussions devoid of practical insight.

When starting this revision, therefore, we began by isolating the material in the first edition that students especially liked. Thus, we begin with a thorough discussion of the nature of human speech because we feel that students still need to be reminded of how special it is to *talk* to another (as opposed to writing a letter). We have retained our discussion of the principles of speech effectiveness applicable across speaking situations, principles that grow out of needs all people have when conversing with others. In addition, our original treatments of audience analysis, credibility strategies, and techniques for persuasion are again prominently displayed in this edition of *Public Communication.*

Much of the remainder of this book, however, is completely new. For example, extensive attention is now given to the important matters of language and delivery. In addition, Chapters 3, 5, 10, 11, and 12 explore, in detail, five common types of public speech experiences. Beginning with "The Initial Speech" in Chapter 3, we discuss the elementary steps involved in speech composition. In Chapter 5, we trace the various stages of developing "The Informative Speech," focusing particularly on how spoken ideas can be made substantive, intense, coherent, and graphic for listeners.

The more advanced types of speeches—persuasive, reinforcing, and occasional—also receive prominent attention in this edition of *Public Communication*. For each type of speech, we try to detail the major roadblocks to effective communication, the special resources available to the public speaker for solving those problems, and the techniques used by other speakers when pursuing their personal and professional goals. Our discussions of these various types of speeches are designed to be sufficiently detailed so that students may be justifiably confident during their trip from chair to podium.

Throughout this edition of *Public Communication*, we have presented the same sorts of lifelike and detailed examples that characterized the first edition. In every chapter, the reader will find numerous and extensive applications of the general principles discussed. As in the first edition, we try to effect here a unique blending of social, scientific, and traditional rhetorical perspectives of speech effectiveness. By drawing upon the most mature thought in both intellectual traditions, we hope to equip the student speaker with the very best advice available.

On developing our ideas about public speaking, we begin each chapter with novel, often amusing, headnotes designed to introduce the student to important concepts painlessly. At the end of each chapter, however, we forsake all manner of subtlety and list 10 concrete and highly candid "Suggestions for Speaking," which the student may use directly and immediately in his or her speechmaking. We feel that these suggestions are among the most practical advice available to the contemporary student of public speaking, and we urge the reader to give them careful attention.

We have retained here (and in many cases expanded) our lists of speaking "tips," our illustrative tables demonstrating speaking strategies in action, and the self-questions a speaker might ask when preparing for a speaking assignment. Thus, while this new edition of *Public Communication* contains many of the same elements found useful by students in the book's previous incarnation, it has undergone major modifications in order to make it as hardheaded and contemporary as the students for which it was written.

Naturally, no major revision of a textbook could be accomplished without the assistance of our students and colleagues. For their advice and encouragement we are truly grateful. We are grateful, too, for the detailed suggestions provided us by Joseph DeVito, Pamela Cooper, Ellen Ritter, Frank E. X. Dance, and John Baird. Finally, we appreciate the love and support of Peggy, Rena, and Margie, who collectively managed to keep their heads when manuscript and page proofs threatened to undo our sanity and good humor. Much of what we know about communication has been learned from them.

R.P.H.
G.W.F.
B.B.

UNIT 1

The Essentials of Public Communication

CHAPTER 1

The Resources of Public Speech

Peg: Hi.

Carolyn: Hi. Did the teacher get here yet?

Peg: No, and I wish he would. I'm nervous as a cat.

Carolyn: Me too. I've put off this speech course for five semesters. Finally had to take it.

Peg: Not me. I'm going to get it over with as quickly as possible. I hate to give speeches.

Carolyn: Yeah. People seem to look right through you when you're giving a speech.

Peg: Yes, and classroom speeches are so darn artificial. I mean who cares about another speech on drug addiction?

Carolyn: Yeah, I know what you mean. Although, I did give a speech in high school about the welfare system. It went over pretty well.

Peg: Yeah, but why a whole course in it? I've been talking all my life! Gee, I wish that teacher would get here and get things started.

Carolyn: Well, at least the kids in here look okay. My roommate said that she really got to know the kids in her speech class.

Peg: Maybe it won't be that bad. I wonder if they'll let us use note cards.

Carolyn: I hope so. I always get so jumbled up when I try to explain something.

Peg: That's what I mean. It's so artificial. I mean, when am I ever going to have to give a speech again for the rest of my life?

Carolyn: Right. Although I guess I'll have to meet the public when I go out and do social work. But that's not the same as giving speeches. . . . Wow, that guy's 5 minutes late already.

Peg: Hey, maybe he got scared too!

Carolyn: Why should he? Teachers don't have to give speeches!

Peg: Well, maybe this course will be good for me. Everybody says I'm too shy.

Carolyn: That's funny, you haven't been shy with me.

Peg: Hey, maybe this course won't be so bad. At least we've got each other!

Carolyn: Oh, by the way, I'm Carolyn Cross.

Peg: I'm Peggy Franklin.

Carolyn: Oops, here he comes. He doesn't look too bad. Maybe . . .

Any of it hit home? Well, at least for Peg and Carolyn, the speech course promises to be quite a chore. Or does it? Beneath the veneer of this rather ordinary social conversation, what can we tell about Peg and Carolyn and, more importantly, what can we say about the problems and pleasures associated with the making and utilizing of human speech?

Let us begin by looking at a few of the somewhat questionable assertions they make from time to time. Peg claims that she hates to give speeches. Yet in the space of 5 minutes, she has given more than a dozen "speeches." You say, however, that these were not real speeches—no standing up, no podium, no note cards, no sleepy audience, no speech teacher writing furiously, and so on. Yet Peg was poised for conversation, she was processing information intellectually (admittedly without note cards), she very obviously was trying to adapt to her audience, and, as we see later on, her audience was evaluating her utterances. So then, when is a speech a speech? Are the standing up, the group of auditors, and the mass of feedback necessary to have a "speech setting," or are there common threads running throughout all of our spoken verbalizations?

We will be arguing in the following pages that the behaviors that Peg and Carolyn will engage in in their classroom speaking exercises are not different in kind from their sometimes mundane, sometimes exciting social conversations. We will be arguing that no spoken interaction can be artificial, as Peg calls it, unless a speaker fails to make a clear investment in her message or does not attempt to demonstrate a semblance of meaningful commitment to her audience. We will contend that all teachers give speeches even though they sit on their desks and often speak in an interrupted fashion. We will try to find out why giving speeches is what makes us human and how speaking makes contact with other humans both possible and pleasurable.

Peg claims that she has been talking all of her life. Yet she does not tell us that many of her talking experiences have been futile, boring, and sometimes, even painful. Most people see a difference between "just talking" and talking effectively. After all, we all have been breathing since birth, yet how many of us, except for the Indian fakir, can control our breathing for biological and (as the Swami would have it) for meditational satisfaction? Similarly, we can learn to control our spoken verbalizations so that they have social impact.

Yet there is much that we can learn from Peg's and Carolyn's casual insights into human speech. Peg pointedly shows us that a certain amount of risk usually attends our talk. In this chapter, we will explore some of the reasons for this phenomenon and try to understand why speech courses initially seem more scary than other academic enterprises. We will also attempt to explain why Carolyn received such a good feeling when communicating successfully with her high school speech class, why people seem to see through us when we speak, and why students seem to know each other well after having survived a speech communication class together. We will try to see why getting "jumbled up" when talking is a very common, natural, and in some senses, a very desirable set of conditions. We will investigate why Peg concluded simultaneously from Carolyn's speech that she was "nice" and how Carolyn was able to judge that Peg didn't "seem shy."

Perhaps most important of all, we will try to understand together why, after only a few short moments of speaking, Peg and Carolyn gave birth to a friendship and why Peg was motivated to say, "At least we've got each other." More than any other statement, this latter one demonstrates how we humans use the pleasures associated with speech to ward off the liabilities that spoken interactions sometimes entail; it also serves to show us that without effective communication, the chances for initiating and maintaining profitable social contacts are, at best, dubious.

To our way of thinking, Peg and Carolyn are unsure about their speech course because they haven't really considered what the act of speaking is all about. Perhaps they would feel less ambivalent about human speech if they knew more about its functions. Let us consider some of them.

Functions of Human Speech

Consider the tale of the lad who, by the age of 5, was yet to utter a single syllable. His parents were beside themselves with worry. Where had they gone wrong in producing a child who would not speak? One morning at the breakfast table, Silent Sam gave vent to his verbalization: "This oatmeal is damned lumpy." Uncontrollably excited, his parents posed the obvious question: "For 5 years you've said nothing, not even baby talk! Why?" The answer came readily: "Until now, everything was all right!"

The implication of this story is not that kids have it too easy these days, but rather that we speak when we have to. We speak because it is one of the few nonviolent ways of changing the social world around us. And being the unsatisfied beasts we are, we do a lot of talking. Our reasons, however, are numerous. Let us examine some of them.

Speech as Humanity

Researchers have yet to find a group of animals that "talks" in a clear way, save one—humankind. By some method of intellectual and physiological happenstance, human beings are unique in their ability to produce meaningful speech. Not only can A produce verbal sounds, but B can comprehend the utterances and react to them. Although the system often breaks down, we are distinctive in that we can create language systems and utilize our creation in the presence of other people, for pleasure, for profit, and, of course, for pain. Put simply, we talk because we are human and we are human because we talk. We talk because we have no other choice. We find ourselves talking to cats, who

cannot return the compliment, and yelling our lungs out at basketball players, who cannot hear a word we say. Yet we do this because, in some sense, talking is our way of soothing, encouraging, and berating ourselves and each other, of displaying our humanness.

And we take our talking seriously. We institutionalize people who continually talk to lamp posts and incarcerate those who use their talking ability to incite riots or to make obscene phone calls. Yet, before we send these latter unfortunates off to the brig, we ask them if they have anything to *say* before sentence is passed. Even if they have committed a more serious crime, we still allow them "a last few words" before the pellet is dropped into the acid.

Although most of our talking is done in less threatening circumstances, human speech is important. Even when alone, we talk in order to simulate social conversation. Who can doubt that Robinson Crusoe spent much of his solitude talking to himself? Or that, as he constructed one of his endless contraptions, he sang, that is, used rhythmic, melodious *speech*, to entertain himself? All of this he (perhaps unwittingly) did to assure himself of his continued humanness.

Speech is the tool we use to describe our worlds, to define our comrades, and to change both our worlds and our comrades. While we can function without speech and still remain human, all reports indicate that a talkless existence is far from pleasurable. An intriguing claim that remains to be substantiated is that the suicide rate among servicemen who went deaf during World War II was higher than the rate among those who were blinded. Even if untrue, the fact that such a proposition seems plausible demonstrates how our "most human" gift penetrates and shapes our existences.

Speech as Self

Can you find anything strange about the following dialogue?

Nancy: Hi, Jack, how are you?

Jack: Things are copasetic. Is the feeling reciprocal?

Nancy: Yeah, I'm fine. Are you going to the game with me?

Jack: Such forms of diversion appear trivial to one mainly concerned with intellectual pursuits.

Nancy: Yeah, but are you going?

Jack: As mentioned previously, one cannot enjoy pastimes that contribute nothing to one's essential self.

Nancy: Oh, I guess that means you're not going with me.

Jack: Correct. Even though such invitations are pleasurable in a sense, one must guard against totally peripheral activities.

Nancy: Good-bye, Jack.

The main item to note here is that Jack is obnoxious. Why? At least one reason for our receiving such an impression is that he seems as if he has stepped outside of his skin and has somehow detached himself from his feelings. There is no "me" in his speech pattern—no "I" or "myself." This, combined with his phony vocabulary, makes his talking seem pompous. Of greater importance for our discussion of human speech is the fact that his words depict him as depersonalized. In other words, Jack's speech is "odd" because it hides him from Nancy.

If asked, "Who are you?" how would you respond? Most likely you would reply by stating your name, occupation, dominant personality characteristic, political party affiliation, or some such objective description. This is not an idle question. With the depersonalization of society, with the myriad social roles each of us is asked to play daily, and with the growing complexities of rapidly changing ideas and mores, "Who am I?" becomes perhaps the only question worth asking. And we ask this question over and over again, always veiling it in some sort of conversational guise ("oh, those other people gave a much better speech than I did, don't you think?") or burying it beneath the cloak and dagger of courtship ("well, now, you probably think I'm just another one of those dumb athletes"). These are attempts to get data about ourselves from the speech behaviors of others—without getting burned.

The fact that we often say things that surprise us probably indicates that we also learn about ourselves by "listening" to our own words. If we were not so egocentric in our speech patterns and concerned with establishing our personal identities, why would 40–80 percent of all our oral statements contain the pronoun "I"? As Brown and Van Riper say, "Listen, if you will, to the staccato of the perpendicular pronoun in the speech about you: 'And I said to him, I said . . . ' 'I'm the kind of person who . . . ' 'I think that . . . ' The 'I's explode like popcorn in the conversational pan."[1] And what could be a more natural way for finding out about ourselves than by listening to our very own speech or to the spoken remarks made about us by others?

Speech as Social Sharing

Whether or not we speak effectively, it is usually a set of social conditions that precipitates our talking—our social sharing. It is not accidental that speaking is the stock-in-trade of psychiatrists, school counselors, politicians, preachers, and teachers. When we are relating our feelings in the psychiatrist's office, we are attempting to share our problems with him or her and, in a sense, *to make our problem the psychiatrist's problem, too.* Our speech is the force that mediates and sometimes demands this sharing.

Oftentimes, the need to share ourselves with others becomes extremely important. Imagine that you have just learned you received an A in a course in which you were sure you would fail. You are uncontrollably excited. What do you do? The answer is obvious. You talk, of course, to your roommate, to your parents, and if they are not around, you corner someone you have not spoken to all semester, who smiles gamely and volunteers, "That's nice. I'm glad for you." However, you are not really interested in that person's response. The important thing is to get the feeling out, to share it with someone.

Sometimes the pressure to talk becomes uncomfortable. Who can ride a crowded elevator from the 20th floor to the street level without feeling the tension generated by the 20 nontalkers as they stare mindlessly at the elevator door? But should some brave soul make a state-

[1]C. Brown and C. Van Riper, *Speech and Man* (Englewood Cliffs, N.J.: Prentice-Hall, 1966), p. 36.

ment, no matter how foolish it is, there's an almost audible sigh of relief from the reticent multitude. People make us talk. Who can endure more than 5 minutes in a small room with a stranger without muttering some inane pleasantry? Just one statement, of course. That's enough to acknowledge that person's humanity and our social responsibility.

Perhaps the most vivid manifestation of the social import of speaking is the decision not to talk. The angry person gives his or her unfaithful spouse the "silent treatment," as if to deny social obligation toward the offending person. Thus, it is not surprising that the ultimate punishment in modern prisons is solitary confinement—a place where talking, where social sharing, is impossible.

We talk because talking is fun. We engage in bull sessions, in talk dates, and in gossip parties simply because it is enjoyable to exercise our speaking capabilities. In *Games People Play*, Eric Berne argues that the ultimate function of human speech is simply to structure time, to have something to do.[2] We talk because we are simultaneously human and social animals. We make small talk because it is rather enjoyable to while away the time "just talking." What else could explain the all-too-human piece of dialogue Brown and Van Riper cite as an example of the very ordinary pleasures associated with human speech?

"Whatcha going to do now?"

"Oh, I dunno. Just take it easy."

"Take it easy, eh? Won't make any nickels that way."

"Who wants nickels? I'm a dollar man, myself."

"Yeah?"

"Yeah."[3]

Speech as Thought

Just as speech is the outgrowth of mental operations, so is it the informer and sustainer of thought. Circular, you say? Precisely. When we talk, we are at once drawing upon what we "know" and at the same time adding to that store of knowledge.

There are those who argue that we never really "know" something until it can be said clearly, lucidly, and articulately. There is much to be said for such a position. After having traversed the campus hundreds of times, can you give a stranger precise, well-phrased directions to the

---

[2]E. Berne, *Games People Play* (New York: Grove Press, 1964).
[3]Brown and Van Riper, p. 121.

Student Union? Or how many times have you found yourself attempting to explain a math formula to a friend, only to discover in the middle of the explanation that you did not know it as well as you had originally presumed? And who can forget the tremendous satisfaction we derive when we are finally able to "put it into words"?

Speech-for-thought also has more serious consequences. For many years, Russian psychologists have been investigating the interrelationships between thinking and speech. Roughly stated, their conclusions are twofold: (1) speech patterns seem to be good indicators of mental development, and (2) the ability to verbalize can assist the individual in growing intellectually. They have found, for example, that patients whose mental disorders have impaired their motor abilities can significantly increase their mobilities by saying out loud what they are trying to get their bodies to do. The same principle of transference operates in the psychiatrist's office. Sometimes by simply putting it into words (which is often a painful procedure in itself), patients are better able to understand the causes and dimensions of their disturbances. Anyone of us who has ever read aloud a self-composed essay to see if "it seems as though I know what I'm talking about" has some feeling for the speech-for-thought phenomenon.

Speech as Communication

In *The Naked Ape*, Desmond Morris discusses why infants cry. According to him, they cry because they are in pain, because they are hungry, because they are alone, because they are in unfamiliar territory, because they want to change their physical surroundings, and because

they are frustrated.[4] What better beginner's list is there to explain why adults attempt to communicate? Common to all of the infant's screams is some kind of built-in knowledge that the infant needs the assistance of others to meet the demands that this world has placed upon him or her.

Communicative speech takes our talk and puts it to work—preaching the Good News; constructing a Third Reich; cleaning up the local polluter; putting pressure on politicians, doctors, lawyers, and other influential members of the community. Communication is the speech of saviors and demagogues, of kings and paupers, of courters and courtees. It is a practical use of talk designed to remove rigidity and lethargy; to modify existing conditions; to right wrongs, or to create new ones in their stead.

Quite obviously, this book will deal heavily with the communicative potentialities of human speech. Communication is an unwieldy process, yet at times it is dramatically effective. Communication presumes an almost computerlike intellectual ability on our parts, yet we take it in stride. Most of all, communication demands a tolerance for individual differences before even elementary social sharing, not to mention social cohesion or social change, can be accomplished. Because all of us are so enamored at times with the egocentric aspects of human speech, speech for communication fights a Herculean battle for its place in the sun.

The Multifunctions of Speech

We should not view these five functions of speech as being mutually exclusive since most of our spoken acts are motivated and guided by more than just one such function. For example, besides providing diversion, our small talk often gives us insight into ourselves and may help us understand something we have never really grasped before. Or, we may sit down for a pleasant evening of chatter and wind up exhorting our guests to join a political cause. There are times when we misperceive the speech function most appropriate to a particular setting, and that creates problems. The businessperson who cannot suppress the impulse to "talk shop" over the dinner table is apparently unaware that dinnertime conversations are usually set up for "sharing speech." And many a popular mobilizer has been accused of primarily seeking ego-gratification with his or her public exhortations rather than adhering to the task of changing public policy. In short, the intricacies and inter-relationships of our speech functions are simply outgrowths of our human complexity.

[4]D. Morris, *The Naked Ape* (New York: Dell, 1971).

To understand human speech is to be in a position to control it intelligently. Speech is a miracle. It makes us unique. It makes us happy. It comforts us. And it gives us social power. It both says things and does things. ("I do" is a good example of the utilitarian power of speech.) Thus, before anyone uses this miraculous tool, it would behoove him or her to know something about it. Now that we have begun to examine human speech, let us examine what happens to it when it and its maker turn public.

Nature of Public Speech

In the public speech situation, the nature and functions of human speech become dramatically apparent. The public speaker is made aware (sometimes painfully) of the amount of personal investment effective speaking demands. The size of the audience vivifies the amount of social sharing that speech entails. The knee-knocking and occasional stammering of the student speaker dramatizes the risks we run when confronting one another in a talking situation. But the sense of controlling our environment that public speaking offers and the emotional and intellectual rewards brought about by such communication experiences can make the whole exercise worth it.

Implicit Messages of Public Speech

Some basic changes are demanded of us when private speech becomes public. One way of reaching such an understanding is to consider the *implicit messages* we send out when we stand to address an audience. That is, when you choose to speak in public, the following "hidden meanings" normally accompany the message you have consciously prepared:[5]

1. *The speaker perceives that some problem exists.* Here, "problem" means any set of conditions that the speaker feels requires change. We talk because we need to alter some portion of the environment in which we function. The "problem" can be as commonplace as the annual need to "rededicate ourselves to the principles of Americanism" on the Fourth of July, or as radical as a plea to nationalize the oil industry.

2. *The speaker perceives that some problem exists that can be overcome by talk.* Not all problematic situations can be resolved through

[5]The senior author is indebted to Professor C. C. Arnold for originally stimulating some of the thoughts presented here.

communication. We cannot, in a single speech, change the eating habits of 200 million Americans. Still, when most sensible persons face a body of listeners, they must have some feeling that their message could at least begin to change a situation that they, the speakers, see as undesirable.

3. *The speaker perceives that some problem exists that cannot be overcome by himself or herself.* Public communication is a pronounced social experience. It implies that collective effort is needed if the speaker is to reorder the environment in the way he or she desires. Although she could regale herself with laughter by "just thinking," comedienne Joan Rivers must realize that her need for self-fulfillment or her need to entertain others (or whatever else motivates a stand-up comic) can only be achieved by engaging some particular others in discourse.

4. *The speaker perceives that some problem exists that cannot be overcome with just one or two people.* This book focuses on public communication—situations in which a speaker addresses a sizable audience. By deciding to do so, a speaker apparently has reasoned ahead of time that speaking intimately to a friend is not sufficient for getting the job done. Such a speaker apparently seeks to influence some sizable portion of his or her social existence.

5. *The speaker perceives that the topic is important enough to risk public exposure.* There are surely better ways of making a living than by standing in front of 60 pairs of eyes, 43 of which close 2 minutes after the speaker has opened his or her mouth. When a person ventures to address a sizable public, he or she must somehow feel that the rewards to be garnered by the effective presentation of a message outweigh the possible "costs" of having self and ideas scrutinized in public.

6. *The speaker perceives that the topic is important to a number of other people.* Many of the things that we feel or know need not (perhaps should not!) be visited upon unsuspecting others, but this does not seem to be part of the ground rules for public communication. A person who presumes to address a body of auditors must have some feeling that a significant number of people can find potential import in what he or she has to say.

7. *The speaker is willing to open himself or herself up to the possibilities of change.* Public communication is not a one-way street. When addressing an audience, a speaker implicitly realizes that he or

she, too, can be affected by the communicative surroundings. The speaker may be shouted down. He may be elected president of the fraternity. She may be encouraged to believe even more strongly in her message. Because communication outcomes are not predictable in any significant sense, change is always a possibility for the enterprising speaker.

8. *The audience is willing to open itself up to the possibility of change.* This proposition is perhaps so implicit that it frequently is overlooked. We seem to forget (as auditors or as observers of communication) that when a group of persons gather together for the purpose of hearing public discourse, they are making an "implicit bargain" with the speaker that goes something like this: "I'm here, and you can try to change me—but you'd better make it good!" Furthermore, speaker and audience "agree" (except in especially turbulent times) beforehand that only symbols (as opposed to physical force) will act as an agent of change in public communication surroundings.

We could probably continue this list of implicit messages of public communication. However, this list should suffice to give you some idea of the complicated dimensions cutting across communicative acts. For the wary observer, there is more than one first realizes in public communication. By being aware of these implicit meanings of public discourse, you can better understand what you have in your favor when you speak publicly. The list presented above is basically an optimistic one. It implies that your decision to speak to an audience is, in many ways, flattering to them. Thus, when composing a speech, you need not worry very much about these implicit messages. Rather, you simply must insure that your *explicit* remarks reinforce the basically positive impression you've already made on your audience when you first decided to speak to them.

Unique Features of Public Speech

The implicit messages just discussed are not part-and-parcel of our private chats. No automatic assumptions are normally made, for example, about a speaker's commitment to a topic in informal conversational settings. The public speaker, on the other hand, operates in a special sphere of influence, a sphere that presents some special communication problems as well as some special opportunities for influence. Let us examine a brief list of these unique features. Compared to private conversation, in public talk we find the following:

1. The public message must be relevant to the group as a whole, not merely to one or a few individuals in that group. In public communication, the "common denominator" must be constantly searched for by the speaker.

2. "Public" language is more restricted; that is, it is less flexible, uses a more familiar code, is less personal in phrasing, and is filled with fewer connotations than is "private" talk.

3. Feedback is more restricted since it is limited to subtle nonverbal responses in many instances.

4. There is greater audience diversity to deal with. In public communication we face the difficulty of entering many "perceptual worlds" simultaneously. (This will be discussed in Chapter 6.)

5. As the size of the audience increases, there is a greater chance of misinterpreting feedback because there's so much to look for.

6. The speaker must do a more complete job of speech preparation because there is so little direct moment-to-moment feedback by which to guide his or her remarks.

7. The problem of adaptation becomes paramount because one message must suffice for many different people.

8. Audience analysis is more difficult and necessarily more inaccurate when many people are interacted with simultaneously.

9. It is sometimes difficult to focus listeners' attention on the message because of the great number of distractions a public situation can entail.

10. A greater amount of change is possible in public communicative settings since the message reaches more people in a given unit of time.

Fear of Public Speech

We would like to conclude this introductory chapter by discussing a topic that probably interests you a good deal—why the public speech experience frightens so many people. Our discussion will be rather detailed for we feel that the more you know about the fear of speech, the better you will be able to cope with it. Death frightens us, after all, primarily because nobody has yet been able to tell us what "becoming dead" involves. Because more people have survived public speeches than have returned from the grave, our current understandings of speech and fear may be of some comfort to you.

Speech and Personality

One of the inescapable aspects of speaking is the inordinate amount of "me-ness" that goes with my spoken words. When I talk, *I* talk. There is not much way of escaping from spoken words, since it is our body that produces them, and it is our eyes that see some of the results of our words on other people. Because there is an inescapable element of the individual speaker in everything he or she says when talking, speech behavior is an especially good mirror of personalities, attitudes, and feelings.

You can easily document the interconnectedness of your speech and your person by trying to carry on a conversation in the third person for 5 minutes. It seems funny. It seems as though someone else were speaking for you, as if your body were being used to convey a message that someone else had created. You feel the impulse to say, "Now, wait a minute, I want to say something." Although con artists, espionage agents, and professional actors can, with practice, "step away from their messages" and speak someone else's part, they undoubtedly feel some tension, at least initially, when choking off *their* feelings and *their* motivations.

When you think about it, you really cannot plagiarize a speech. Oh, you can take your roommate's old outline into speech class and read it, but it is you, not your roommate, who will feel the exhilaration of having communicated successfully. It is you who will feel the increased social acceptance precipitated by the speech. On the other hand, if you have chosen the wrong roommates, it is you who will feel the boredom. It is you who must deal with the negative feedback from your audience. It is you who must feel embarrassed when your listeners perceive your lack of personal involvement. All of this occurs while your roommate,

the creator of another message, is completely uninvolved in the way that your message is received.

As Arnold points out, a speech is an action, not a product.[6] We do not "make" a speech as we do an essay. We *are* our speeches. Business executives will attest to the fact that the easiest way to dismiss a troublesome subordinate is to tell the employee, "Put it in writing and I'll send you a memo." This allows the executive, when responding, to think through the available options carefully and to castigate a disembodied product rather than engage in the personal, human activity that spoken confrontations necessarily entail. It is probably for this reason that the late psychologist Haim Ginott advised parents who have "had it" with their kids to write but not show occasional "hate letters" to them rather than to display their resentments in spoken confrontation with their children.[7] Because our talk is us in a very real sense, it is usually the warmest and most tender vehicle for saying "I love you," and often the most cutting and cruel way of saying "Get lost."

Speech and Fear

Once one fully appreciates how "personal" the act of speaking is, it becomes easier to understand why so many of us are fearful of speaking situations. Some of our most common daily experiences center around the mild (sometimes not-so-mild) fear associated with the speaking act:

> "I'm scared to death to give this speech. I know I'll just fumble all over myself."

> "But I've never had a job interview before; how will I know what to talk about?"

> "I just know how they're going to react. I'm really afraid to tell them."

> "But I've never been to a wake before. What should I say?"

All of these are common situations, and not very grueling when you think about them. Most of us grit our teeth, put our brains in gear, and get through the experience somehow. Nevertheless, talking necessarily entails risks for all persons. Some readers may find our use of "necessarily" puzzling. After all, we all have had many enjoyable conversations where fear, tension, and risk did not seem to be present. Our

---

[6]C. C. Arnold, "Speech as Action," *The English Record*, 20:36–43 (October, 1970).
[7]H. Ginott, *Between Parent and Child* (New York: McGraw-Hill, 1965).

rejoinder may sound like just another professorial equivocation. It does seem true that all of our oral communicative activities involve some sort of risk or tension, but it is our capability of dealing with the tension that varies greatly. In many cases, the pleasures of the communicative experience minimize our perceptions of the tensions. Knowing why such tensions exist in the first place, however, seems to be the first step in developing an ability to cope with these unpleasant, but necessary, portions of the speech experience.

Consider the melodramatic proposal situation, a situation where risk, tension, and fear traditionally are present. He, by asking for her hand, risks not only rejection but also being thought foolish or presumptuous. She is his one true love, and hence tension is produced because a valued relationship hangs in the balance. And because all of this is so tenuous and uncertain, because he cannot totally predict her response, the fear of the unknown looms large.

This example gives rise to two propositions about the risks of talking. The first is that *the fear associated with talking will be high when we are acutely aware of being evaluated.* What increases our awareness of this evaluation procedure? There are several factors. Tension seems to increase when

1. *The person we are talking to is especially important to us.* This is one way of explaining the tension some students feel in a public speaking exercise. The teacher is grading, the peer group is sizing you up, and you yourself are especially conscious of your words.

2. *The size of the audience is larger than normal.* The application to the classroom speaking situation is obvious. Here, a great number of evaluations of us are being made simultaneously, and the complexity of monitoring such judgments becomes difficult. However, another variable to be taken into account here is the composition, not only the size, of the audience. After all, we would much rather speak to a roomful of friends than face one irate employer!

3. *There is an imbalance in the status of those engaged in conversation.* This probably explains why it takes us so long to "warm up" when talking to some of our teachers. Because they have a certain amount of power over us, we cannot help but feel that they are judging everything we say—even our hellos and good-byes!

All these situations have one thing in common—a sudden consciousness of the judging of our verbalizations and, ultimately, of our very personalities. The "risk" involved is that the judgment will be negative. This is perhaps why lulls in conversations, those awful "dead" spots during an otherwise convivial evening, are especially painful. Suddenly, we are made to realize that people have been sitting back and judging us, and that these judgments were previously camouflaged by the very chatter we now so passionately desire to have resumed.

The second proposition is that *the fear associated with talking will be high when we are not able to predict the outcome of the interaction.* This springs from the very nature of fear itself. When in doubt, fear! This is reasonable, since for most of us maintaining the status quo will suffice if our only other option involves embracing a hazy and possibly painful future.

The unknowns in the speaking situation are many. In addition to the sometimes tortuous search for things to say and ways to say them, we also have to decide what our feelings on the subject are and how the listener will react. Thus, unpredictability seems to be the nature of communication. We can try to control as many factors as possible, but the tensions connected with speaking seem high when

1. *We do not know (or are unsure of) how we feel about ourselves.* This may seem like a strange proposition, but one of the most unnerving of human prospects is to find out something about ourselves that others have long since observed. It is probably for some such reason that many persons fear psychiatric counseling sessions. This situation presents two risks: (a) "I'll find out something about me that I'd rather not deal with" and (b) "You'll find out something about me that I'd rather we didn't discover simultaneously."

2. *We don't know or are unsure of how we feel about the audience.* The archetype situation involves conversing with strangers. Because each of us lives in a very unique world, we necessarily meet and engage an "unknown quantity" whenever we talk with another. Strangers simply add to the unpredictability of the situation. First meetings are often awkward for us, for we are never quite sure what we might be risking by talking to this new addition to our lives.

3. *We are unsure of the dynamics of the speaking situation.* Life is filled with examples of this type of talking tension. How does one behave when meeting "Her" parents for the first time? What do you say to a professor outside of the classroom? How do you manage yourself when speaking to your boyfriend and to your parents simultaneously? The many unknowns that an unfamiliar speech setting sometimes involves can wither the hardiest of us.

At this point, two questions should puzzle most readers: (1) With all these risks and tensions present, why should I ever open my mouth? and (2) How do I cope with these risks and fears? The answer to the first question is obvious from our initial discussion in this chapter. As humans, we have no other choice but to speak. The second question is a bit more difficult to answer. We could, of course, simply avoid talking to people who are important to us, whose status is higher than ours, whom we do not know. Obviously, such a solution is patently impractical.

Like all human problems, the antidote to fear seems to be knowledge and experience. By reducing the "unknowns" in the speaking situation, we will increase our chances of having a pleasurable interchange. Becoming aware of our own uncertainties and limitations will better enable us to deal with them. We will begin to get a feeling for the range and complexity of human behavior only by meeting different people. By thrusting ourselves into various types of interactions, we will be in a position to meet the challenges of new and strange speech settings. And last, by knowing as much as possible about the nature of human auditors, about both our self-image and our social image, and about the practical demands placed upon all speakers, we will be able to put the tensions associated with talking in their proper perspective —as necessary, but conquerable, portions of the speaking experience.

Thus, the psychology of the speech classroom is not very different from the psychology your mother used with you when, as a 4-year-old, you felt sure that a gaggle of goblins lay in wait in your closet, ready to spring out when the shadows lengthened. If she was sensible, she invited you to come with her, hand in hand, and investigate the nature of dark closets. While the closets are just as dark in spoken interactions, experience (in the form of sensitive classroom speech activities) still seems to be the best handmaiden.

Suggestions for Speaking

Because we feel that *everything* in this book—including our "theoretical" discussions—can contribute directly to your speaking effectiveness, we shall conclude each of our chapters with advice you might find useful when speaking in public. In all cases, these tips will be drawn from the material in the chapter just concluded. Thus, our "Suggestions for Speaking" will also serve as a practical summary of the chapter's content. Listed below, then, are some things to keep in mind when speaking:

1. Since speech is personal, explain to your listeners why *you* care about your speech topic; don't strive to sound like a disembodied "expert."

2. Because speech is social, tell your listeners (directly or indirectly) why they are important to you and what you want of them.

3. Rehearse *out loud* any speech you are going to give; by listening to yourself, you can gauge your own clarity and convincingness.

4. Be candid about the specific forces precipitating your speech; always "assist" your listeners in determining your motives for speaking.

5. Project an image of mutuality. Tell your listeners (directly or indirectly) that you are interested in their opinions on the topic.

6. In *public* speaking, be especially careful not to use undefined words early in the speech.

7. Remember that you will have to sustain a public audience's attention; save some of your best material for when attention lags.

8. Presume that you will be slightly nervous when speaking; if *you* accept your nervousness, your audience won't be bothered by it.

9. Presume that something unplanned might occur during your speech; save your favorite example or anecdote for just such a rough spot.

10. Presume that one or more persons in your audience will be bored or confused; if they continue to be unresponsive to you despite your best efforts, don't look at them.

CHAPTER 2

Principles of Effective Speech

Knowing something about the other persons in the class is good because I can at least try to gear my speeches toward them, talking about something they will understand. I can also somewhat anticipate their reactions. However, I will never know exactly what they will do or say. No one can. There's always some element of a person that we don't know. That's what makes people so interesting.

I have found that in the future I will have to be more explicit in order to get people to understand me. This assignment really showed me how differently people think and interpret ideas.

The speakers who made the biggest impact on me were the ones who shared parts of their own lives. Telling stories of one's own experiences, especially if they are personal like Debby's, gives me the feeling that they trust me. If people trust me enough to think I will not attack their innermost feelings, I will give them my best attention. I really hate to hear people talk about something that they are either bored with or don't know anything about.

I was more confident than last time. I was able to look everybody in the eye. I glanced around the room continually. I had more confidence in myself and more confidence in my subject. I also had more confidence in everyone listening. They all know what it's like to talk in front of the class and how they all like everyone else to listen.

The feedback cards showed that most of the people knew what my main idea was, but I felt as if they weren't very interested, or if they were interested, they didn't show any response.

When the speech started, I experienced about the same type of tension a person might experience while waiting in a doctor's office for a shot. The shot doesn't hurt as much as the anticipation of what's going to happen. Surprisingly enough, I became very relaxed during the speech itself. Because I was fairly well versed in the subject, the tensions were kept to a minimum.

I found out that it's easy to sound good to yourself and for the rest of the class to be totally indifferent.

The remarks you have just read were made by students who had just completed classroom speaking exercises. We do not present these observations because they are theoretically trenchant (though some are), nor because they open new vistas in the study of communication (though some might), and certainly not because they are dramatic, earthshaking statements about speaking and listening. Rather, we have included them here because they speak to some of the essential, very human issues that many of us are concerned with when conversing with others.

There are, perhaps, no startling insights to be found in these written "debriefings" of speech experiences, but lurking beneath the surface of these casual remarks are a host of intriguing ideas about human communication. For example, in these short excerpts we find echoes of both the "highs" and the "lows" of talking. Some of the students reflect a growing confidence in their ability to manage successfully the demands placed upon them by their own ambitions, by their ability to construct intelligent messages, and by their listeners' often irrascible modes of responding. We also see the frustration that an apathetic or confused audience can generate in a speaker, as well as the continual struggle that speakers wage when attempting to assess the effect they are having on their hearers. In other words, it is easy to sound good to yourself whereas the class is totally indifferent!

If asked, most of us could probably come up with an intuitive list of communication basics—you must have something to say, some way of saying it, and someone to hear you say it. Needless to say, this triad of necessities leaves something to be (practically) desired. So, too, does the oftquoted but rather vacuous set of communicative prescriptions we have all heard countless times: "Tell 'em, tell 'em what you said, sit down!" On the assumption that something intelligent can be said about the essential demands of communication, we hope to illuminate the following requirements that listeners place upon speakers:

1. In some fashion, a speaker must demonstrate commitment to his or her *message*.

2. Through some means, a speaker must demonstrate commitment to his or her *audience*.

3. Somehow, a speaker must attempt to *balance* these "commitments."

We are not suggesting that these three mandates are all we need observe in winning friends and influencing people. But, if pressed, we might be so bold as to assert that friends are rarely won and people are seldom influenced by a speaker who disregards these ABCs of communication. Or to put it another way, these principles of effective speaking constitute necessary but not sufficient conditions for profitable interaction with others.

Thus, in every sense this is a chapter about principles. Now, before you throw down the book in disgust, we want to suggest that not all principles are as trite and overblown as your experience with them may have led you to believe. Principles have acquired a bad reputation largely because they have been misused by preachers, teachers, parents, and other "busybodies" during our younger, and less tolerant, days. Normally, principles are stated in a grand and all-encompassing manner, as if they were true for all times under all circumstances. Principles typically sound gluttonous. They consist of overly large statements about too many things that can never be known for sure. No wonder they leave such a bad taste in so many mouths.

Yet talk about principles we must. We shall try to keep our discussion from sounding overly moralistic, but you should be aware that we will indeed be talking about *principles* here; that is, guidelines for use in all communication situations. Our basic position will be that whereas "talking" is eminently natural, effective communication comes as a result of hard work and only after we have made some rather difficult intellectual and social choices. The principles we will discuss are, like all worthwhile principles, easier to talk about than to follow in daily life. We feel, however, that unless the matter of communication is raised to the level of *principle*, it is too easily treated as a mechanical and hence not particularly worrisome matter. We would like you to begin *not* to think, in optimistically American fashion, that communication can be had for the mere asking. Effective communication must be paid for dearly. The principles we will discuss here may well prove to be the coin of its realm.

Commitment to the Message

My fellow Americans. It is with great pride and a sense of gentle humility that this speaker stands before this magnificent convention audience with a message of welcome and a clarion declaration to this great nation, to our children, and to our children's children that this political party will henceforth take its place in the sunlit and glorious future that is our party's rightful destiny, a destiny replete with the splendor of governmental accomplishment, with the blessings of our distinguished political ancestors, and with a burning sense of national purpose that will serve this country in good stead in the days that lie beyond.

Even the kindest among us will label this passage as unadulterated nonsense! Yet it is just this sort of thing to which many speakers at political conventions have subjected us for years. Such speakers seem to feel obligated to eschew their personal feelings, to search for the most abstract of metaphors—in short, to divorce themselves from their messages. In the fictitious (but painfully familiar) passage cited above, we see the verbal rantings of a man bent on treating his audience to a kind of speech-by-formula. The speaker makes no reference to himself nor to those he is addressing; he does not detail his personal convictions or his reasons for speaking. In short, our imaginary speaker seems to be compromising his medium—human speech—for, as we observed in Chapter 1, speech is a phenomenon attended by me-ness.

Perhaps we should pity rather than censure this convention speaker, who is probably the product of years of the abstract, formulary, impersonal discourse that is the conventioneer's stock-in-trade. Nevertheless, there are those who object to this emasculation of human speech and who insist on making the medium work for them.

Consider the case of Lawton Chiles, then a first-term senator from Florida, who was once called upon to give a welcoming address to the Democratic National Convention. From a national standpoint, Chiles was unknown, and he knew it. Apparently, he perceived his main communicative challenge at the convention to be one of explaining why he was talking to the assembled delegates and why he was worthy of having their attention. In attempting to satisfy such rhetorical demands, Chiles attempted to demonstrate his commitment to his message by revealing his personal stake in the interaction. In so doing, he steered well away from the communicative claptrap that was his "rightful destiny":

> Since I learned I'd been selected to make the welcoming talk on behalf of the great State of Florida, I've been thinking about how it happened that I was given this opportunity.
>
> Two years ago I was just half-way through my walk from one end of Florida to the other. The first statewide poll showed only 5 percent of the people recognized my name. I had no money in a race that required a million-dollar stake and I was running against two millionaires. . . .
>
> Before my walk ended, I met thousands and thousands of others who never had had a chance to see or talk to an office-holder or a candidate running for office. They had only seen them on TV.
>
> Because I was out there where people could see me and talk to me, they hoped that I would be different—that I would listen—so they elected me. That's how I happen to be here to welcome you.
>
> But it's not quite that simple because the people that I listened to got to me. I found they love this country—that they were way ahead of their leaders

—that they wanted to have a part in solving problems. They looked at me in the eye and asked me:

"Will you come back—will you be different—will you listen?"

So because of how I got elected, I carry a burden of how to keep faith with the people and that burden has only increased since I have been in the Senate. Because of that burden I do welcome you as delegates to this Convention— but with the same challenge that the people gave me—Will you listen? Will you be different?[1]

Now, some might argue that Senator Chiles went beyond the limits of demonstrating personal involvement in his message and, in effect, merely produced an egocentric speech, unfit for the occasion or the audience. This may be the case, but many would judge otherwise.

For instance, Chiles did not continue on in this very personal vein, and later in the speech focused on national and international matters. In doing so, however, he never strayed far away from explaining why these issues were important *to him*. When a speaker (like Chiles) attempts to demonstrate commitment to the message, the speaker really says two things: I know what I'm talking about, and I mean what I say. Chiles's command of the "facts" in the passage cited above as well as his attempt to say "I know because I've been there—I've made an investment" were his attempts to show that he stood with his message.

Any number of everyday examples will serve to point up how interested we as listeners are in assessing a speaker's commitment to his or her message. We are generally intolerant, for example, of one who pays lip service to an idea but who fails to indicate what he or she has done, is doing, or will do on behalf of the proposition advocated. In a similar vein, many TV buffs are especially annoyed by "lip-sync-ing," the process by which a popular singer on a variety show simply "mouths" the words to her current hit, while her previously recorded voice wails plaintively in the background. Upon seeing such antics, the TV viewer might mutter, "Doesn't she care enough about that song to make a real-life, here-and-now investment in her message?" On still another front, some of us are especially bothered by persons who frantically search for million-dollar words, only to wind up mispronouncing them badly. Ostensibly, we feel that such a person is making someone else's message and would be better off saying it in his own words.

In this era of ghostwritten speeches, dubbed foreign films, and the televised college lecture, people are becoming cynical about others' commitment-to-message. In some senses, listeners have been inundated

[1]L. Chiles, "Address at the 1972 Democratic National Convention," July, 1972. Reprinted by permission of Lawton Chiles.

by the Ford salesperson who drives a Chevrolet; hence, listeners seem to hold speakers guilty of noncommitment to their messages until they can prove themselves innocent. A wary speaker, therefore, is often wise to demonstrate *initially* his or her stake in the interaction and what behavior he or she has engaged in on behalf of the proposal. Perhaps this is why the introduction to Senator Chiles's speech was so heavily laden with demonstrations of his personal commitment to the message he was carrying to the convention.

When striving to demonstrate commitment to a message, speakers' options seem somewhat limited. We can envision two traditional means by which speakers can indicate that they know what they are talking about and mean what they say: first, by revealing the self and second, by presenting "the facts."

Personal Revelation

If the audience and occasion permit it, one of the most dramatic ways of displaying that we have a stake in the message we are presenting is to recount what we have done on behalf of the proposition we are advocating. Listeners seem to treat a speaker's personal experiences as one of the best indicators of message commitment. Thus, speakers are wise to demonstrate that their personal experiences are accurate and relevant to the propositions they are advocating.

Naturally, demonstrating the authenticity of our personal experiences can be as difficult at times as, say, the angler's "one that got away" stories continue to remind us. Likewise, the sociology professor who goes off on a tangent about a summer vacation will probably not be perceived as providing relevant data to support a point on the sociological impact of Marx's theories of collectivism. Personal revelation has its communicative liabilities.

Using personal revelation in an attempt to demonstrate commitment to a message seems most appropriate when the audience views the speaker favorably. After all, why should a respected speaker attempt to marshall a mass of facts when he or she simply can draw upon the very basis of his or her credibility—the audience's perceptions of the speaker's past accomplishments? Thus, the speaker who uses personal revelation should do so if (1) the audience is generally favorable toward the speaker or the speaker's proposal, and (2) the speaker's accomplishments can be easily verified.

Let us consider an example. Several years ago, James Snavely gave what might have been the first and only public speech he had ever given. He addressed the Philadelphia chapter of the American Civil Liberties Union in order to thank the membership for their assistance in a series of court battles he had been fighting. He did not come to the meeting armed with statistics or lawyers' briefs. He came only to tell of the rather painful series of events he had experienced over the previous six years. Needless to say, he was facing a friendly audience, one that had no reason to suspect him of dishonesty or irrelevance. Perhaps knowingly, then, he chose a very wise rhetorical course—the simple and direct presentation of his personal experiences:

> *Approximately 5½ years ago, I sent my oldest child for her first day to school; my child was given, by the teacher, a card for my signature. This card was for my permission to attend religious training in a nearby fire hall under the guidance of Child Evangelism Inc. Needless to say, I made the un-christian move of not signing it. Several days later I received a letter on school stationary, signed by the principal, that explained why I should sign the card. The letter proceeded to tell me how last year 500 and some odd children, out of 500 and some, had attended regularly every Wednesday, and of the work that was being done by this training, that the school fully endorsed and supported this Bible study, and further told me of the large financial contribution made by these children last year to the missionaries overseas. On the second Wednesday of this Bible study, I asked my child how many of the 37 in her class attended. She told me, all but her. I naturally became worried. I asked my child what she and the teacher do while Bible study is in progress. She told me the teacher goes to the fire hall to teach Bible study while she stays alone in her room and plays blocks. The following Wednesday I went to the school and verified this with my own eyes. I was now becoming disturbed. . . . I then contacted the superintendent of the jointure, and after much argument he promised me that the teacher would not leave my child alone again. Several Wednesdays later I checked with my child to see if this situation had been corrected. She told me it had. I asked her what she and the teacher do while the other children are at Bible study. She told me her teacher reads her Bible stories.[2]*

Snavely went on to tell of the social and financial persecutions he and his family suffered at the hands of his community and concluded his speech by urging the group to continue to work for greater human tolerance.

Snavely's speech is not an oratorical masterpiece, but it is a good example of the kind of communicative impact the detailing of personal experiences can bring about. Besides revealing a very intense commitment to his message, Snavely's tale has a number of additional benefits:

1. *Removing impersonality.* Many communicative situations, especially public ones, tend to foster "third-person speech," in which

[2]J. Snavely, "Address at the Philadelphia Branch, American Civil Liberties Union, December 12, 1964. Reprinted by permission of the A.C.L.U. of Pennsylvania.

the speaker refers neither to self nor audience. Mentioning personal experiences helps to break through this wall of estrangement by depicting the speaker as a real-life, definable individual.

2. *Flattering to the audience.* Especially for a private man like James Snavely, revealing personal experiences can be quite threatening. But by such personal presentations, a speaker can tell the audience that they are somehow "special" and worth his risking his privacy.

3. *Intensifying the message.* Whenever we open our personal lives to another, there is some element of risk involved, even if our presentation is not as personally painful as Snavely's. Thus, when Snavely digs deep into his own life for supporting material, he is, in effect, telling his audience that his message is more important than any discomfort or embarrassment he might suffer.

4. *Tapping readily available resources.* From the standpoint of searching for things to say, our life experiences obviously provide us with an efficient source of information retrieval. We are the experts on our own lives, and hence our experiences present a handy body of materials from which to draw in communication. It is for this reason that speech teachers have always urged student speakers to speak on topics with which the students have had experience (the very advice we shall give you in Chapter 3).

Factual Presentation

Despite the many dividends to be derived from using personal experiences when speaking, there are a number of liabilities to this approach. As many cynics have observed, personal experiences are fine, as long as they are *our* experiences! Thus, speakers rarely find themselves in a position where the presentation of their life events is alone sufficient for effective communication. Someone, somewhere, always seems to want the "facts." Often, these "someones" are members of a skeptical or hostile audience. Sometimes, these "someones" are simply people who have little sympathy for a speaker who sees himself or herself as the only body of resource material available for communication.

Research in communication has documented again and again that a presentation of cold, hard evidence is often helpful in speaking situations.[3] In fact, there is one dominant theme in the research literature: When the speaker is unknown or held in questionable regard by an audience, a presentation of factual evidence is mandatory.

[3]M. Karlins and H. Abelson, *Persuasion: How Opinions and Attitudes Are Changed,* 2nd ed. (New York: Springer, 1970).

Intuition itself would probably force us to this conclusion. For example, who would be naïve enough to doubt that it was Ralph Nader's command of the facts that allowed him to launch and sustain the consumer movement? As long as lethargic bureaucrats could dismiss Nader's assertions as his opinions or as the product of only his experiences, they could hardly be expected to take action on his proposals. Perhaps because he appreciates the universality connoted by factual evidence, Nader employs almost exclusively lawyers and scientists—persons capable of gathering and intelligently disseminating "the facts."

In the handbook *Action for a Change*, Nader and Donald Ross are careful to urge even campus consumer groups to speak primarily from a factual base when directing their persuasion at hostile audiences:

> *Take for example the corporate polluter. Sit-ins and marches will not clean up the rivers and the air that he fouls. He is too powerful and there are too many like him. Yet the student has unique access to the resources that can be effective in confronting the polluter. University and college campuses have the means of detecting the precise nature of the industrial effluent, through chemical or biological research. Through research such as they perform every day in the classroom, students can show the effect of the effluent on an entire watershed, and thus alert the community to real and demonstrable dangers to public health—a far more powerful way to arouse public support for a clean environment—than a sit-in.*[4]

In the less dramatic world of the speech class, there is nothing inherently valuable in showing up for your speech with an armful of note cards. Factual knowledgeability is simply one way of demonstrating that you have made a special commitment to your message, that you mean what you say and know what you are talking about. Still, whereas the Vietnam vet in your class can easily draw upon his past experiences when speaking on the dangers of nuclear proliferation, you, who have spent most of your life in school, must search for other ways of signaling to the audience that you have made a full-scale investment in your message of nuclear disarmament. Opinions are fine, but some audiences demand more.

Our remarks in this section are tempered by the inevitable caution: All communicative approaches should be situationally determined. Commitment to the message can be shown in a number of ways—through personal history, through factual presentation, and sometimes even through the simple expedient of taking a firm stand on the issue

---

[4]From *Action for a Change* by Ralph Nader and Donald Ross with Joseph Highland. Copyright © 1971, 1972 by Ralph Nader. Reprinted by permission of the Viking Press, Inc.

in question. But all such communicative choices must pass through the "filter" of audience expectation.

Commitment to the Audience

If you are a particularly hardy person, you might want to try a little experiment. The next time you walk through a college dormitory, take a cassette recorder with you. Find four or five of your friends engaged in a rap session. Enter the room, sit down, and simply turn on the tape recorder. What happens? The first thing you will probably notice is the silence or "shock" stage, which is quickly followed by the "outrage" phase—"What the hell are you tape-recording us for?" That's your cue to leave—quickly!

Now why would a group of adults get so upset about a tape recorder? After all, they were undoubtedly committed to their messages; they knew what they were talking about and meant what they said. They were probably generating great thoughts that were just meant to be recorded for posterity, weren't they? Of course, they were not. Your friends were simply engaging in speech-for-pleasure and were doing so for each other, not for parents, steadies, teachers, or outsiders.

By invading the group with your tape recorder, you introduced a potentially new and unknown audience into the dynamics of their conversation. As humans, we seem to have a built-in desire to adapt our messages to particular others, not to anyone who happens by and captures our words on tape. One need go back no further into history than to the Watergate affair to verify such a doctrine. Presidents, like all of us, want to know "who out there" will be listening to their taped remarks.

In communication, commitment to our messages is simply not enough. We can know all the facts in the case, but if this information cannot be efficiently adapted to particular others, it will have little social impact. Similarly, your revealed personal experiences and gut feelings can possess both richness and depth, but if others do not perceive such qualities in your remarks, your feelings and experiences are of little *social* value.

In an elementary sense, commitment to an audience involves two things: (1) *demonstrating that we are making messages for the particular audience we are addressing,* and (2) *demonstrating in some fashion that our audience's attention and adherence are important to us.* Actually carrying off these gyrations in everyday communication is difficult, especially when we are attempting to affect group attitudes, values, and levels of information. But anyone who has ever been invited to have an old-fashioned, heart-to-heart talk with his or her parent, only to be lectured at, knows how much we like to be catered to individually in communication.

One research study has documented how important particularizing our communication can be in helping us achieve effective social interaction. An authority on communication patterns in the family, J. G. Stachowiak, discovered that fathers of well-adjusted children sent "targeted communications" (i.e., messages aimed at particular persons— "Good job, *Johnny*") to their children, while fathers of disturbed children sent more "general" messages.[5] This conclusion does not imply that a failure to adapt to particular others will engender mental illness in our listeners; it should imply that all listeners in any context desire to have their immediate worlds dealt with in communication.

Perhaps this "demand of adaptation" explains why Richard Nixon visited each and every state in the United States during his 1960 presidential election bid. Apparently, he reasoned that by demonstrating a willingness to engage in interaction with particular others, he would be making the kind of adaptive responses necessary to show his commitment to his various audiences. By actually setting foot in each state, and targeting his communications for particular segments of society, he hoped to "be with" his audience both physically and psychologically. However, as writer Theodore White notes, this tactic caused him to spread himself too thin in the campaign and may have cost him the election.[6] Despite this, it was a good *communicative* thought.

Commitment to Public Audiences

In speech settings, the problems of adaptation become paramount. The public communicator must make essentially "one" message work for great numbers of people—each person with his or her own attitudes, expectations, and interpersonal needs. In public communication, segments of a given audience must be adapted to individually, but such adaptations occur in the presence of and are observed by other sectors of that same audience. To resolve such a dilemma, many speakers adopt the "smorgasbord" approach, including a little something for everyone. Such a strategy has its drawbacks because a speaker using it might be perceived as having no real message of his or her own.

However, problems of adaptation in public speech settings can be solved. Let us consider for a moment the communicative techniques of

[5] J. G. Stachowiak, "Decision-Making and Conflict Resolution in the Family Group," in *Perspectives in Communication*, eds. C. Larson and F. Dance (Milwaukee: Univ. of Wisconsin, Department of Communication, 1968).

[6] T. White, *The Making of the President: 1960* (New York: Atheneum, 1961).

the Reverend Jesse Jackson, one of the most intense spokespersons of today's black movement, and one who many contemporary observers judge as being perhaps the most "situationally sensitive" speaker for the black community.

Jackson was once called upon to speak to a group of Operation Breadbasket workers in Milwaukee. While the audience consisted of many older, long-time civil-rights workers, there were also a good number of youthful activists present; similarly, blacks and whites were almost equally represented, as were men and women. To compound Jackson's problems, his audience was also composed of both well-educated, rather wealthy citizens as well as unskilled members of the poverty class. Jackson had to adjust simultaneously to all these situational demands, while conveying a forthright message. In many senses, he did remarkably well. Consider, for example, the following two passages from his speech:

> There was a farmer in South Carolina who had an old wood stove, and he finally got a new range—Tappan—so he moved the old wood stove out in the barn. He put some hay under it, and the dog took up residence under the stove, and the cat took up residence in the oven. So anyhow, the cat had some kittens (by some other cat). But just because they were born in the oven didn't make them biscuits! (laughter and applause) And just 'cause black folks are born in the American oven don't make them American, 'cause Americans can live all over Milwaukee, and black people can't. (applause)

> Everytime some newsman asks me about the question of welfare, I always get the impression they're asking me what I think the nation's going to do about black folks. And it immediately becomes my obligation to let them know something about the history of welfare. The first thing is that welfare came into existence for white people. Black folks came out of slavery and were promised 40 acres and a mule, which amounted to an economic base at that time, but that never did come forth. And black folks had to struggle with no state support. Whereas when the Depression came in the late twenties and early thirties—when the whites were unemployed—emergency acts were passed as depressionary measures. So welfare came into existence for white people. There are numerically in America more poor whites on welfare tonight than poor blacks.[7]

In reading these two passages, did you recognize that they both essentially carry the same message? Yet note how the supporting material and especially the language of both passages are markedly different. Appar-

[7] J. Jackson, "Address at the Milwaukee Chapter of the Southern Christian Leadership Conference," July 1971.

ently, Jackson was attempting to meet the communicative demands placed upon him by subsections of his audience.

Commitment to the Audience: Some Techniques

Let us turn our attention away from the public platform of civil rights to consider some of the options open to the student speaker when he or she attempts to demonstrate some sort of commitment to listening classmates. Unlike Jackson, most of us do not have the inborn intellectual and linguistic capacities necessary to make on-the-spot adaptations necessary to "particularize" an audience. But modes of public adaptation can be learned, and we have probably already learned some of these modes in our everyday "private" conversations. A list of methods for demonstrating audience commitment might include:

1. *Allow the audience to interact.* As far as we know, there is no heavenly ordained reason for listeners not to dialogue with a speaker. Many contemporary speakers are now beginning to realize that some verbal participation by an audience can produce highly favorable effects. Naturally, it is difficult for a speaker to "channel" dialogue in a public speech setting. Still, there are many cases in which a question directly asked of an audience can instill in listeners the feeling that their worlds are being dealt with at the time of the interaction. What greater way is there to inculcate a feeling of particularity than to ask a person what he or she thinks?

2. *Adjust to the subtle responses of the audience.* It is not always feasible or even wise to encourage actual responses from a group of listeners. After all, there is always the chance that an ambitious listener might hog the stage and divert attention from the speaker's proposal. We can, however, notice and, more importantly, adapt to the subtle (often nonverbal) information which an audience always supplies the speaker. The attempt to adjust for feedback is often judged by an audience as a sign of commitment to them ("you look a bit confused. Let me put it another way . . . ").

3. *Indicate that the audience can affect you.* In a sense, both (1) and (2) suggest to an audience that their attitudes and behaviors can and will affect the attitudes and behaviors of the speaker. Yet there are more dramatic ways of indicating that mutual influence will occur in a public speech situation. For example, when attempting to launch his presidency on a populist note, Jimmy Carter

scheduled numerous "town meetings" across the country and even participated in a "Call the President" show whereby he dutifully attended the White House phones for a day, all in an attempt to generate a sense of give-and-take.

4. *Openly acknowledge speaker-audience similarities.* This may appear to be a totally commonsensical proposition. Yet, often communicators only imply elements of speaker-audience commonality instead of making them explicit. It is better to make obvious the information and attitudes the speaker and his or her audience potentially have in common. Even such elementary devices as analogies and examples drawn from the experiences of the audience can indicate that a speaker is seeking to individuate the audience.

5. *Adjust to situational changes.* Again we happen on a straightforward but oftentimes elusive rhetorical device. Being the ever-changing phenomena they are, spoken interactions involve moment-to-moment alterations in both the psychological and physical forces that surround them—the audience tires, the room gets hotter, the speaker loses his or her place. All such factors impinge on the audience and create on-the-spot problems for the speaker. Situational changes are noticed by the audience and are oftentimes psychologically proximate to them. Perhaps this is why students often are disgusted with the college lecturer who reads notes.

6. *Urge the continuity of the speaker-audience relationship.* Perhaps the subtlest of all, this proposition may well be the most important feature in signaling commitment to an audience. In essence, it encourages a speaker to regard the spoken interaction as *part* of his or her relationship with the audience. Because they have been bombarded with fly-by-night salespersons, contemporary listeners seem especially worried about being "used" by a speaker. Thus, the speaker who rushes through the interaction, fails to connect his or her proposal to the future well-being of the audience, or neglects to mention his or her future intentions might well seem like a hit-and-run specialist. As Ray Bradbury says in *Fahrenheit 451*, "The difference between the man who just cuts lawns and a real gardener is in the touching. . . . The lawn-cutter might just as well have not been there at all; the gardener will be there a life-time."[8]

[8] R. Bradbury, *Fahrenheit 451* (New York: Simon and Schuster, 1967), p. 143.

Balancing Message and Audience Commitment

If you are like some students, you were perhaps a bit disturbed by the general tone of our remarks in the last section. "What's with all this adapting business?" you might ask angrily. "I'm my own person. I say what I feel. I'm not going to 'make strategies' and 'put on a mask.'" While we do applaud the rough-hewn quality of your feelings about strategizing, we would like to stop for a moment to ponder a question that all of us have asked ourselves many times: When we communicate, should we be brutally honest or should we be diplomatic and even reticent at all times?

Instrumental Communication

Although this is an intriguing question, we are bothered by the "or" in this query. We do not feel that communication forces us to choose between adapting and not adapting, but rather that there are ways of sticking to our principles and still making those views palatable to others. We do not believe that communication forces us to sacrifice deeply held beliefs in order to placate others, nor do we feel that our only choices are between being egocentric rugged individualists and chameleonlike manipulators.

We feel that there is a range of options open to us as adaptive communicators, and that commitment to our message and commitment to our audience can and must be balanced. In other words, we are advocating an instrumental approach to human speech, one that sees audience adaptation, audience analysis, and choice among communicative options as central to effective speaking.

As you probably already know, there is another way of approaching spoken interactions. The expressive view of communication sees adapting as antagonistic to individuality and views the speaker's feelings as the only important judge of what should be said in a given encounter. In contrast, Hart and Burks have specified the characteristics of instrumental communication.[9] These characteristics include the following:

1. *Adaptation to others is vital in communication.* Because people are so extraordinarily complex and because each of us is unique, communicators simply must adjust to the constraints placed upon them by individual listeners. This implies that our actual

---

[9]R. Hart and D. Burks, "Rhetorical Sensitivity and Social Interaction," *Speech Monographs,* 39:75–91 (1972).

remarks in communication are often quite different from what we might say on impulse and from what we might say to another person in the same situation.

This does not imply that we must make endless adaptations to others. Some people, after all, have a capacity to push us to the brink of exasperation. However, in instrumental communication, the speaker is charged to consider making adaptations before the interaction is broken off. Adapting is difficult as, say, our kid brother's endless questions continually remind us, but it is rare to find a prosperous society where the mutual adaptation of its members is not present.

2. *Some things are best left unsaid in communication.* Who among us has not at one time had the impulse to tell a particularly obnoxious person to get lost? Sometimes we do, of course. But oftentimes we swallow our invective and avoid future contacts with that person. In other words, we operate instrumentally, reasoning that little good could be derived from a hot-and-heavy spoken confrontation at that point in time.

When deciding what to say, instrumental communication gives us two guidelines: (1) What would I like to say? and (2) What can my listeners handle? Some persons, of course, never go beyond the first stage—if they feel it, they say it. However, we feel that it is often wise to think twice (Stage 1 plus Stage 2) before telling off someone or before concluding that careful *preparation* of a speech takes too much of the spontaneity out of life. Once the decision to say or not say has been made, one final principle of instrumental communication becomes operative.

3. *The same idea can be communicated in countless ways.* Just as human beings are complex, so, too, are their abilities to phrase the same fundamental conception in a variety of ways. Needless to say, some ways of saying things are better than others. For example, it is oftentimes not difficult to determine that we are attracted to the person in our Psych 212 class. After much cogitation, we decide that something must be said. Then comes the hard part. How do you express your attraction without appearing trite, conceited, super-cool, too reserved, and so on? While the tenets of instrumental communication are not going to tell you how to meet someone, they do suggest that human encounters usually present us with a range of communicative choices. Jesse Jackson knows, as you know, that his fundamental idea of black solidarity must be argued for differently when he speaks to a caucus of young black activists than when he addresses the old guard of the Democratic party.

We do not present the tenets of instrumental communication as a panacea for all your communicative ills. What we are arguing for here is a way of thinking, which suggests that commitment to our messages and our audiences need not be antagonistic forces in our daily encounters with others.

Balancing Our "Commitments" Practically

Admittedly, the preceding remarks have been a bit preachy. Let us now consider the practical reasons for attempting to maintain balance between our perceived commitment to the message and our commitment to our listeners.

What would you say is the ultimate barrier to effective communication—too much talk? not enough talk? no empathy? too much empathy? We would like to suggest that the root problem is when our message commitment and audience commitment are "out of sync." In other words, when listeners perceive that we as speakers are more concerned with appearing firm and knowledgeable than we are with adapting to their values, they turn us off. Likewise, when listeners see us as having no real stake in what we are saying, but only as trying to curry favor with them, they are equally put out by us.

Psychologist Haim Ginott made much the same points in two passages from his book, *Between Parent and Teenager:*

> *The phrase, "When I was your age" brings instant deafness to teenagers. They defend themselves against our moralistic monologues by not listening. They do not want to hear how good we were, and how bad they are by comparison.*

> *Says Belinda, age sixteen: "My mother tries hard to be a teenager. She dresses in mini-skirts, wears beads, and talks hip. When my friends come visiting, she asks them to "ooze her some skin" (shake hands) and to tell her some "groovy" news. It makes me sick to see her act so foolish. My friends pretend that she is one of us, but they laugh at her behind her back, and they make fun of me."*[10]

In the first passage we see a very common problem—that of regarding the production of "our" message as being of greater concern than our listeners' favorable reception. When a teenager complains that she is being treated paternalistically by a parent, she says, in effect, two things: Her father is engaging in ego-gratification in his daughter's presence, and she is being treated as an abstraction of members of her

[10]H. Ginott, *Between Parent and Teenager* (New York: Avon, 1969), pp. 33, 41. Reprinted by permission of Haim Ginott.

class, not as the unique individual she is. To regard our messages as more important than the people to whom they are addressed is to erect a communicative barrier that can prove insurmountable in later interactions with those same listeners.

If we dislike the arrogance and self-righteousness of the speaker who gives little regard to his or her audience, so, too, do we distrust the pandering speaker who seems to have no personal message and is willing to bend whichever way the wind blows. Ginott's second passage is a rather poignant example of a woman who has sacrificed her "messages" in order to reach a very fragile sort of rapport with her "audience." Similarly, the baseball umpire who declares, "Well, it's a strike but I don't want you to be upset with me so I'll call it a ball," is also allowing his or her commitments to be "out of phase."

Sacrificing message commitment is really quite naïve when you think about it. After all, listeners know full well when they attend a speech that they are there to be influenced, that the speaker is desirous of changing their attitudes, values, or levels of information in some fashion. For a speaker patently to deny any personal communicative intent is to forsake the very rationale behind communication—that of mediating our and others' world through talk. Thus, we become suspicious of the car salesperson who reverently asserts, "I'll probably lose my job for this, but okay, you can have it for your price and I'll sacrifice my commission." In this rough-and-ready world, listeners realize, implicitly at least, that communicating implies mutual influence and risk, a situation in which both they and the speaker are attempting to accrue dividends.

The speaker, then, is constantly in a double-bind situation. He or she must attempt to particularize listeners, often by demonstrating how their lives will be affected advantageously by the discourse. Equally, the speaker must show an investment in his or her message by appearing knowledgeable and forthright. Any other set of conditions will present interminable problems, problems that an instrumental communicator should not have to face. While we do not urge the principles of instrumental communication upon all persons in all circumstances, we do think they are the best general guide for speaking success. We trust that your own experience with speaking will attest to that.

Suggestions for Speaking

In many ways, we feel that this chapter is the most important in the book. Here, we have tried to present a *philosophy* of speech effectiveness. The principles of communication discussed are broad-based but are also rather practical guides, useful for making decisions about what to say and what not to say. We also feel that unless you adopt some sort of overall game plan of speaking effectiveness, you must resign yourself to a life of uncertainty and ad hoc decisions. The game plan discussed in this chapter is, we feel, eminently practical and capable of generating advice such as the following:

1. Examine your speech outline to see if you have included any personal examples; ask yourself if you have given enough detail to make them understandable to the audience.

2. Give the audience an idea of the steps *you* are willing to take to insure that your proposal becomes reality.

3. Eliminate from your outline personal remarks that might seem gratuitous or too self-revelatory to an audience you don't know well.

4. Check to see if your phrasing sounds mechanical or dehumanized, and eliminate any unnecessary technical terms.

5. For every piece of factual evidence you include in your speech, have available another piece for use in the question-and-answer session.

6. Avoid being overly familiar with your audience; nobody wants a speaker to pander to them.

7. From time to time, try engaging the audience in *restricted* dialogue by asking questions that can be answered quickly and helpfully.

8. If you find a natural opening to do so, refer to some concrete event about which you and your audience have special knowledge.

9. Try to approach the golden mean in speaking by being candid without being blunt, flexible without being spineless, and graceful without being pompous.

10. Remember the Great Double Law of Speaking: The more you concentrate on your notes, the less you'll notice your audience; the harder you try to impress people, the emptier your ideas will sound.

CHAPTER 3

The Initial Speech

There was a man with nothing to say
  And no way of keeping still.

"I like to listen to my own voice,"
  Said he, "And so I will."

"If I had to wait for something to say,"
  Said he, "I would be so old

Before I got to make a speech
  That everything would have been told

A thousand times. Then who would come
  To listen, and rejoice

At the nothing at all I have to say
  In my rather remarkable voice?

I can sound it high. I can sound it low.
  I can say 'harrumph!' so loud

It booms like a ton of TNT
  Set off in a thundercloud.

I can whisper and hiss as soft as sleet
When it falls in the silent sea.

I can wink and imply on the sneak and
The sly—
So slyly and sneakily

That the people I bribe to listen and cheer
Are so thoroughly overawed

By my artistry that they look at me
And no man dares applaud.

—For fear, of course, they might break
The spell

Of the truly remarkable way

I fill the room with the boom-boom-boom
Of my nothing-whatever-to-say.

With the whisper and hiss and the sneak
And sly

And the ever rising swell

Of my boom-boom-boom as I fill the room
With the nothing I tell so well."[1]

If you are like most people, you're probably a bit envious of a person who can sound good even when he or she has nothing to say. Most of you have quite the opposite problem: You spend a good deal of time carefully writing a speech and practicing it until you become convinced that you have a truly great oration on your hands. Then you discover that those ideas that seemed so clear and exciting to you in private somehow seem much less compelling when actually expressed. You march up to the front of the classroom on the day of your speech, put your notes on the podium, look confidently at your fellow students in the audience, but then something goes awry. Perhaps during your speech you wonder if you are making any contact with the audience at all, or you feel that you are trying to shout your message across the Grand Canyon. Novice orators often discover that those speeches that looked so good on paper the night before seem to generate

[1] J. Ciardi, "About Making Speeches: For Little Spiro," Copyright 1971 by Saturday Review Co. First appeared in *Saturday Review*, February 6, 1971. Used with permission.

nothing but blank faces, fidgeting, and audible sighs when actually delivered before an audience. Why, you might ask, is it sometimes so hard to find effective and interesting words for our ideas, and why do speeches that look good on one's note cards sometimes sound so dull and lifeless when actually spoken? Why can't *we* fill the room with boom-boom-boom?

Perhaps this chapter will help you do so. It will be, we hope, a practical adjunct to the general ideas advanced in Chapters 1 and 2. Our purpose in this chapter is to help you prepare for the first speech experience. We do not know, of course, what your personal history of public speaking has been like. Probably, you were asked at some point in your early youth to recite a piece, present an oral book report, or make an announcement to members of a religious group. More than likely, these speaking experiences were informal and were not etched into your memory. Rather than dismiss these childhood experiences as irrelevant, however, we urge you to contemplate them anew and to discover in them the pleasures and pains of speech sketched out in Chapter 1.

We also urge you to think about them in connection with the present chapter on "initial" speech experiences. In this chapter, we shall address the basic problems and resources all of us face when first attempting to master the art of public speaking. Our discussion will be practical rather than theoretical, and we shall offer our opinions freely about what constitutes speaking effectiveness. We shall not, of course, cover all of the nuances of public speaking in this chapter, but we will mention how to select, develop, and organize speech topics. The advice we offer you will not be foolproof. We will not insure you against confusion or frustration. But we do trust that you will find our advice sensible—ideas you probably would not have thought of on your own. We shall, as always, try to detail the *reasons* supporting our suggestions to you. This chapter is meant to be a primer, not a catechism. We would prefer that you regard our remarks not so much as *our* answers but as questions *you* would be wise to ask yourself.

Speaking and Writing

Most people today are taught at great length the art of writing essays. Stop for a moment and ask yourself how many English courses you've taken in high school and college in which you have been asked to write essays. Although many of us may still find it difficult to write a good essay, at least we have received a good deal of training and practice in that form of communication. The trouble begins, however, when you are asked to give a speech, and you prepare that speech as if you were writing an essay. A speech is a unique animal. Being unaware of the difference between a speech and an essay causes many problems for people interested in getting their ideas across to an audience. So before you ever sit down to think about your first *speech*, let's be sure that you don't "think essay" inadvertently. What are some of the differences between a speech and an essay?

A Speech Is Time- and Situation-Bound

One major difference between a speech and an essay is that a speech is given at one time in a particular place, whereas an essay can be read whenever and wherever we choose. Some essays, of course, may respond to some particular problem or occurrence. For instance, a sudden revolution in a South American country or an upcoming vote on a school bond issue may call forth letters to the editor of the local paper. But by and large the best essays are those that retain their relevance and interest for many kinds of people in many different times and places. A good essay on the structure of the federal government, for instance, can be read in Boston in 1800, in Atlanta in 1863, and in Washington in 1950, and it will still be interesting and valuable for the different persons who choose to read it. A good essay is *timeless*; if it refers only to what is happening in Poughkeepsie, New York, on October 3, 1962, then its value will often diminish outside of that time and place. Such an essay would become, in effect, a piece of journalism.

A speech, however, is given at a particular time in a particular place before a particular group of people. Although some speeches also deal with timeless issues, they typically consider and respond to immediate problems and solutions. Suppose, for example, that you wish to give a speech about the high tuition at your school. It will matter considerably who hears the speech and when you give it. Will you speak to a group of administrators or a group of students? Will you time the speech early in the term, when tuition has just been paid, or later, when money matters may seem less pressing? A good speech must be adapted to the immediate time and place, and must be seen as relevant to the specific audience you'll be addressing (as we suggested in Chapter 2).

For instance, if you are speaking on the problems of pollution, you might use as examples the factories in your town or perhaps the power plant at your school or the mines nearby in your state. Perhaps because listeners hear so much talk in their daily lives, they become more impatient with irrelevant speech than they do with a remotely interesting essay. A speaker speaks to contemporaries, whereas an author often writes for the ages.

A Speech Is a Personal Contact

Another major difference between a speech and an essay (already hinted at in Chapter 1) is that speech presumes personal contact between living, breathing human beings, whereas an essay is rather antiseptic in contrast. Often, one can read a good essay, enjoy it, and still have no idea who wrote it. And it may not matter who the author is either, because the ideas and information expressed in the essay compel one so strongly. An essay is *topic*-centered; it discusses and develops a particular idea. The attractiveness of that idea is somewhat independent of its promulgator. Or, to be more precise, its promulgator's credibility is *not an ever-present consideration* for the average reader. An author does not always "stand with" his or her book or article.

A speech, on the other hand, is *audience*-centered, and a speaker is always "on the line." Except for rare times when a speech is broadcast over television or radio, most speeches bring together people in close proximity. A speaker, unlike an author, always "goes with" his or her words. Because people are in each other's physical presence in spoken interaction, a speech must be somewhat different from an essay if it is to be successful.

One important practical implication of the "personalness" of speech is that good speakers typically talk about subjects with which they are personally involved. People can read essays on space technology, but *they attend speeches to see space technologists.* A speaker who attempts to hide his or her feelings about a topic when speaking is thereby refusing to use one of the built-in assets of human speech.

Another practical implication is that the speaker must adapt his or her remarks to the specific people who have come to listen. Suppose, for example, that a speaker wants to give a speech on agricultural pest control. Is he or she speaking to a collection of farmers or a group of English majors? Such a speaker could be more technical for the farmers but would have to adjust the topic to more general aspects of pest control for the English majors (e.g., speak about disease-bearing pests). A speech that ignores its intended audience is an ungracious, and ultimately unsuccessful, speech.

Because a speech involves personal contact between people, speakers must assume responsibility for not abusing the control they have over audiences. When they speak, speakers take up the time of a number of people and thus incur the obligation of using their audiences' time well. They should speak on significant and challenging topics. They should attempt to "stretch" themselves and their listeners intellectually. Speakers who have been asked to speak for particular lengths of time should observe those requests. Anyone who has suffered through a speech that lasted twice as long as it should have knows how insulting a public speaker can be. Thus, to engage in the act of speaking is to incur very real—and very personal—responsibilities.

Finally, speakers who remember that *a speech is a personal contact rather than a performance* should feel much more at ease while speaking. Stage fright is a universal problem (as we noted in Chapter 1). Typically, people feel uneasy when speaking if they feel that they must "perform" for the audience or give a razzle-dazzle display of oratorical prowess. A better approach to take is to view a speech as a chance to communicate with people, to establish or reestablish a personal relationship borne out of concern for a topic of manifest importance. Speakers who remember that a speech provides an opportunity for them to talk to people and to share ideas, rather than a chance to display verbal pyrotechnics, will make better use of their personal contact with their listeners and as a result probably will feel more at ease when speaking.

A Speech Uses the Aural/Oral Channel

The most obvious difference between a speech and an essay is the different communicative channels involved. A "channel" is a way of getting a message across to someone—a blackboard, a signal flare, a radio broadcast. Essays use the channel of written or printed communication, whereas speeches use the "aural" (hearing) and "oral" (speaking) channels.

Because an essay uses the written channel, communication proceeds almost entirely at the choice of the receiver. If a person becomes bored or tired while reading a book, he or she can put it down, thus ending the communicative interchange. The communication is resumed only when the reader feels motivated to do so. If the book is unclear, the reader can reread portions of it. If unfamiliar terms are encountered, the reader can stop to look up the definitions of those terms in a dictionary. In written communication, the reader controls the action.

Because speech is spoken and heard, however, the sender's responsibility for communication increases dramatically. For that reason, a speaker must be careful to design the speech so that it can be easily heard and understood by the audience—*upon first and only hearing.* If a speaker goes along at a tremendous pace, he or she may leave the audience behind. If the speaker uses unfamiliar terms or concepts, the speaker may lose the audience's attention because of their inability to look up the ambiguous words while listening. Ideas in a speech must be organized with listeners in mind. Spoken words, unlike written ones, are highly ephemeral. Because this is so, listeners become more easily confused and frustrated than do readers.

Practical Implications

As will be stressed later, the very special channel through which speech passes requires that a speaker watch carefully for certain things. First, work for *simplicity* of language and organization; a ten-syllable word is nobody's friend. Try not to cover every angle of a topic but focus on two or three main points. Use plenty of concrete examples and illustrations to let the audience "see" what you mean; unlike a writer, a speaker *must be* the reader's eyes. Give the audience *signposts* in the speech: Tell your audience where you are going, which main point you are currently dealing with and, at the end, where you have taken them. Because most of us have had so much experience with writing essays and less occasion for speaking in public, it is easy to forget the functional differences between speaking and writing. To forget these differences, however, is to produce a speech that is less than it could be. Orality, we are suggesting, is a demanding master indeed.

Choosing and Developing a Topic

The first problem that confronts most speakers is finding something to say. Actually, most of us have plenty to say; we just have trouble putting those ideas into a form that can be handled in the short time available for speaking. Speakers should settle on a topic that is interesting and challenging, as well as one that they would really like to talk to other people about. Thus, the first step in the process of finding a topic is to determine a general topic area.

Discovering General Ideas for a Topic

Few things in the world of public speaking are more depressing than sitting alone in a room at 2 A.M. on the morning before a speech is scheduled to be delivered, trying to think of a topic. So, our first piece of advice is to start thinking of topics *now*. Don't try to force a topic at the last minute. Make communicative life easier by giving yourself time to think through your thoughts carefully and completely.

In addition to planning ahead, try *brainstorming*. By that we mean writing down all of the topics that come to mind without rejecting any of them at first blush. The time for dismissing ideas comes later. Initially, speakers should let their minds run free; they should jot down any idea that comes to them, measuring neither its interest nor its complexity. Many good but difficult topics are lost by being rejected too soon for the wrong reasons.

So, you find yourself sitting in the library trying to brainstorm a topic. Where can you turn for inspiration? One good source of speech topics is your public speaking class itself. Think about the public speeches and informal comments other people have already presented in class. Perhaps you disagreed vigorously with a position another student took; try presenting the opposing viewpoint in your next speech. Perhaps another student began an idea that was never really developed; you might expand that idea into a speech of your own.

Here is a rhetorical law: A good speech deals with a topic that the speaker cares about. One good way to think about speech topics is to ask yourself the last time you felt strongly about something—something that excited or depressed you, that made you feel very angry or very happy. Were you upset at being unable to finish your racketball game because your court time had expired? Perhaps you could speak on the need for more athletic facilities at your school. Were you elated over the latest peace initiatives in the Middle East? Perhaps you could speak about America's role in that part of the world and what it might mean for the average American. Emotion, we are suggesting, is an infallible guide to a speech topic.

Sometimes, speech topics can be found in the communications other people address *to us*. For instance, consider what you have been told recently by television, radio, magazines, books, and so on. Has any of it angered or exalted you? What if you happened to see elderly people portrayed as senile, incompetent, or harmfully saccharine on a television commercial? That commercial may prompt you to speak on the problem of prejudice against the elderly in our society. Things you have heard in your everyday interactions with others might also be a source of ideas. For instance, most people find it difficult to accept compliments gracefully. Perhaps you could give a speech on the need to be able to do so in society. By listening carefully to the world around you, you can learn much about what interests people generally, what ideas are in the wind. Speech topics generated from such sources have the added advantage of having been "pretested" for social relevance.

Generating Specific Ideas Within a Topic

Once a speaker has settled upon a general topic area that seems interesting and compelling, generating subideas becomes important. Eventually, it will become important to narrow this list of ideas so that one's speech has manageable proportions. Initially, however, it is important to do nothing that could cause the creative juices to stop flowing. But how can one go about generating such a large supply of ideas? How can a speaker be assured that he or she has pulled together a sufficient amount of information for public presentation? Now, if he or she "just thought about the topic" for a while, an appropriate number of ideas might emerge. But we would like to encourage the use of another method for generating communicable ideas, a procedure that operates somewhat systematically.

Opposed to the "Method of Just Thinking" is what has been called a "Topical System for Generating Thoughts."[2] Now while this system is no press-a-button-get-a-thought twentieth-century monster, it is a system for recalling information that a speaker may not have thought of otherwise. By thinking of a particular subject matter in terms of universal topics, a speaker can "retrieve" information previously "stored" within him or her. Thus, the topical system works in an auto-suggestive manner—the aspiring speaker becomes his or her own conscious computer. Research has documented that more and better ideas can be generated with its use than without it.

Though scary at first, the system is not all that complicated and it just might help you to answer that nagging question, "Well, how am I going to come up with something to say about welfare rights in speech class on Tuesday?" The topical system includes the following themes, which can be developed in any speech:

1. Existence or nonexistence of things

2. Degree or quantity of things, forces, etc.

3. Spatial attributes, including adjacency, distribution, place

4. Attributes of time

5. Motion or activity

6. Form, either physical or abstract

7. Substance: physical, abstract, or psychophysical

8. Capacity to change, including predictability

9. Potency: power or energy, including capacity to further or hinder anything

10. Desirability in terms of rewards or punishments

11. Feasibility: workability or practicability

12. Causality: the relation of causes to effects, effects to effects, adequacy of causes, etc.

13. Correlation: coexistence or coordination of things, forces, etc.

14. Genus-species relationships

[2]J. F. Wilson and C. Arnold, *Public Speaking as a Liberal Art*, 2nd ed. (Boston: Allyn and Bacon, 1968), p. 115. Reprinted by permission of Allyn and Bacon, Inc.

15. Similarity or dissimilarity
16. Possibility or impossibility[3]

To illustrate the use of the system, consider the speech pathology major who decides to present an address on hearing disorders. She is aware of the facts, understands the theories, is familiar with the research, but really is not sure of what to say and what not to say in a speech on the subject. By using the categories in the topical system, our speaker may be "reminded" of the essential features of hearing disorders and can then develop these features by making recourse to more specific research material. Let us consider each of the "generators," and see how it might work to "remind" our speaker of the salient features of hearing disorders, features that may have been "forgotten" had the topical system not been used:

1. Existence: over 50 percent of the elderly have hearing disorders, workers in a noisy environment are especially prone to hearing problems

2. Degree: mild ringing in ears, total deafness, death

3. Space: intimate connection between brain and ear, ear covers only small area

4. Time: can lose hearing overnight, many middle-ear infections occur between 4 and 7 years of age

5. Motion: fast movement can cause dizziness because of inner-ear problems, rapidly moving sound waves can cause temporary loss

6. Form: some hearing losses are surgically correctable, some can be helped by hearing aids

7. Substance: roots of hearing loss can be physical, psychological, psychophysical

8. Capacity to change: inner ear can improve itself, surgery can correct middle-ear damage

9. Potency: can cause death, inability to discriminate any sort of speech

10. Desirability: hinders social interactions, can adversely affect employment opportunities

[3]W. Nelson, "Topoi: Functional in Human Recall," *Speech Monographs*, 38:121–126 (1970).

11. Feasibility: auditory training for those with residual hearing problems, lip reading training

12. Causality: abnormal growths in ear cause problems, high fever and infection can also cause damage

13. Correlation: related to disease, psychological problems

14. Genus-species: types of hearing losses are middle-ear infection, vertigo, partial deafness

15. Similarity: distinction between middle-ear and inner-ear problems, middle- versus outer-ear maladies

16. Possibility: inner ear cannot be corrected by surgery, hearing aid can help those with inner-ear damage

There is every reason to suspect that our speaker will come up with these ideas by just sitting down and contemplating the subject of hearing disorders. The value of this system, however, is that it efficiently systematizes the search for discussable thoughts and hence may relieve the speaker of searching through old notes, reference books, and so on. If used conscientiously, the system can save the speaker time, effort, and very possibly might add to the inclusiveness and impact of the speech itself.

Naturally, in any given setting, some of the topics will be more helpful generators than will others. For example, one speaker might get more mileage out of time, space, form, and feasibility in preparing for a speech on bridge stresses, whereas another speaker may be assisted more by desirability, similarity, and possibility when discussing the plays of Molière. One of the handy features of this system is that it can be used over and over again each time a different topic is used in connection with it.

Adapting the Topic to the Audience

By now, a speaker should have generated a good deal that *could* be said about a topic. But speakers need to be able to narrow their scope since audience fatigue and the time available for the speech limit what can be said about the matter in question. Because you don't want to bury your audience under too many points, careful consideration must be given to what *actually* can be said.

In narrowing the scope of a topic, the best guide in making one's choices will be the audience. Remember that you are not just talking to anyone; you are talking to a particular group of people. Furthermore, adapting a topic so that it interests and influences that particular audience is the main business of a speech. In choosing what to say on a topic, then, a speaker should consider what an audience needs to hear, what they will be able to understand, and which ideas they can accept (given their current ideas and beliefs).

We have already discussed the notion that a speaker needs to adapt his or her ideas to the listeners at hand. Adaptation means that, sometimes, what a speaker would very much like to say may be something that the audience will not understand or cannot accept. Often in our lives, we will want to express our feelings without reservation. But to be an effective speaker, you cannot say anything you please unless, of course, you enjoy talking to yourself. Thus, let us discuss some of the ways of winnowing the ideas already generated about a given speech topic.

A topic must be interesting. Obviously, one way to narrow a topic is to select exclusively those issues that will interest the greatest number of people in the audience at hand. This is a natural impulse. A speaker wants to insure that people find something to think about in a speech, that they see the speech as relevant to themselves, and that they pay attention to him or her.

The problem with setting a goal of interesting the greatest number of people possible is that for nearly any topic a significant percentage of an audience will not be very interested *initially* in what a speaker has to say. It is sad but true. You may feel that you have the most fascinating topic in the world, but it probably isn't going to capture the hearts and minds of everyone in the audience when you first announce it. Even though every member of your audience would be devastatingly affected by such a disaster as nuclear war, not everyone will find that topic interesting. Thus, we can posit another law of communication: *No speech topic has inherent interest.* It is your job as a speaker to create or build interest in it.

Although some people may not be interested in a topic like nuclear war, they are certainly interested in something. If a speaker can link a topic to these other issues in which people are interested, he or she can capture the attention of those who don't initially care about the topic at hand. In other words, for every focused, specific topic, there are also broader issues potentially relatable to that topic.

For instance, let's suppose that you want to persuade listeners to take adult education classes after they graduate. Because such a topic lacks inherent interest for all persons, you must search for "neighboring" ideas that already interest listeners. One such issue might be career success. You might argue that people who take adult education classes go further in their jobs. Or you might relate adult education to one's need for social contacts and suggest that one can meet interesting people in adult education classes. In making the topic interesting, then, good speakers maintain a balance between a sharp focus on the topic itself and the broader issues that might expand the appeal of the topic.

Don't be too focused. One pitfall to avoid is being so narrow in your scope that few people find the topic interesting or worthwhile. For instance, suppose a student wants to argue that the paper wrappers surrounding fast-food hamburgers should be outlawed. Such a focus is quite narrow and hence not likely to pique listeners' curiosity initially. How might such a topic be broadened? Although people might not care about hamburger wrappers, they may care a good deal about keeping the environment unsullied. By relating the matter of wrappers to the environmental issues of littering and tree preservation, a speaker might avoid the pitfall of being so focused that his or her subject appears arcane and hence irrelevant in a social setting.

Don't be too broad. On the other hand, grand generalities are to be avoided as well. A speech might fall into such a trap if its topic were "Honesty" or "Why You Should Have Friends." In such cases, the speaker needs to narrow the discussion to a specific core of issues. If listeners do not see explicitly how a speech applies to their everyday lives, if they don't understand what the speaker is asking them to do or to think, they are likely to ignore it. Perhaps speakers are tempted to talk on subjects like "The Need to Be Successful" because they assume that such a topic will interest everybody. But listeners are a bit on the lazy side and a bit selfish to boot. They seek to know how a topic is relevant to their particular circumstances and life situations. Knowing this, perhaps a speaker bent on talking about "Honesty" should do so at income-tax time, thereby "situationalizing" an otherwise obscure topic.

A topic must be challenging. We have already discussed the idea that speech involves personal contact. In addition to occupying the time of several people, speakers ask their audiences to risk changing their minds to adopt new behaviors as a result of listening to the speech. Because speakers are making such demands of their listeners, they should favor worthwhile and challenging topics. What do we mean when we say that a topic should be challenging? A challenging topic is one that both speaker and audience care about and in which they are involved. A speech on the design of eighteenth-century snuff boxes, for instance, is not likely to generate much audience attention and support because it fails (on its face, at least) to open new and immediately relevant vistas for its hearers. To insure that a topic is challenging as well as interesting, then, speakers should ask themselves three questions about the topic:

1. *Why do I care about this topic?* The best speeches are those in which the speaker becomes personally involved in the topic. One of your authors once heard a classroom speech by a woman who urged her listeners to eat insects as part of their daily diets. The very first question she was asked after the speech was whether she, herself, ate insects on a regular basis. She had to reply that she never had done so and, of course, the impact of her speech was lost entirely. She failed to answer the question, "Why do I care about this?" Similarly, a speech on the challenge of sports is likely to be more effective when given by an athlete than when delivered by a Saturday afternoon beer-and-popcorn sideliner.

2. *Why should the audience care?* It is difficult to challenge an audience or to educate them significantly if your topic is remote, relevant only to you. For instance, suppose that you were raised on a hog farm and that the science of raising swine is your life's work and ambition. You can answer the first question of "Why do I care about this topic?" but many audiences will greet a speech on this topic with something less than unbridled interest. Such listeners may not see what feed mixes, temperature control, and antibiotics have to do with the lives they lead. And if the speech focuses mainly around how to get a pig into a truck, you may lose the audience entirely! Perhaps, instead, you could discuss hogs by mentioning the quality of their meat, their important by-products, or the significance they have for your state's economy. Sometimes, of course, the search for such "relatable" ideas can be taxing. Without that search, however, communication often ceases.

3. *Why should I care whether they care?* In most speeches, a speaker asks the audience to think or do or see something in his or her way. Perhaps a speaker wants an audience to ride bicycles instead of cars, to vote in local elections, or to support a new design for carburetors. This prompts yet another law of communication: Any time you ask something of someone else, you risk being thought a *busybody*; you risk sounding *preachy*. Few of us like to have others tell us what to do. Imagine, for example, that your neighbor knocks on your door one evening and announces that he has found a new way to brush teeth and that he wants you to brush your teeth that way from now on. You would probably be offended by such an intrusion. It is none of your neighbor's business how you brush your teeth, unless, perhaps, you live adjacent to a dental hygienist. The same implicit principle holds true in a public speech: I don't want to be told what to do or think unless you have established that it is your business to do such telling.

How does one get the audience to do or think certain things without being preachy? Our answer: by speaking about those subjects in which the speaker really has some personal stake in what the audience thinks. Even if you have found some fabulous new way of tying your shoes, for example, and even if your audience will suffer the agonies of the ignorant without your revelation, it is probably impossible for you to convince them that *you* have a right or obligation to lift the scales from their eyes on this matter. The pitfall of preachiness lurks in many topics. Speeches that ask the audience to lose weight or to avoid obesity border on preachiness, especially when delivered to an audience of strangers.

While many topics run the risk of making the speaker sound like a busybody, most topics include some set of issues out of which *common concern* can be fashioned, out of which a speaker's right to make requests of an audience can be established. Consider the topic of smoking, for instance. A speaker who urges the audience to give up smoking because it undermines their health risks being thought a busybody—if the audience becomes ill from smoking, that's their business. On the other hand, a speaker who asks the audience to refrain from smoking *because it affects the health of others, including the speaker,* is on firmer ground. That angle on the topic of smoking is very much the speaker's business.

What have we learned about selecting and narrowing speech topics? A truly interesting topic has something to offer the greatest possible number of people in the audience. The topic must have a specific focus, but it must also be related to broad human issues. The topic should be one in which the speaker and audience are personally involved and about which the speaker has a right to talk to the audience (and to ask for their help or cooperation in some way). Remember, speakers can rarely say anything they please or talk about any topic that springs to mind. To presume the contrary is to engage in a kind of communicative arrogance, which listeners rarely forgive.

Organizing the Speech: Principles

By now, you should have chosen a topic that both you and your audience can be made to care about, and you should have some idea of what you can say that will make that topic interesting to the greatest number of listeners. Now it is time to shape those ideas so that the audience can follow you easily. A speech will be clear if the audience can think along with it, if they know which point the speaker is on, and which general ideas the speech will be covering and when. Let's start at the beginning and talk about what to do in the *introduction* of a speech.

Getting an Audience's Attention

The very first priority in a speech, of course, is to get the audience's attention. After all, in the first minute of a speech, the audience decides whether to pay close attention to the speaker or retreat to the privacy of their own thoughts. If an introduction promises nothing more exciting than a detailed description of how to boil water, the audience will resign themselves to a mental nap. But what sorts of things generate and maintain listeners' attention?

1. *Examples and illustrations.* A detailed example is often a clear and easily understood method of introducing an audience to the meat of a speech. People normally grasp examples immediately. The best introductory example is one that is directly related to a topic and is sufficiently detailed and vividly presented. Liveliness in an example usually comes from adding *detail*. For instance, in a speech on the joys of skiing, a speaker might begin the speech by describing the fragrance of the pine trees, the sun sparkling on the snow, the wind whistling past one's face, the awesome grandeur of the mountains, and the intense pounding of one's heart while zooming down a mountainside. Examples containing this amount of detail rarely fail to rivet the attention of listeners.

2. *Strong but simple ideas.* The audience is not ready for a complex, difficult argument when a speech commences. They must be eased into the topic in an attention-getting way that is strongly and clearly expressed. For instance, suppose that you wish to defend the notion that in our economy there is a direct trade-off between unemployment and inflation. If you begin such a speech by droning on about supply and demand curves and the Federal Reserve system, you will tuck the audience in bed without question. Instead, how about saying this: "We have a choice in our country today—either we see prices go skyrocketing right through the roof or else some of us relinquish our jobs." Having started on such a controversial note, the speaker can then develop those ideas in greater detail.

3. *Humor.* Humor, if appropriate to the topic, is often an effective way to begin a speech. All of us like to laugh; audiences are no different. This does not mean that you are called upon to do your Johnny Carson imitation; the point is to introduce the topic, not

merely to entertain people. But humor relevant to your topic is often helpful. Another positive result of humor is that it helps you as a speaker to relax by loosening the vocal and breathing mechanisms. Thus, even if nobody else laughs at your joke, it helps you to bridge the gap between quietude and public talking.

What to Include in the Introduction

After the audience is informed of the topic, the speaker must prepare them for listening to the remainder of the speech. One way to do that is to forecast briefly what will eventually be asked of the audience. If the audience knows where the speech is heading and where it will terminate, they can follow it more easily in process. The specific request a speaker will eventually make of an audience is often called the *thesis statement*.

A thesis statement should clearly state the speaker's purpose, what the audience will be doing or thinking if it adheres to the speaker's remarks. For instance, the statement "I would like to discuss how to improve housing around this university" is a thesis statement, but not a very good one because it fails to tell the audience what *they should think or do as a result of listening to the speech.*

A better thesis statement would be, "I hope this speech convinces you to apply pressure to our city council for improved housing on the perimeter of the university." Such a thesis statement should come *after* the topic has been introduced and after favorable attention has been secured. Good speakers do *not* make the thesis statement the first matter of business: "I want to talk to you today about . . . " Such a manner of starting a speech is not attention-getting, does not introduce the topic in a way that makes the audience want to listen for more, and sounds formula-ridden as well.

Another thing to include in an introduction is the *central idea* that the speaker will pursue throughout the speech. A central idea is an idea or concept that helps tie the speech together, the idea that the speaker especially wants to impress most upon his or her audience. Often, the central theme is mentioned in connection with the thesis statement itself. On the housing topic, for instance, a central theme might be, "Conditions are intolerable around campus because students don't use their political power." Each main point in the subsequent speech would then be linked to that central idea and developed further.

Another component of the introduction should be a brief *overview* of the main points to be covered in the speech. An experienced speaker often groups ideas into just a few main points. If the speaker forecasts those points for the audience, the audience will be more likely to listen for the ideas and hence follow the speech more easily as the various points are addressed. An overview that would dovetail with our thesis statement about housing conditions might go something like this: "We need to look at three important issues related to student housing: insufficient housing, available housing that is too expensive, and available housing that is unsafe and poorly maintained." The issues of availability, cost, and safety then become the three main points of the speech.

The introduction of a speech is also the appropriate time to begin to show audiences how the topic is relevant to them, how it is relevant to the speaker, and how it relates to other, broader issues that may concern listeners. Our student speaker, for example, might mention how many students live in off-campus housing to show how the topic relates to the audience. And since our speaker also wants to maintain the interest of students living in dormitories, he or she could briefly mention that the deplorable housing conditions signal unsavory attitudes toward all students by the city council, a *broad issue* that should interest students whether they live on or off campus.

The Body of the Speech

We now come to the body of the speech which contains a speaker's amplified arguments. The first step is to insure that the speech has but a few main points; even though there may be dozens of things one *could* say on a topic, a speaker will only be able to cover a few main issues in the modest time normally available. No absolute number of points can be recommended for all speeches in all circumstances, but for speeches lasting 10 minutes or less, three main points are normally just about right. Once the main points have been determined, several other important decisions must be made.

What to put under main points. The next step is to start fleshing out the main points you've selected by asking yourself which subsidiary issues, arguments, and examples seem appropriate to each main point. It may be easier for you to do so if you think of ideas as being boxlike structures. The first box in the housing topic bears the label "Housing is not available"; the second, "Housing is too expensive"; and the third, "Housing is unsafe." The speaker can then "deal" the more detailed issues, arguments, and examples into the appropriate boxes. Thus, if our speaker wants to tell the audience about a friend whose building caught fire three times last year, he or she will subsume that example under point 3. Describing the difficulties experienced by students from out of town who undergo long searches for housing will fit neatly under point 1. As a speaker sorts through the more detailed information he or she has assembled and puts them in the appropriate "boxes," the speech will begin to take shape.

In fleshing out the main points of a speech, speakers should avoid two temptations. One tendency is to put a great many subideas or examples under one main point. Such an impulse will surely lead to listeners' confusion, for subsuming a dozen subpoints under a single main point is nearly as problematic as having a dozen main points in the first place. The solution? Cut back and simplify.

A second temptation is to place the same idea under more than one main point. For example, a speaker may want to argue that it is especially deplorable that housing is so *unsafe* given its *high cost*. Such an argument might well be placed under either main points 2 or 3. But to do so would be to clutter up the speech, to risk confusing listeners as to the proper subordination of ideas, and to place a burden on the speaker of constantly reorienting his or her audience. It is far better to make arbitrary designations of subpoint placement than to jump back and forth to the same point several times in the same speech. Once a point has been dealt with, the speaker should move on.

After the speaker has sorted subpoints under the appropriate main points, he or she should insure that examples, explanations, or arguments are placed under each main point as well. Above all, a speaker should not construct a main point out of nothing but examples. The third main point about unsafe housing, for instance, could easily turn into a long and pointless tirade about "the dumps I have lived in." Thus, be sure to combine examples with *arguments* so that the speech draws lessons and memorable conclusions from those examples presented. On the other hand, a speaker should not just argue in the abstract (say, under main point 2) that housing costs are too high. It is helpful to give concrete examples of what it costs to live in particular buildings around campus. Good speakers let their arguments and explanations work with examples to prove the main points they are presenting.

How to move between main points. Moving between points, especially between major points, is particularly tricky. Speakers want their listeners to know that they are moving to a different idea because if the listeners don't "change gears" at the appropriate time, they'll try to associate what the speaker is saying now with his or her statements of a few minutes ago. Thus, the transition from one point to another should be smooth and obvious. Avoid simply ending one point, taking a deep breath, and pitching on into the next point. Instead, move between points smoothly by using *signposts* and *transitions*.

A signpost is an announcement of a new point, a way of signaling to the audience that the speaker is changing ideas. The most effective signposts are those that clearly state the new main point using words similar to those used in the overview. The overview for the student housing speech was, "We need to took at three important issues related to student housing: insufficient housing, available housing that is too

expensive, and available housing that is unsafe and poorly maintained."
A good signpost will remind the audience of each of those three main
points as the speaker comes to it—successively—by repeating key words
already used in the overview. The first signpost can repeat the wording
of the overview by saying, "Let's first discuss the idea that *not enough
housing is available* here in Phillipsville." The second signpost could say,
"Another important problem is that *housing is too expensive.*" Your final
signpost could be, "One last issue is the *unsafe and poorly maintained
housing* here in town." When the signpost repeats key words from the
overview, the audience will remember the words and will better realize
that the speaker is announcing a new point.

A *transition* contains the signpost but moves smoothly from the
previous point to the new point. Good transitions explain *why* the
speaker is going from one point to another and thereby links the two
points together. Here is how one might make a transition between
points 2 and 3 in our student housing speech:

> It's clear, then, that the prices of housing here in Phillipsville are way out
> of line. (This sentence sums up the preceding point.) But if we are going to
> spend so much for rent, at least we should get a good, decent apartment for
> our money. (This sentence ties together cost issues from point 1 with safety

and maintenance issues in point 2.) One last issue is how unsafe and poorly maintained most housing is. (That's your signpost, and you're into the next point.)

Concluding the Speech

The conclusion of the speech is important because it is the last chance to influence the audience, to tell them what the speaker wants them to remember above all else. The first part of the conclusion should refer to the thesis statement mentioned in the introduction and remind the audience what they should do or think, given the argument presented thus far. In the student housing speech, the speaker might ask the audience to write letters to members of the city council or perhaps to pressure university officials to ask the city council to take action. A speaker should clarify for the audience exactly *how* they can respond to the speech. That is, a speaker should be specific if he or she asks for some kind of action. For instance, if the speaker asks the audience to write to the city council, he or she might give names and addresses of some members on the council and even suggest some of the phrasings such a letter might contain.

After the speaker makes clear what is wanted of the audience, the speech can be closed. One thing to do here is to *summarize* the speech. That can be done in two ways.

1. If the speech has covered issues that were previously *familiar* to the audience, the speaker can summarize the speech by stressing one main point that he or she wants the audience to remember. That point could very well be the *central theme* set up in the introduction.

2. If the speech covered issues that were *new and unfamiliar* for the audience, then the conclusion should probably restate the main points of the speech very briefly, again repeating the key words used in the overview and in the signposts. Whichever technique the speaker uses, the goal of a conclusion is to remind the audience of the main idea covered in the speech.

Finally, the conclusion should present a final persuasive "pitch" to the audience. This appeal may take the form of one last argument or a recasting of the strongest argument presented in the speech. Perhaps a strong, vivid example or illustration might be most persuasive here. Whichever technique is chosen, the speaker should leave the audience with a good, easily remembered reason to accept what he or she has said.

Organizing the Speech: An Example

On September 15, 1910, Woodrow Wilson accepted his party's nomination for governor of the state of New Jersey. Wilson eventually won that office and went on to become president of the United States. The speech Wilson delivered upon accepting the gubernatorial nomination was his first major political address. Those giving first speeches may feel some sympathy for him! Wilson's speech is remarkably well organized and will be used here as an example of the ideas we've been discussing in the latter part of this chapter.

Acceptance Speech, Democratic Nomination for Governor of New Jersey. Woodrow Wilson, September 15, 1910

(1) You have conferred upon me a very great honor. I accept the nomination you have tendered me with the deepest gratification that you should have thought me worthy to lead the Democrats of New Jersey in this stirring time of opportunity. Even more than the great honor of your nomination, I feel the deep responsibility it imposes upon me; for responsibility is proportioned to opportunity.

(2) As you know, I did not seek this nomination. It has come to me absolutely unsolicited, with the consequence that I shall enter upon the duties of the office of Governor, if elected, with absolutely no pledges of any kind to prevent me from serving the people of the state with singleness of purpose. Not only have no pledges of any kind been given, but none have been proposed or desired. In accepting the nomination, therefore, I am pledging myself only to the service of the people and the party which intends to advance their interests. I cannot but regard these circumstances as marking the beginning of a new and more ideal era in our politics. Certainly they enhance very greatly the honor you have conferred upon me and enlarge the opportunity in equal degree. A day of unselfish purpose is always a day of confident hope.

(3) I feel confident that the people of the state will accept the promises you have made in your platform as made sincerely and with a definite purpose to render them effective service. That platform is sound, explicit, and businesslike. There can be no mistaking what it means; and the voters of the state will know at once that promises so definitely made are made to be kept, not to be evaded. Your declarations deserve and will win their confidence.

(4) But we shall keep it only by performance, by achievement, by proving our capacity to conduct the administration and reform the legislation of the state in the spirit of our declarations with the sagacity and firmness of practical men who not only purpose but also do what is sensible and effective. It is toward this task of performance that my thoughts turn as I think of

soliciting the suffrages of my fellow citizens for the great office of governor of the state.

(5) I shall do so with a very profound sense of the difficulty of solving new and complicated problems in the right way. I take the three great questions before us to be reorganization and economy in administration, the equalization of taxation, and the control of corporations. There are other very important questions that confront us, as they confront all the other states of the Union in this day of readjustment: the question of the proper liability of employers, for example, the question of corrupt practices in elections, the question of conservation; but the three I have named dominate all the rest. It is imperative that we should not only master them, but also act upon them, and act very definitely.

(6) It is first of all necessary that we should act in the right spirit. And the right spirit is not a spirit of hostility. We shall not act either justly or wisely if we attack established interests as public enemies. There has been too much indictment and too little successful prosecution for wrongs done; too much talk and too few practicable suggestions as to what is to be done. It is easy to condemn wrong and to fulminate against wrongdoers in effective rhetorical phrases; but that does not bring either reform or ease of mind. Reform will come only when we have done some careful thinking as to exactly what the things are that are being done in contravention of the public interest and as to the most simple, direct, and effective way of getting at the men who do them. In a self-governed country there is one rule for everybody, and that is the common interest. Everything must be squared by that. We can square it only by knowing its exact shape and movement. Government is not a warfare of interests. We shall not gain our ends by heat and bitterness, which make it impossible to think either calmly or fairly. Government is a matter of common counsel, and everyone must come into the consultation with the purpose to yield to the general view, the view which seems most nearly to correspond with the common interest. If any decline frank conference, keep out, hold off, they must take the consequences and blame only themselves if they are in the end badly served. There must be implacable determination to see the right done, but strong purpose, which does not flinch because some must suffer, is perfectly compatible with fairness and justice and a clear view of the actual facts.

(7) This should be our spirit in the matter of reform, and this our method. And in this spirit we should do very definite things. It is obvious even to a casual observer that the administration of the state has been unnecessarily complicated and elaborated, too many separate commissions and boards set up, business methods neglected, money wasted, and a state of affairs brought about of which a successful business concern would be ashamed. No doubt the increase of state expenditures that has marked the last decade has been in part

due to a necessary and desirable increase of function on the part of the state; but it is only too evident that no study of economy has been made, and that a careful reconsideration and reorganization of the administrative processes of the state would result in great savings and in enhanced responsibility on the part of those who are entrusted with the important work of government.

(8) Our system of taxation is as ill-digested, as piecemeal, and as haphazard as our system of administration. It cannot be changed suddenly or too radically, but many changes should be inaugurated and the whole system by degrees reconsidered and altered so as to fit modern economic conditions more equitably. Above all, the methods of assessment should be changed, in order that inequalities between the taxes of individuals and the taxes of corporations, for example, should be entirely eliminated. It is not necessary for the maintenance of our modern industrial enterprise that corporations should be indulged or favored in the matter of taxation, and it is extremely demoralizing that they should be. Such inequalities should be effectually removed by law and by the action of the tax-assessing authorities of the state and of the localities. This is a matter which will require dispassionate study and action based, not upon hostility, but upon the common interest.

(9) The question of the control of corporations is a very difficult one, upon which no man can speak with confidence; but some things are plain. It is plain, so far as New Jersey is concerned, that we must have a public service commission with the amplest powers to oversee and regulate the administration of public-service corporations throughout the state. We have abundant experience elsewhere to guide us in this matter, from the admirable commission so long in successful operation in Wisconsin to the latest legislation of sister states. We need have no doubt of our right course of action here.

(10) It is the states, not the Federal authorities, that create corporations. The regulation of corporations is the duty of the state much more directly than it is the duty of the Government of the United States. It is my strong hope that New Jersey may lead the way in reform by scrutinizing very carefully the enterprises she consents to incorporate, their make-up, their objects, the basis and method of their capitalization, their organization with respect to liability to control by the state, their conformity to state and Federal statute. This can be done, and done effectually. I covet for New Jersey the honor of doing it.

(11) And so, also, gentlemen, with every other question we face. Let us face it in the spirit of service and with the careful, practical sense of men of affairs. We shall not ask the voters of the state to lend us their suffrages merely because we call ourselves Democrats, but because we mean to serve them like honest and public-spirited men, true Democrats because true lovers of the common interest, servants of no special group of men or of interests, students of the interest of the people and of the country.

(12) The future is not for parties "playing politics," but for measures conceived in the largest spirit, pushed by parties whose leaders are statesmen, not demagogues, who love, not their offices, but their duty and their opportunity for service. We are witnessing a renaissance of public spirit, a reawakening of sober public opinion, a revival of the power of the people, the beginning of an age of thoughtful reconstruction that makes our thought hark back to the great age in which Democracy was set up in America. With the new age, we shall show a new spirit. We shall serve justice and candor, and all things that make for the right. Is not our own ancient party the party disciplined and made ready for this great task? Shall we not forget ourselves in making it the instrument of righteousness for the state and for the nation?

(13) When I think of the flag which our ships carry, the only touch of color about them, the only thing that moves as if it had a settled spirit in it— in their solid structure, it seems to me I see alternate strips of parchment upon which are written the rights of liberty and justice and strips of blood spilled to vindicate those rights, and then—in the corner—a prediction of the blue serene into which every nation may swim that stands for these great things.[4]

The Introduction

When he gave this speech, Wilson commanded the attention of his audience in a way that few people do in college classroom speaking. But notice that he still begins his speech with forceful, direct, yet simply stated ideas. He states those ideas in the first paragraph. Wilson explains in the second paragraph what his involvement in the topic is: He did not actively seek the nomination, but since he won it he intends to serve the people's best interests unselfishly. In the third paragraph, Wilson argues that the party's platform and principles are indeed relevant to the audience and to the people of New Jersey; he asserts that these principles are "businesslike" and therefore useful to the audience.

The last sentence of the fourth paragraph contains Wilson's thesis statement. Obviously, his purpose is to persuade people to vote for him on the basis of the performance he promises. He clearly states that he will ask the audience for their votes ("suffrages") on the basis of his "performance."

Wilson's fifth paragraph contains an unusually clear, simple, and direct overview: "I take the three great questions before us to be reorganization and economy in administration, the equalization of taxation, and the control of corporations." After announcing the main points he

---

[4]W. Wilson, "First Political Address," in *A Treasury of the World's Great Speeches*, ed. H. Peterson (New York: Simon and Schuster, 1965), pp. 686–689.

will cover, he wisely limits his topic by making clear to the audience what he will not mention so that he can devote more attention to his well-chosen focus.

Paragraph 6 sets up a central theme in the speech that will serve to tie the main points together. That theme is the idea of governing in the "common interest," seeking "common counsel" so that no single group in the state is especially favored or injured. This idea ties together much of the rest of the speech.

The Body

Paragraph 7 contains Wilson's first signpost following a good transition from the preceding paragraph. The first sentence of that paragraph restates the "spirit" of the preceding one. The next sentence constitutes a bridge between that spirit and the "definite things" Wilson pledges to accomplish. And the third sentence is the signpost. Notice that the sentence refers to the "*administration* of the state." "Administration" constitutes a repetition of one of the key words from the overview and thus effectively reminds the audience that this is a main point.

The first sentence of paragraph 8 signposts the "system of *taxation*," and because "taxation" was a key word in the overview, the audience realizes also that this is one of Wilson's main points. Notice that the first sentence of paragraph 8 is also a good transition because it links together and moves smoothly between the previous idea of administration and the present idea of taxation. Paragraph 9 also contains a clear signpost, calling our attention to the key words "control of corporations" (also contained in the overview).

Paragraph 11 asks for the specific action Wilson wants, the approval of "the voters of the state" on the basis of his Democratic principles. Paragraphs 11 and 12 also bring the speech back to the theme of the "common interest," which was sounded early in the speech and which helped to tie the main points together. The very last paragraph is the final persuasive appeal.

Wilson's speech is surely not perfect. Few are. But as a well-organized speech that shows the speaker's involvement in the topic and its potential relevance to the audience, Wilson's address can serve as a model for anyone's best efforts at speech composition.

Writing and Delivering the Speech

At long last, you are ready to sit down to write the speech you have carefully conceptualized. In another couple of days, you will actually deliver it before an audience. You've gathered together your ideas and placed yourself at your desk with a clean page of paper, two sharpened

pencils, a gooseneck lamp peering down at the paper, and a confident mien on your face. But what do you do now?

Writing the Speech

Do *not* start by writing an essay with complete sentences or by working from the beginning to the end of the speech all at once. Of course, *we* won't know how you write the speech, nor will your instructor. But students who write the speech in full sentences, completely fleshed out from the start, generally come to grief. Such a method of writing prevents the speaker from seeing the forest for the trees. That is, a speaker is unlikely to have a clear idea of the main points, of the bare bones of the speech, if he or she is overly concerned with adding in the finer points all at once. Another problem with the "all at once" approach is that it reduces a speaker's flexibility in changing the speech. If a speaker decides to reverse points 2 and 3, it becomes harder to do that when they have been spread over several pages.

Instead of writing the speech all at once, start by putting down the main points. That will serve as the anchor for your thoughts, and you will then be more likely to organize the speech around those clear main ideas. Now, take out another sheet of paper, again write your three main points, but underneath them jot down some of the subpoints they subsume. Take out a third piece of paper, fill it out as you did the second, but include more detail, such as examples and illustrations. By following the "progressive outlining" method, a speaker will have a clearer sense of the organization of the speech, of how the main points gather up the other ideas and hold them together. A speaker who writes in outline will also be blessed with greater flexibility of conceptions and less shuffling of paper. Compose your introduction and conclusion last, because you won't know what to preview or review until the body of the speech has been clearly formulated.

Using Notes

Unless the class instructor has reasons for preferring a particular method of using notes, we recommend that speakers use whatever method they are comfortable with. Three attitudes toward using notes in actual speaking are common. The first is not to use them and to memorize the speech. That technique lets the speaker maintain a good deal of eye contact with the audience, but it is also quite taxing intellectually and psychologically. Also, if a speaker forgets a word or two under such conditions, the entire speech might become derailed because no back-up notes are available. A second way of using notes is to write the speech out word for word (after it has been worked up to that point by progressive outlining). This method allows a speaker to plan carefully what he or she is going to say. But quite often, people who use fully written manuscripts become too dependent upon them. Such people often bury their noses in their notes, reading to the audience instead of talking with them, with the resulting speech sounding as if it is being recited from the telephone directory.

The method *we* prefer is to have notes take the form of a detailed outline. A speaker can use these notes by glancing down at the paper from time to time to see the idea or example to be discussed next. Then, the speaker explains the idea to the audience in a more or less extemporaneous fashion. This method means that each time the speech is given, it will take on a different flavor. The speaker will therefore stay fresh and spontaneous in the delivery but will still have a definite plan to follow in the speech. The flexibility afforded when using notes allows the speaker to maintain eye contact with the audience, much as he or she would in informal conversation. Becoming tied to your note cards prohibits this.

When using an extended outline, we recommend writing, word for word, three important parts of the speech. The first part is the introduction, because precise wording in the beginning of a speech is important for getting the attention and interest of the audience. The second parts of the speech that should be written carefully are the transitions and signposts; careful attention to these insures that the speaker can move smoothly and clearly among ideas. Finally, write out the conclusion. Nothing is more frustrating for a listener than a speech that doesn't know how to end; it resembles an airplane circling the runway in a dense fog, desparately searching for a landing spot. A polished conclusion allows the speaker to finish his or her remarks gracefully and cleanly. If you do follow our advice and write out the introduction, transitions, signposts, and conclusion, know them well enough so that you aren't tied to your notes, thus eliminating awkwardness and insuring precise phrasings.

Practice!

Your best ally in public speaking is practice, and a great deal of it. Speech anxiety is a problem that affects everyone who speaks in public, and disciplined practice can make one more familiar with the speech situation and hence remove that portion of the fear generated by the unknown. You might ask your friends to listen to you practice the speech, or you might tape-record yourself during practice. Student speakers might go to the room in which their class meets to practice the speech when the room is unoccupied. *Practice will build confidence.* That, too, is one of the few laws of communication.

Delivering the Speech

As the speaker practices the speech, he or she needs to keep in mind a few simple rules for delivery (a discussion that we will expand greatly in Chapter 7). *Go slowly in important places.* Of course, nobody should absolutely crawl along when speaking, but speakers should slow down in the introduction. At that point, the audience is still adjusting to the sound of the speaker's voice and to the new topic; by speaking slowly, speakers give their listeners time to "warm up." Slow down, too, during the transitions, because the audience needs to observe the signposts. Finally, slow down in the conclusion so that the audience hears and understands the last important ideas presented in the speech.

Use delivery for emphasis. When a speaker is announcing a main point, he or she should pause before the point and then express it with somewhat more force than is used in the rest of the speech. This approach will help the audience see that the speaker has reached a main point. When the speaker is merely briefing the audience on some simple facts or listing some quick examples, he or she can back off in the delivery. Use the delivery to emphasize some points and not others by varying the speed and force of the delivery.

Use delivery to give impact to ideas. Think about the feelings and attitudes involved in what is being said, and let those feelings come through in the delivery. Put the sort of expression into the voice that matches the content of the words. If you tell the audience about the horrors of child abuse, for example, you should *sound* horrified and angry. If you tell the audience about your grandmother's miraculous recovery from surgery, the tremor in your voice should project a feeling of joy. The voice and body are tremendous assets in speaking and should be used as such. While the essayist must be content with the subtleties of language, the speaker has a wide range of verbal and nonverbal resources at his or her command.

Some students wonder what to do about gestures when speaking. Do *not* plan them out; the best gestures are the most natural and spontaneous ones. Speakers who feel self-conscious about their hands, though, might place them on the top edges of the speaker's podium. That position looks natural, and it allows natural gestures to develop as the speech progresses. Natural gestures will not emerge if the speaker is holding notes, pens, visual aids, and so on, so leaving the hands empty is normally a good idea.

Gestures—like voice intonation, speech organization, topical development, and the myriad things that make up public speaking—are most effective when listeners see them as natural and appropriate to the moment of dialogue. All of the advice we give you here about speech preparation is not an attempt to make a "new you" but to make the "best you," the natural but thoughtful you, the most effective advertisement for your ideas. The more you practice, the more likely it will be that the "best you" will find favor with the listeners in your life. This, we promise you.

Suggestions for Speaking

In the preceding pages, we offered a host of practical suggestions for preparing your initial public speech. It is, of course, difficult to remember the many and varied practical hints given and more difficult still to execute all of them in your first public speech. Eventually, you will probably be able to master those and many others. Right now, however, we would like to suggest some ideas that you might find useful as you prepare for your first major speech. We mix a bit of philosophy with our pedagogy here, so be sure to examine our assumptions carefully.

1. Consider all of the things you would like *not* to speak about and determine *why* you wouldn't want to do so. Such "negative" thinking may suggest positive options.

2. Never give a speech about something that is unimportant to you; life is too short for such dissembling.

3. Never assume that something is unimportant to you until you have investigated it thoroughly in connection with a speech assignment.

4. Have a friend use the topical system to help you generate thoughts about a speech topic; "communal inspiration" is a time-honored aid to creation.

5. Without appearing to pander, find a way of signaling your awareness of your audience's current experiences and values.

6. Indicate to your audience, explicitly if possible, your experience with the speech topic and why you feel as you do about that topic.

7. There are no boring topics, only boring speakers; interesting examples can vivify the driest of subjects.

8. To be convincing, be specific without being tedious, clear without being obvious, organized without being mechanical.

9. Presume that listeners can listen for no longer than 3 minutes without forgetting what you have just said and what the overall purpose of your speech is.

10. Our bodies don't lie well. Use gestures, vocal intonations, and speech rate to signal accurately the content and strength of your feelings about your subject matter.

UNIT II

The Informative Challenge in Public Communication

CHAPTER 4

Techniques for
Audience Analysis

The indoor speaker loses as many crowds as we
do, but he never finds out because their bodies
are still there. We of the outdoors cannot fool
ourselves: if the audience is not there it is plainly
not there, and talking to no one in public has
more than a hint of nightmare. Its ever-present
possibility forces us to study the crowd and our
subject, and ourselves. I write of what I have
thus learned—in Hyde Park London, Times
Square New York, Franklin Park Washington,
the South Side of Chicago, Sydney's Domain, on
the bank of Melbourne's Yarra, and in several
dozen other spots.

One way or another the crowds have taught
me a vast amount—directly by reminding me of
things I had not sufficiently dwelt on, indirectly
by forcing me to go deeper than, but for the
pressure of their questioning, I should have
gone. To have everything one utters subjected to

crowd scrutiny, every word liable to challenge on the spot, is very concentrative.

Crowds can be maddening—spoiling your best effects by interjections; shouting you down (this is true in Australia and England; I've never had it in America); worst of all, walking away and leaving you talking to no one. As you grow in experience, the proportion of the disagreeable diminishes; but it never wholly vanishes. And, be you as experienced as you may, there are still meetings in which the disagreeable has a carnival. When it has, there is no consolation in putting the blame on the crowd. They don't invite you; you invite them. Whether a party has been a success or a failure, there is no appeal against the judgment of the guests.

Listeners arrive with no objections sizzling and leaping inside their heads; their questions arise out of what they have heard us say in our speech. So that what we talk about is entirely up to us; but they can still walk away the moment they are bored. We still have to interest them sufficiently to keep them standing there.[1]

For many years, F. J. Sheed spent much of his time as a sort of roaming religious lecturer—buttonholing people on street corners, collaring whatever large or small crowds he could, and (to complete our metaphor) losing his communicative shirt all too often!

Sheed's remarks are compelling. Here is a man who seems to have come up with a theory of how communication works—or ought to work —and has learned it from real-life experience. From his years of lecturing, Sheed seems to have concluded that public speaking is very much a *transactive* experience, a continual giving and taking between speaker and audience, a phenomenon that continually defies any casual attempt to define, regulate, or control it. He has found that in public communication the best chance for success is making a series of intelligent guesses about the people he'll be addressing.

But the primary value of Sheed's remarks lies not only in his acute analysis of human behavior but in his vision of the nature of communi-

[1]F. J. Sheed, "My Life on the Street Corner." First appeared in *Saturday Review*, May 10, 1969, pp. 22, 23, 66, 67. Copyright 1969 by Saturday Review Co. Used with permission.

cation itself. He seems to have, as Bonnie Johnson would call it, an "implicit communication theory."[2] In her study, Johnson found a number of such implicit theories of communication operating in the minds of everyday talkers. Some persons, for example, believe that in order to communicate effectively, we must find the appropriate weapons to use on our auditors. Others think that communication is sort of magical, a process that "just happens." Still others see communication as a kind of mechanical procedure whereby we pull the appropriate lever in order to get the desired response—as if people were but so many cigarette machines.

According to Johnson, the important thing about implicit communication theories lies in how they affect the individual's spoken behavior. For example, if I believe that communication basically is a mechanistic process, I will live my life trying to find the appropriate "button" to push for each person with whom I come into contact—a mode of thinking that can lead to dehumanization. On the other hand, if I believe that communication is nothing more than an interpersonal magic act, I will either not treat my communication contacts seriously, or I will not try very hard to improve them. (It's all magic, after all!)

We can, of course, think of still more common implicit communication theories. Preachers often see themselves as "shepherds leading their flocks"; hence, the very paternalistic tone of many contemporary sermons. Ralph Nader, as another example, seems to see his communicative job as that of "attacking the fortress of public opinion," a state of mind that probably does much to contribute to the hard-charging, usually negative manner in which he approaches those in power.

In this chapter on audience analysis, we would like to follow a *transactional* theory of communication. That is, like Mr. Sheed, we feel that communication is best conceived of as a process through which people, possessed by varying levels and types of "potentials," come together by pooling their motivational, experiential, and attitudinal resources. To our way of thinking, audience analysis is crucial in each and every speaking situation: Speakers are not pinball players and listeners are not pinball machines. Rather, listeners are very active, somewhat mysterious creatures who can only be *induced* to behave in particular ways, never directed to do so. Our implicit theory was delineated many years ago by the storyteller Aesop:

The Wind and the Sun were disputing which was the stronger. Suddenly they saw a traveller coming down the road, and the Sun said: "I see a way to decide our dispute. Whichever of us can cause that traveller to take off his

---

[2]B. Johnson, "Implicit Communication Theory," unpublished paper, Department of Speech, Pennsylvania State University, 1972.

*cloak shall be regarded as the stronger. You begin." So the Sun retired behind
a cloud, and the Wind began to blow as hard as it could upon the traveller.
But the harder he blew the more closely did the traveller wrap his cloak
around him, till at last the Wind had to give up in despair. Then the Sun
came out and shone in all his glory upon the traveller, who soon found it
too hot to walk with his cloak on.*[3]

Let us consider, for a moment, the implicit "communication" theories of our two protagonists. Wind, being the rugged individualist that
he is, assumes that a forceful presentation of his message will win the
day. Sun, on the other hand, remembers that travelers (listeners, if you
will) have certain "sets of potentials" within them (e.g., body temperature tolerances) that he, as "speaker," must reckon with quite seriously.
By insightfully assessing, and then adapting to, these "potentials," Sun
emerges the victor. And he does so because of his perception of the
interaction, not because of any gimmickery he employed. In other
words, *his attitude toward communication determined, in large part, his success.*
Who could blame Traveler for resisting the callous, overpowering messages of Wind, a communicator who treats his fellow interactants with
disdain, without regard to the gifts *they* have brought to the communicative festivities, without concern for even elementary audience analysis.
By learning more about audience analysis, you will begin to see that
public speaking is *more interaction than performance.* By coming to understand that proposition, you will be earning your own intellectual place
in the Sun.

Timing of Audience Analysis

While the goal of audience analysis and adaptation is similar for all
communication situations (how can knowledge of my listeners be used
to increase the probability of making them understand me and accept
what I have to say?), approaches for achieving this goal must vary from
setting to setting. As stated in Chapter 1, public settings differ from
other communicative circumstances in a variety of ways. Let us relist
just a few of them:

1. The public communicator must attempt to analyze and adapt to
   many diverse people simultaneously.

2. In doing so, the on-going feedback he or she receives is more
   restricted and subtle, and, hence, more likely to be misinter-
   preted.

[3]C. W. Eliot (ed.), "Aesop's Fables," *Harvard Classics,* vol. 17 (New York: Collier,
1909), pp. 35–36.

3. Therefore, public communication requires a higher degree of advanced speech preparation than is required by more private settings.

Given what we know about such settings, then, how can a public communicator cope with the formidable task of analyzing and adapting to the many diverse people that compose his or her audience?

When thinking about audience analysis, we can profitably arrest the process at three points in time:

1. *Prior to communication.* The speaker is most concerned with discovering aspects of his or her auditors that will predispose them to accept or reject the message.

2. *During communication.* The speaker is most concerned with monitoring audience feedback so as to discover whether previously selected communicative options need modification.

3. *After communication.* The speaker attempts to discover whether or not the message actually achieved the goals specified ahead of time.

Let us consider each stage of the process separately.

Prior Audience Analysis

Because public communication usually demands that a speaker bear the brunt of the talking burden, advanced preparation is the key to success. To start such a process, you could simply get a list of your audience members and learn every conceivable thing about each of

them. But the people making up your audience are so multifaceted that you could not possibly hope to use such volumes of data (which would be incomplete under any circumstances) even if you did manage to compile them before speech time. Thus, another option would be to look at the whole audience. For example, you determine that they all belong to the Lions Club and are male. Satisfactory? Not really, since we can seldom treat an audience as if it were a single entity. Even though people behave distinctively when brought together (e.g., because of group pressures), they still retain much of their individuality.

Thus, when speaking, we must compromise between conducting a psychiatric interview and a shot-in-the-dark foray. If we think about the members of the audience in such a way as to cluster them in terms of similarities and differences, we might generate useful data. A happy medium would be to regard neither one nor all but small clusters of people (overlapping, possibly) who have something or some things in

common. Table 4-1 depicts our necessary compromise in conducting prior audience analysis.

Helpful as such an approach to prior audience analysis might be, we are still left with a more burning question: What do you look for in such "clusters" of people? One answer lies in an attempt to understand some aspects of the psychological makeup of people in general and then to use such "searchlights" to discover relevant aspects of the actual audience we will be dealing with. Later in this chapter, we will attempt to lay out some of these pertinent resources residing within most all listeners.

As a sort of preview to that section, we might list four of the most common questions a speaker might ask when speculating about his or her intended auditors:

1. What information do I have about their attitudes and values?

2. What kinds of beliefs will I be addressing myself to in this communication situation?

Table 4-1   Audience Analysis in Public Communication

Options	Analyze each individual in audience.	Treat audience as "clusters" of listeners.	Analyze audience as if it were a single listener.
Example	"That lady in the gray hat looks uncomfortable with my last statement."	"I've got to remember that the audience is composed of both young people and their parents."	"They're all white Protestants and hence should respond similarly to my remarks."
Commentary	Audience analysis becomes an exercise in futility.	Audience analysis becomes both precise and manageable.	Audience analysis provides little data to guide us in creating messages.

3. What sorts of experiences have these listeners had that may add to or subtract from my communicative impact?

4. What kinds of general listeners' needs will be brought to bear on this speaking situation?

Modest though this "starter's list" is, answers to such questions can do much to direct a speaker's mind in the search for things sayable.

Process Audience Analysis

Prior audience analysis always is a gamble because the speaker can never be certain that his or her inferences about the audience are correct. As a result, public speakers must necessarily consider how their listeners are responding from moment to moment during the speech. In its literal sense, of course, this is impossible. Still, speakers need to know whether their audiences are, in some fashion, interested, understanding, and accepting of the messages with which they are presented. If an audience does not respond positively, the speaker will need to modify his or her original strategy in order to produce the desired results.

But again the question appears, What is it that the speaker should observe? Moreover, how can the speaker immediately interpret what he or she notices? How is feedback used to make intelligent adaptations to auditors? Unfortunately, perhaps even more so than in the case of prior analysis, there are no easy answers.

Oftentimes, all a speaker has to work with when speaking are the nonverbal responses of the audience. Thus, what the speaker must do is to maintain close visual contact with the audience as he or she attempts to monitor and interpret their behavior. In so doing, the speaker must strike a balance between ignoring important feedback and becoming overly sensitive to the negative or positive feedback of one or two individuals. The public communicator must be concerned with the major trends present in the audience.

While such bromides may be obvious to you, it should be stressed that when process-analyzing our listeners, we are making inferences about their internal states. Sometimes such inferences may prove to be incorrect, but more often they are right. Research suggests that most speakers can identify reliably the following clues as being either positive or negative.[4]

[4]For additional insight on such matters, see J. C. Gardiner, "A Synthesis of Experimental Studies of Speech Communication Feedback," *Journal of Communication*, 21:17–35 (1971).

POSITIVE AUDIENCE FEEDBACK

Constant eye contact

Smiling

Positive head nods

Comfortable but erect posture

Note taking

Little or no movement of the body or limbs

NEGATIVE AUDIENCE FEEDBACK

No eye contact (or eyes rolled up)

Slouched posture

Manipulating or examining objects or parts of the body

Looking around the room at others

Doodling

Shaking head

Yawns

Tapping fingers

Eyebrow movements (down and together)

Questioning facial expression

Again, we must caution you to interpret this kind of information carefully. When speaking in public, you will be receiving a great amount of information at once. It makes little sense to become fixated by one or two inattentive listeners. The most important thing is to demonstrate to your listeners that *you are paying attention to them*—not so much that you've forsaken your message but not so little that you have given them "license" to disregard you.

That such "process feedback" can be of great import to the speaker seems undeniable. If, for example, listeners signal lack of acceptance or understanding, the speaker may have to provide additional clarification or even move back to a preestablished point of mutual agreement. The success or failure of public communication depends to a great extent on our ability to "read" an audience and to modify our behavior to account for on-the-spot problems. We perhaps should apologize for making such obvious comments, but each time we encounter a college lecturer who has not peered past the podium in 30 years, we feel compelled to renew such preaching!

Especially for the beginning speaker, process audience analysis may seem somewhat frightening and hence more trouble than it's worth. But to forsake the *experience* of communication is to forsake the *interchange* of ideas and to turn talk into mere mechanism. A good speaker learns as much from a good speech as does a good audience. That's why it's called *co-mmunication*.

Postaudience Analysis

After the speech is over, most speakers would like to know the effect of their message. If they specified their goals in a meaningful way ahead of time, they are well on the road to discovering their impact. A meaningful goal statement might ask, What would I like my audience to do as a result of listening to my speech? Postaudience analysis, therefore, consists of gathering evidence relating to goals specified in advance.

The public speaker has a variety of tools for gathering such data. Audience behavior during and immediately following the speech can provide many clues as to its effectiveness. Applause, questions, compliments, and wholesale criticism may indicate which points were not understood, which points needed greater support, and to what extent members of the audience favored or understood one's remarks.

Questionnaires, interviews with audience members, and follow-up conversations can sometimes provide the speaker with a precise assessment of effectiveness. For some speeches, very precise measures are available: Did they sign up for the proposed project? Did they contribute to the Will Rogers Clinic? Can they build a weather vane?

When you know that you will be addressing the same audience several times—as you would in a speech communication class—postaudience analysis may suggest options for use in future presentations. If approached dispassionately, feedback from the instructor, from friends and class members, and from audio- and videotape recordings can lead to an accurate assessment of our strengths and weaknesses as public communicators. And the great advantage of postaudience analysis is that cool, appropriately strategic thoughts often come to us after the excitement of the moment has passed and taken with it the little tensions and blindnesses that speaking sometimes brings.

Complications of Audience Analysis

No discussion of audience analysis would be complete without some mention of one of the most distinctive features of public speech settings. Intra-audience effects, a network of messages sent and received by audience members themselves, constitute one of the most interesting facets of public speech. As an example, picture yourself in front of the television set ready to watch the "Tonight" show. Johnny Carson makes his appearance and amidst the polite applause, we clearly hear the refrains of Loud Clapper and Shrill Whistler. Quite simply, these characters serve to induce their fellow auditors in the studio to respond favorably and to join in the fun. But that's not all. The laughter and clapping of the studio audience serve, in turn, to encourage the TV audience to similarly enjoy the proceedings—a kind of rippling effect.

Desmond Morris describes this phenomenon when he discusses the responses of teenagers to their idols:

> *As an audience, they enjoy themselves, not by screaming with laughter, but screaming with screams. They not only scream, they also grip their own and each other's bodies, they writhe, they moan, they cover their faces and they pull at their hair. These are all the classic signs of intense pain or fear, but they have become deliberately stylized. Their thresholds have been artificially lowered. They are no longer cries for help, but signals to one another in the audience that they are capable of feeling an emotional response to the sexual idols which is so powerful that, like all stimuli of unbearably high intensity, they pass into the realm of pure pain. If a teenage girl found herself suddenly alone in the presence of one of her idols, it would never occur to her to scream at him. The screams were not meant for him, they were meant for the other girls in the audience.[5]*

As can be seen from these examples, the effects of auditors on one another can be powerful forces in public speech settings. Naturally, such listener-listener interaction does not always operate in a direction favorable to the speaker. The ways in which these intra-audience responses can complicate the speaker's job are represented in Figure 4-1. A politician, candidate King, is giving a campaign speech to an audience

[5]D. Morris, *The Naked Ape* (New York: Dell, 1971), p. 98.

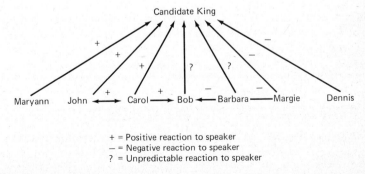

+ = Positive reaction to speaker
− = Negative reaction to speaker
? = Unpredictable reaction to speaker

Figure 4-1   Intra-audience Effects in Public Communication

of seven people. The following model indicates some of the communicative reactions and interactions that result from his speaking.

Although in reality intra-audience effects are much more complicated, our model depicts some of the adaptive demands forced upon our plucky politician by his very "busy" audience. The following shorthand comments are made available by our diagram:

1. From the speaker's point of view, Maryann is a "good listener." She is totally enthralled with the candidate's speech; she hangs onto every word he says and is oblivious to her fellow auditors.

2. John and Carol, on the other hand, are "perfect listeners." Like Maryann, they are really "into" the speech but in addition are reinforcing the speaker's remarks (for one another and for Bob) by their approving chatter and applause.

3. From the candidate's viewpoint, Bob is inscrutable. Bob is quite interested in overhearing Carol's positive reactions to the speech and the negative reactions of Barbara; hence, he may not be paying much attention to the political oratory itself.

4. Barbara's reactions are also difficult to assess. She is being greatly affected by Margie, who appears to be really turned off by the speech. Because she needs immediate social support (she and Margie are members of the same sorority), Barbara is probably tending in Margie's direction. Because her feedback to the speaker is minimal, it is difficult to tell how Barbara will eventually react.

5. Margie is obviously a lost cause, what with her scowls, sarcastic laughs, and so on.

6. Dennis is equally disturbed by the speech but is just grimacing, not overtly expressing his displeasure.

This little diagram shows how tricky process audience analysis can be. Audience analysis is not just a matter of "toting up" listeners' individual reactions to us as speakers but one of assessing the reactions and *interreactions* of our listeners.

But how should our hypothetical speaker above adapt to his set of conditions? He can probably afford to direct his attention away from Carol, John, and Maryann for a while (since they are "with him" for the moment) and concentrate instead on Bob, Barbara, and Dennis. By soliciting their opinions for example, King might draw them into the conversation and hence discover and adapt to the sources of their disagreement (a technique that grade-school teachers often wisely use with unruly children). The remaining problem is, what is he to do with Margie?

Not all members of an audience have the same social power. There are, for instance, *opinion leaders* who have a great deal of influence on an audience. Thus, if Margie is a person of considerable clout, King might ask for her comments on an issue, hoping that this amount of personal attention will reduce her hostility. If Margie is not an opinion leader, the speaker is probably best advised to ignore her and to concentrate instead on more viable possibilities, hoping that the group of auditors he has "hooked" will then sway the one he has not yet been able to reach. The tireless, but tiresome, adage "ya' can't win 'em all" seems to be especially true of public communication, a situation in which the complex, dynamic, social geometry of an audience can do much to advance and retard speakers' efforts. The issue of intra-audience effects, although interesting in and of itself, serves better to point up the complex adaptations forced upon a speaker who takes audience analysis as seriously as he or she should.

General Questions for Audience Analysis

A complete list of everything that would be useful for a speaker to know about an audience would be a very long list indeed. Students of collective behavior and scholars in the area of communication have, however, often agreed that five fairly standard questions are useful to the public speaker. Although these questions are not exhaustive, they do help a speaker determine areas where communication problems might arise. Let us consider each of these audience probes briefly.

What Is the "Demographic Style" of the Audience?

Demographics refer to the sociological facts that distinguish an audience. Sometimes, such matters as the *sex* of the audience, their *socioeconomic* status, their *occupational* or *political* preferences, or their *ethnic* background may have major impact on how they will respond to you as a speaker. Determining such features becomes more than a matter of "cultural snooping," however. That is, it is not so important to determine how many persons of British ancestry are in your audience as it is to discover whether any ethnicity based feelings *will affect* how they relate to you as a speaker. Knowing how many women there are in your audience is really rather irrelevant unless your speech topic bears directly on your audience members' status as women (as it might when speaking on the topic of abortion, for example).

Thus, when making such demographic determinations, it is good to keep the following points in mind:

1. All members of a demographic "category" do not necessarily *believe* in similar things nor do they necessarily share relevant *information*.

2. The only demographic information that is relevant to a public speaker is that which points up attitudinal or informational *problems* he or she might have with listeners.

3. Great caution must be exercised when making inferences about appropriate communication strategies when one *only* has demographic facts to go by.

Naturally, a speaker would be foolish not to consider such powerful factors as demography when preparing speech materials. But countless research studies have demonstrated how hazardous it can be to trust such facts to tell us what to say in all cases. The practical conclusion would be to collect as much demographic data about your audience as you can but monitor your inferences with more than normal caution.

What Is the "Psychological Style" of the Audience?

One useful dimension along which audiences may be classified is the degree of similarity or "togetherness" imbedded within them in a speech setting. A useful classification of this sort (provided by Hollingsworth[6]) groups audiences into five psychological types:

1. *The pedestrian audience.* Typified by those who stop to watch the person selling vegetable slicers in a supermarket. Except for the fact that each listener has interrupted what he or she has been doing for the moment, the individual auditors have no obvious ties with the speaker or with other members of the audience. The salesperson's first task, therefore, must be to capture attention or at least divert it from the other marvels of the supermarket.

2. *The passive audience.* Exists when the speaker has already claimed attention. Such audiences are most frequently "captive" listeners: for example, students who inhabit lecture halls because they want to pass a course that requires attendance. Since the audience has already directed their attention toward the speaker, his or her main task is to sustain and direct their interests.

[6]H. Hollingsworth, *The Psychology of the Audience* (New York: American Book, 1935).

3. *The selected audience.* Shares with the speaker a common and known purpose but may not be in agreement as to how to achieve certain goals. For example, all members of the PTA audience might agree that a problem exists but may not be in agreement as to how to solve the problem. Since the audience has chosen to attend the speech on the basis of their inherent interest in the topic, the first task of the speaker in such situations is to take sources of motivation and channel them in some preconceived direction.

4. *The concerted audience.* Members share a pressing, active need to achieve some end, oftentimes accompanied by sympathetic interest in the topic and speaker. Usually, however, no clear division of labor or rigid organization of authority is embodied in such audiences. While the inclination of such an audience normally is to go along with the suggestions of the speaker, they must be convinced. The difference between the selected and concerted audiences may be explained by the following comparison. While the delegates to the World Council of Churches Convention (selected audience) may agree on their combined purpose for convening, each represented denomination (concerted subaudience) brings individual concerns to bear on the communicative situation.

5. *The organized audience.* Typified by military gatherings and many extremist political groups. Such audiences are oftentimes completely devoted to the speaker and his or her purpose. The "doctrine" is known and accepted. The lines of authority are clear. The speaker's main job in such situations is to specify and help implement the action to be taken.

Although no research has yet been done on the question, it is probably true that communication itself helps to create and to disband such audience types. Thus, speakers launched the women's movement in situations involving pedestrian and passive audiences, and, through persuasion, eventually built and sustained concerted, and later, organized audiences. While much of your classroom speaking will be done in the face of passive (maybe, on some issues, selected) audiences, there is much reason to be aware of the communicative options and demands residing within such collections of individuals. More than one speaker has failed to win the day because he or she has misperceived the motivations and orientations of assembled hearers. The Bible-toting campus crusader who talks to all others as if they were "one of us," and succeeds only in insulting his passive audience, is but one example of the failure to adapt to the psychological style of an audience.

What Reference Groups Does the Audience Prize?

Reference groups are composed of those persons we respect and admire, and who can exert significant force on our potentials-for-response as listeners. Reference groups are voluntary groups to which a listener actually belongs (Black Cultural Center) or aspires to (the In-Crowd). Reference groups set standards that determine "acceptable" behavior for members of the group. Typically, such reference groups make us feel better about ourselves by giving "strength in numbers" to our beliefs and self-images.

Reference groups are important to the public speaker because, if correctly identified, they provide a handy set of "clustered values" that can be used to bolster a speaker's arguments. Obviously, an individual listener may have many reference groups that are not always relevant to the topic or purpose for speaking. Thus, in analyzing an audience we should look for only those reference groups that appear to embody knowledge and beliefs *relevant* to the demands of the situation.

Knowing your audience's reference groups can also help you determine which of your *own* features you might like to emphasize when speaking. It is a wise corporation attorney, for example, who plays down her lawyer's role in negotiations with the union and emphasizes instead her history as a union member or leader.

Most of us rarely take the time to conduct such a role inventory, but if we did, we would find that the number of roles we can use when speaking is much larger than expected. One of your writers attempted to take such a role inventory and found that, from time to time, he was a child, sibling, spouse, parent, card player, employee, employer, advisor, committee member, writer, photographer, swimmer, bicyclist, tennis player, subscriber, contributor, insuree, driver, pedestrian, and a Minnesotan. A knowledge of such potential reference group identifications allows us to determine the roles which members of an audience share with us and then to capitalize on such commonalities when speaking.

In attempting to locate reference groups within yourself and your audience, you might keep in mind two types of questions:

1. What will such information tell me about my audience's attitude and knowledge concerning both me and my topic?

2. What will such information tell me about how I might best adapt my message to this particular audience?

While knowledge of your audience's reference groups will add immeasurably in preparing a speech, be wary of stereotyping. Not everyone fits the mold that popular opinion may ascribe to certain groups (e.g., would a liberal or a conservative be more likely to contribute to the United Fund?).

Another caution to keep in mind is that public audiences will usually identify with a great number of oftentimes competing reference groups. Thus, your job as public communicator is to focus again on the largest common denominator. In public communication, you cannot reach all of the people's groups all of the time.

How Large and How "Dense" Is the Audience?

Audience size—both absolute and relative—has an impact on speech preparation. Obviously, as the absolute size of an audience increases, the necessity for using mechanical devices such as microphones, amplifiers, and projected visual aids also increases. Thus, the speaker who faces a large audience must be prepared to master the workings— and failings—of public address systems and other devices made necessary by a large audience. Psychologically, such mechanical mediators can sometimes work against your attempts to create intimacy in the public setting.

More importantly, however, as size increases, the give-and-take of communication is made less obvious, and the feedback you receive is less useful because it is prodigious, yet subtle, in so many cases. Thus, for example, although an instructor of a small class may allow students almost complete freedom to ask questions, interrupt remarks, and make comments of their own, such behaviors become less possible as the class size increases. As a result, with large classes lecture materials must be prepared more thoroughly in advance, the instructor must accept the major portion of the speaking burden, and the amount of interaction a class member may have with the instructor or with fellow students is reduced. Because of these features, it becomes doubly important for the public speaker to *demonstrate* the commitments to message and audience we discussed in Chapter 2.

Related to audience size is the matter of audience density, which is said to have impact on the suggestibility of listeners. The few studies that have investigated this phenomenon of "packed togetherness" have been inconclusive, but there is reason enough to suspect that the speaker cannot afford to ignore the potential import of audience density. As Minnick states,

> *A communicator who wishes to attain maximum suggestibility and strong emotional response often tries to seat his audience elbow to elbow and to fill clusters of vacant seats or vacant rows between the audience and the rostrum. Since a person's emotional responses are heightened and facilitated by awareness of the response of others, a communicator who assures crowded seating provides a condition of maximum effectiveness.*

A standing audience is superior in this respect to a seated audience, since the members of it can be more tightly compressed and thus exposed to an even greater number of facilitating stimulations. It was no accident that the audiences of Adolph Hitler and Benito Mussolini invariably stood packed shoulder to shoulder in an arena or public square. Nor was it an accident that these audiences were notably noisy and demonstrative.[7]

Naturally, this matter of density does not always work in favor of the speaker. A person addressing a tightly packed, hostile audience may be undone by the interactions of his or her assembled hearers.

What Situational Expectations Does the Audience Have?

When people come to hear a speech, their minds are never clean slates ready to be written upon. Rather, listeners have "sets" or expectations about what they will be hearing. Naturally, these sets will differ depending on whether they are attending a revival meeting, an acceptance speech by a Nobel Prize winner, a keynote address at a political convention, or a lecture in Physics 101. Audience members have expectations in all cases, and the public communicator must try to calculate the shared expectancies of his or her listeners. While it is not always necessary for a speaker to meet each and every expectancy, it is necessary to acknowledge the importance of most of them.

Factors that may influence audience expectations include the time of day or the month of the year, attractiveness and comfort of the room, the use of music, and the display of objects and symbols. A Fourth of July audience in the heartland of America, for example, may be disappointed and confused if they do not meet in a scenic location; hear the familiar strains of marches and patriotic melodies; and are not surrounded by red, white, and blue bunting. Along these same lines, in fact, some religious groups, during their tours of college campuses, have been unpacking both their Bibles and their twelve-strings and amplifiers. All of this is done on the assumption that "since they're looking for rock, we can slip in a little old-time religion on the side!"

When attempting to locate the situational expectations of your listeners, you might find it helpful to ask such questions as the following:

1. Why did the members of the audience select to be here? (out of habit? because they were compelled?)

[7]W. Minnick, *The Act of Persuasion*, 2nd ed. (Boston: Houghton Mifflin, 1968), p. 70.

2. What do they usually expect to hear in a situation like this one? (humor? many facts?)

3. What previous knowledge (and hence expectations) do they have of me? (Have they heard me speak before? Did they like my last speech?)

4. What do they expect to hear someone like me say about the topic in question? (top-of-the-head opinion? personal examples?)

5. How will the local environment affect my audience's expectations? (Did they like the person who preceded me on the platform? Are they getting tired?)

There are many situations, of course, where we as speakers might find it wise not to meet audience expectations. For example, when you announce to your classmates that you will be speaking on capital punishment, you should not be surprised to hear a few groans, so common is the topic in speech communication classrooms. These negative "sets" can do much to undermine your own potential impact. Thus, you might want to make it clear in the beginning of your speech that you will be approaching the topic in a novel manner, that their previous biases toward the topic might not be operational here, and that your commitment to the topic is such that this will not be just another speech given by just another student for the sake of a B grade and a pat on the head.

Finally, it is important to remember that listeners' expectations change *during* interaction as well. You cannot expect your hearers to switch quickly from a humorous introduction to a fact-filled and technical explication of nuclear power's dangers. Also, you must be careful not to promise anything early in your speech that you fail to deliver later. Situational expectations, in other words, should be part of both prior and process audience analysis.

Specific Questions for Audience Analysis

So far, we have talked rather generally about the "things" that individual listeners bring to bear when assessing a speaker's remarks. We have talked obliquely about such mavericks as beliefs, attitudes, motivations, and needs. In this section, we hope to remedy that situation a bit by discussing two forces that lie at the very root of our listeners' personalities. When conducting audience analysis, it is imperative that we learn about our audience's *beliefs* and *needs*, although actually doing so is a process fraught with hazard.

What Are the Audience's Beliefs Relative to the Topic?

Have you ever stopped to ask yourself how you know what someone else believes? Why, anyone knows that you find out what someone believes by . . . by . . . well, you just have to. . . . Actually, there is a very simple response to the question—you guess!

Not a very telling answer but about all we have to go on in normal, everyday speech. This is not to say that our bets cannot be precise and sophisticated. While we cannot really know what someone else believes, we can make some intelligent guesses. And we do have data upon which to make our rather fragile assessments. We can get an inkling of the shape and magnitude of another's belief system. As we are using the term here, a *belief system* incorporates what we would do (if the opportunity presented itself) about a certain object, person, or idea. As such, a belief system has a number of components; they are depicted in Figure 4-2.

You will note immediately that we actually "see" only about half of what makes up a person's belief system—we guess about the other half. All we have to go on when assessing others' attitudes and values is what they say they believe (opinions) and what they actually do (physical behavior). In order to have tools for exploring this question, let us consider some definitions.

Attitudes are beliefs that are target-specific—that is, oriented to a specific object, person, or idea. Thus, "Ronald Reagan was truthful" or "*Star Wars* was a great movie" are both attitudes. Values are beliefs that represent general, abstract, idealized conceptions of objects, people, or ideas; for example, "People should be truthful" or "Humans are inher-

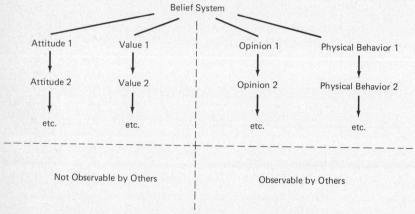

Figure 4-2   Components of Our Belief Systems

ently bad." Another's attitudes and values are not directly observable by us and thus can only be inferred on the basis of others' opinions or physical behaviors.

Opinions are verbalized beliefs (observable by others) that may or may not represent attitudes or values. Thus, I can say, "I like Don" (opinion), even if my "real" attitude is quite the opposite. The same holds true for physical behavior—actions or artifacts that may or may not represent attitudes or values. I may, for example, drink beer at a party (physical behavior) even though I find beer distasteful or go to church each week even though I no longer believe in organized religion.

When viewed from this perspective, then, audience analysis is a process of making inferences about the internal states of a group of auditors and then using such information to guide us in our thinking about responses to the communication situation.

In trying to find out what a person believes, what his or her "potentials for response" might be, we have a number of directions in which to go. We can, for example, use

1. Opinion 1 to predict opinion 2 ("you say you love me. I suppose that next you're going to say you want to marry me") or physical behavior 1 ("he said he loves me. Maybe he's going to try to kiss me").

2. Physical behavior 1 to predict physical behavior 2 ("oh, no, the boss didn't smile at me today. Maybe she's going to bawl me out") or opinion 1 ("he kissed me! Will he now tell me he loves me?").

3. Opinion 1 to predict attitude 1 ("he says he voted for Reagan. That means he must like the dope"), which may, in turn, predict attitude 2 ("if he likes Reagan he probably also likes Goldwater") or value 1 ("anybody who likes Reagan probably believes in superpatriotism").

4. Physical behavior 1 to predict attitude 1 ("she's reading the newspaper at the table. She must not love me"), which may, in turn, predict attitude 2 ("if she doesn't love me, she must want a divorce") or value 1 ("anyone who doesn't want to make love to me must be a religious nut").

5. Opinions or physical behaviors to predict value 1 ("anybody who talks and acts like that must be a fascist"), which may, in turn, predict value 2 ("anyone who believes like that must also be an isolationist") or attitude 1 ("one who believes in superpatriotism probably thinks Reagan is great").

Complex though this "systems" view of beliefs may be, a speaker who does not seriously reckon with such complexity when analyzing and adapting to an audience might find himself or herself in serious trouble. Thus, we offer the following list of practical cautions about assessing listeners' beliefs:

1. Obtain a sufficient amount of information about your audience. Any information, no matter how seemingly irrelevant, is desirable because by understanding the overall structure of a belief system, you are then in a position to speculate about the specific beliefs relevant to the topic you are addressing.

2. Observe opinions and physical behaviors that are relevant to your communicative purpose whenever possible. Ask questions constantly. You never know when your soon-to-be listeners will reveal something important about themselves.

3. Note consistent modes of behavior and opinion-giving in particular because *patterned* responses tend to give us the most important information about a person's basic attitudes and values.

4. Be especially aware of opinions and physical behaviors exhibited under stress by listeners. After all, it is what we do and say under stress that often reveals our gut beliefs and motivations.

5. Keep a diary of how your listeners have responded to other speeches and how they react to one another informally. Trying to remember such details without recording them is unwise.

What Needs Appear to Motivate the Audience at Hand?

Needs are the basic forces that motivate us to accept or reject a speaker's remarks. Such a perspective views the human (in part) as a need-fulfiller, one who sees the certain needs as being basic to survival, other needs as pertinent to happiness, and still other needs as irrelevant to both survival and happiness.

We all have needs. You might have a need at the moment to skip to another chapter. You might have a need for a Coke. While interesting, these are not the needs with which we are concerned here. Rather, we will focus on the needs shared by groups of people, for it is only *group* needs and aspirations that are of prime relevance to the public speaker. You can be sure, however, that if chapter-skipping and Coke-drinking were shared consistently by a significantly large number of people, they would be included in Figure 4-3. But to include them would be to mislead you as a public communicator—one who is looking for safe

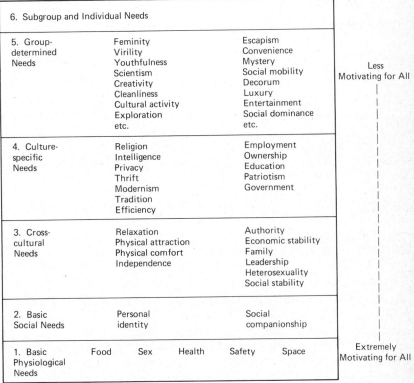

6. Subgroup and Individual Needs			
5. Group- determined Needs	Feminity Virility Youthfulness Scientism Creativity Cleanliness Cultural activity Exploration etc.	Escapism Convenience Mystery Social mobility Decorum Luxury Entertainment Social dominance etc.	Less Motivating for All
4. Culture- specific Needs	Religion Intelligence Privacy Thrift Modernism Tradition Efficiency	Employment Ownership Education Patriotism Government	
3. Cross- cultural Needs	Relaxation Physical attraction Physical comfort Independence	Authority Economic stability Family Leadership Heterosexuality Social stability	
2. Basic Social Needs	Personal identity	Social companionship	
1. Basic Physiological Needs	Food Sex Health Safety Space		Extremely Motivating for All

Figure 4-3   Hierarchy of Needs for Public Audiences

ways to lay bets about the majority of his or her listeners. Take a look at Figure 4-3, which depicts some common human needs.

As you can see, we have grouped the needs of people in general into five levels.[8] Level 1, Basic Physiological Needs, includes those things we require in order to live a life of any sort. We cannot get along very well unless our basic needs for shelter, health, and so on, are satisfied in some fashion. Next, we are told that life would not be worth living unless our Level 2 Basic Social Needs are attended to in some fashion. Unless we have some inkling of "who we are" (personal identity) and someone else to explain ourselves to (social companionship), life does not promise to be very satisfying.

The public speaker usually can count on the existence of other needs in his or her auditors, and, if perceptive, can draw upon such needs when speaking. Level 3, Cross-Cultural Needs, includes those requirements that persons of all societies crave to have satisfied. If anthropologists are right, some sort of need for physical comfort (above and beyond the satisfaction of our basic physiological needs), independence (not to be confused with democracy), economic stability (not capitalism), family ties, and the like, are common to most people of most cultures.

We are obviously motivated by even more. Level 4 needs, those that are Culture-Specific, must also be satisfied in some fashion. Here, we have listed needs especially relevant to modern, westernized society. The American values of privacy, thrift, ownership, education, religion,

[8]The basic portion of this model is similar to that of A. Maslow, *Toward a Psychology of Being* (New York: Van Nostrand Reinhold, 1962).

and a curious combination of modernism and tradition (among others), have become the stock-in-trade of countless public speakers in our culture. Appeals made to needs at this level are often strongly motivating.

Finally, Level 5, Group-Determined Needs, is also included. Here, we find needs that are held strongly by certain sizable segments of our society; we find the forces that motivate us to accept or reject women's liberation, the space program, the middle-class ethic of social dominance, and the prospects of a Majorcan vacation. Here we see the needs that impinge most directly on our day-to-day experiences. Here we see the beautiful blonde selling underarm deodorant via a perverse combination of femininity, youthfulness, cleanliness, and even social mobility!

We were not able to include chapter-skipping or Coke-drinking in our chart, although such needs would probably fall in among the thousands of Subgroup and Individual Needs that motivate some of us quite strongly. To include them, however, would be to detract from our emphasis on the needs of public audiences. So we leave it to you to fill in the blanks in Level 6 with your own preferences for pepperoni pizza and punk rock.

Undoubtedly, there is much to quibble with in our categorization of specific needs. Some of you, for example, may feel that religion is much more a cross-cultural need than we have given it credit for here. Indeed, you may be right, since needs often "move" from level to level as societies grow and express their own aspirations and desires. We hope, however, that you will not allow your quibbling to offset the essential points we are trying to make here:

1. Public audiences have certain needs that vary significantly in motivating power. The wise public speaker tries to assess which needs are most important to his or her audience at the time of speaking.

2. People listen to public speakers in order to assure themselves that their needs can be fulfilled more fully than they are at present or that valued needs will continue to be satisfied at their present levels. Be *specific* when showing the value of your ideas.

3. Public audiences require a speaker to show how his or her proposal can meet the needs they feel are of immediate importance. "Long-range" appeals are seldom attractive to listeners.

4. Public audiences generally distrust speakers who urge abandoning basic needs in favor of desires that only a few of them share. Never trifle with basic needs unless you've got a good alternative.

5. The speaker's own individual and subgroup needs may not be appropriate for mentioning in a public communicative environment. Be sure that you don't confuse *your* needs with those of your listeners.

6. This list of needs can provide sources of insight and argument to you during speech preparation. They might be used as a sort of "checklist" when looking for supporting materials.

Sample Audience Analysis

As a way of tying together our discussion of audience analysis, Table 4-2 presents a message that bears the earmarks of some very careful audience analysis. It is just a rather ordinary public message, one that you would find in almost any popular magazine. As you read this selection, note the remarks we have made in the left column— remarks that indicate how we feel the speaker is attempting to analyze and to direct the motivating forces residing within her intended audience.

Table 4-2 Effective Audience Analysis: An Example

Commentary	Sample Message
Taps real or vicarious experiences; appeals to personal identity and "familial" needs as well as an important reference group.	"Ever go to a company picnic and find you've got competition? I did. I looked at those petite girls my husband works with and I suddenly saw myself: the fat wife. That's when I turned into 160 pounds of fear and jealousy."
Taps real-life experience of audience; builds rationale for exploring an unknown product. Uses television example because of her large and diverse audience.	"I had always loved to cook and bake and my Larry could put it away without even gaining. Some husbands are like that. But me? I just blossomed out—on submarine sandwiches, pizzas, cakes and pies. Why, that fellow on television who said, 'I ate the whole thing!' had nothing on me."

Table 4-2 (Continued)

Commentary	Sample Message
Reinforces personal identity and hetero-sexuality needs; introduces appeals to physical attraction and femininity. Uses a great amount of detail to keep her pedestrian audience interested.	"Sometimes Larry and I would even get up in the middle of the night and go out for ice cream. Next day, though, I'd hate myself. Larry never said anything about my gaining. He didn't want to hurt me, I guess. But I got the message another way. When he saw me in the cow-size clothes I had to buy, he just stopped giving me compliments. That crushed me. But it really took those slender, attractive women at the picnic to convince me that a wife can't sit back and get fat."
Eliminates conflict between need for habit and need for physical attractiveness.	I had tried to reduce a number of times with liquid meals, grapefruit diets, reducing pills. But they didn't work for me, especially the liquids. I needed something to chew on."
Reassures audience that need for health will be satisfied; "proves" the scientific validity of the product. Slowly gets into the proposal so as not to jar the audience's situational expectations.	"Thank goodness I'd read those stories of people who had taken those reducing-plan candies, Ayds. I finally decided to try them so I went to the drugstore and bought the plain chocolate fudge kind. I carefully read the direction folder in the box and learned that Ayds contained vitamins and minerals but no drugs. That made me feel even better about starting the Ayds plan."
Asserts that pattern and stability can be preserved with product; introduces appeal to efficiency. Emphasis on family links her closely to demographics of her audience.	"At breakfast, I took a couple of Ayds with tea—you can have any hot drink—about 15 minutes before eating. Cereal or an egg and toast for me. At lunch, I'd take my Ayds and tea again and have soup, sometimes a sandwich or salad. Then at dinner, Ayds and tea again and a small portion of whatever the family was having."

Table 4-2 (Continued)

Commentary	Sample Message
Reinforces efficacy and health arguments.	"I'll tell you, those Ayds really helped me curb my appetite. They're so good, I'd eat a couple between meals, too. They contain only 26 calories apiece, which was much better than a slice of my own chocolate frosted 'Wacky' cake."
Begins to satisfy need for distinctive personal identity; introduces fulfillment of social dominance need. Direct linkage to audience's presumed values.	"The plan worked beautifully for me. I lost pound after pound. Each time I went down, I'd run out of the bathroom and say: 'Come look, I've lost again!' When I hit 101 pounds, everybody in my home town, York, Pa., was looking. That's when the truth really comes out. Like this friend of mine. I used to complain about being fat. But she'd say: 'Oh, you're not heavy.' Now she introduces me this way: 'Would you believe that Shirley was once pudgy?'"
Summarizes satisfaction of family, heterosexual, and physical attractiveness needs.	"Larry, of course, is just as proud as he can be. Picks me up these days like I'm one of the kids. I'd never let him attempt it when I was fat."
Encapsulates the fulfillment of social dominance need; final reinforcement of femininity need.	"The company picnic changed for me this year, too. Thanks to the Ayds plan, I heard someone say: 'Wow! Here comes Larry and his "new" wife.'"[9]

Suggestions for Speaking

We have covered a good deal of territory in this chapter. We hope you now feel somewhat comfortable with the notion of audience analysis and see it as a vital part of the speaking enterprise. In this chapter, we tried to provide you with a number of suggestions for studying listeners

[9]"I Didn't Want to Lose Him, So I Lost 59 Pounds," by Shirley Gallagher (as told to Ruth McCarthy), *Family Circle*, August 1972. Reprinted by courtesy of Ayds.

but tried to avoid making it seem like some sort of mechanical process. At its best, audience analysis requires you to think in a semiorderly fashion about your listeners—what they know, what they feel, what elates and depresses them, what they have done, what they are hoping for.

In a sense, audience analysis can never be done badly if it is done at all. The more you think about your listeners and their potential reactions to your speech, the more likely you will be to compliment them, to make them feel that you have come to talk with them rather than to perform for them like some sort of dancing bear. Audience analysis keeps us humble. It reminds us that communication brings together essentially alien minds. Speaking, like all things worthwhile, requires effort. Painstaking audience analysis is part of that effort. Careful consideration of the fruits of audience analysis results in thoughts like the following:

1. Be especially attentive to the audience's moods and experiences that transpire just prior to your speaking; adjust your remarks accordingly.

2. Remove anything from your speech that makes it seem that you know the audience's minds better than they do.

3. Don't be overly self-conscious about your speaking; continual apologies for personal ineptness become tedious.

4. Make a list of the other speakers who have bored or irritated this audience; spot the likely reasons for their failures.

5. Be sure not to become overly responsive to one or two members of the audience and thereby insult all other listeners.

6. After speaking, go over your speech outline and make marginal notes about audience reactions received; save these notes for later use.

7. When possible, use examples that depict real people; try to insure that the persons depicted are congruent with your audience's demographics.

8. Feel free to mention your audience's reason for attending the speech; whether they are "captives" or highly motivated, they will appreciate your empathy.

9. If you violate your audience's expectations of you, be prepared to satisfy their resulting curiosity or to suffer the consequences of their disjointedness.

10. Never produce tension in your listeners by threatening their need satisfaction unless you *also* show them how to resolve the ambiguities you've created for them.

CHAPTER 5

The Informative Speech

"Write your own letter of recommendation," said Charlie, "and I'll sign whatever you write. I'll stop at your house on the way to the airport. . . ."

I was touched. Good old Charlie! What a friend! He had given me a blank check. All I had to do was write an unforgettable letter and my life would be changed from that of a lowly advertising copywriter to that of an exalted advertising-agency creative director. I went to my typewriter and began. . . .

This is to recommend Mr. James R. De Foe. He is a workhorse who would be an asset to any company. I have seen him work 12-hour days, 7 days a week, month in and month out. You have a winner in this gentleman who isn't afraid to roll up his sleeves and dig in. Sign him up quick whatever his price.

"You sound like a grind," my wife said. "If you get the job, they'll dump every kind of problem on top of you and expect you to live at the office."

"You're right," I said, getting myself another drink. "But I don't have much time. Only twenty minutes."

I wrote:

This is to recommend James R. De Foe, a charming, quick-witted and talented gentleman who isn't afraid of work. In the midst of the biggest crisis, Jim will come up with a jest that will break the tension. If you want to laugh, hire him. But don't be deceived by Jovial Jim. When the chips are down, he delivers with a smile. He's worth whatever price he asks.

"That's awful," my wife said. "I wouldn't trust such a clown to carry my groceries. You're applying for a top executive position, not office jester. You need a more balanced approach."

"You're right," I said, hating her. "Please pour me a drink."

I made another try.

This is to recommend James De Foe, a well-balanced man. He works hard; he plays hard; he's a delightful guy. Whether it's solving a problem or shooting out of a sandtrap, Jim's your man. You can't go wrong with well-balanced Jim De Foe. Meet his price, whatever it is.

"There's too much with the 'well-balanced,'" my wife said. "It sounds as if your sanity were being questioned. It also sounds fictitious. I can't picture such a person. There's no firmness, no character to the person. . . ."

"This is my last try," I said in the tightly controlled voice of a man about to explode. "Whatever I write now goes into that letter."

And I wrote:

It is my pleasure to recommend De Foe. He is adequate.[1]

Sometimes, it just isn't easy to explain our thoughts to others. It becomes especially difficult, as we see above, to explain *ourselves* to others in unfamiliar circumstances. Ignorance of the audience, lack of familiarity with certain communicative rules (e.g., propriety), failure to understand the scope of one's subject matter—all these can interfere with successful communication. It is small wonder, then, that so many of us throw in the towel from time to time and settle for mediocrity.

In this chapter, we would like to discuss how information can be shared with others. We will consider five tasks the informative speaker is especially advised to tackle and will suggest practical methods for so doing. Our hope is that when you set out to inform others about yourself and your ideas, you will be able to resist the several attractions of adequacy. Excellence can be had for such a modest additional investment.

Making Ideas Substantive: Research

To begin, let us presume that you are an afficianado of bluegrass music, that native American, toe-tapping, but not-quite-country music that has been "rediscovered" in the past two decades. Given your interest in bluegrass, your special attraction to performers like Earl Scruggs, and to instruments like the five-string banjo, you decide to make these matters your informative speech topic. There is more than a bit of a gap, however, between making this decision and delivering a successful informative speech. Although you may indeed have a burning "impulse" to tell others about your musical interests, your earnestness alone will hardly win you garlands. Getting another to understand some new concept normally requires that you search diligently for helpful and stimulating information. One begins such a search by looking inside oneself.

Self-Knowledge

What do you already know about bluegrass music? What experiences with the topic have you had that may prove fruitful for your speech? Undoubtedly, you already know a good deal. The real trick, of

[1]J. R. De Foe, "This Is to Recommend, Well . . . Me." Reprinted with permission from *The Saturday Evening Post,* January 28, 1967. Copyright, 1967. The Curtis Publishing Company.

course, is (1) retrieving these ideas from the storehouse of your mind, and (2) writing them down as quickly as they surface. As a retrieval aid, Wilson and Arnold have suggested using a systematic approach, labeled the Topical System for Generating Thoughts, which we described in Chapter 3.[2] For sake of illustration, let us consider your informative speech on the history of the five-string banjo to see how you might retrieve some of the information already "stored" within you:

1. *Existence.* The true American banjo was not invented until 1831, when a banjo enthusiast named Joel Sweeney made a small but revolutionary modification. He added a fifth string, higher in pitch than any of the others, right next to the lowest pitched string and secured by a peg mounted halfway up the neck.

2. *Degree.* No other instrument in the world was strung like the five-string banjo, which was plucked solely by the thumb.

3. *Space.* Black slaves brought the first banjos to the United States; before that the origin is disputed. Possibly, the Arabs brought banjos to the African west coast; possibly, the Arabs themselves picked them up from civilizations further east.

4. *Time.* Throughout the nineteenth century, the banjo held its place in America's affections, but around the turn of the century a decline set in.

5. *Motion.* The index finger of the right hand should pluck up, sounding the first string only. Then, with the other three fingers, brush down across all five strings.

6. *Form.* Earl Scruggs developed a new playing style, now known as "Scruggs Style Picking," which he introduced on the Grand Ole Opry in 1945.

7. *Substance.* The distant ancestor of the banjo, an instrument called the rebec, originated in Arabia a thousand years ago and consisted of a skin head stretched over a gourd or hollow body with a neck holding three gut strings.

8. *Capacity to Change.* Whereas in the basic method of strumming the right hand goes up, down, up, down, in frailing, all notes are plucked by the back of the fingernail as the hand moves downward. Whereas the notes are exactly the same on paper, they sound quite different when one method rather than another is used.

[2]*Public Speaking as a Liberal Art,* op. cit.

9. *Potency.* You can get a good deal more incisive punch and attack when you frail a banjo—a technique also called "beating" a banjo, "rapping," or "framing" the banjo.

10. *Desirability.* During the 1940s, a few folklorists discovered the five-string banjo and recognized it as one of America's most remarkable contributions to the world's music.

11. *Feasibility.* The tenor banjo, which used heavier strings and was tuned differently to better compete with the loud bass instruments of ragtime and jazz, had its heyday in the 1920s.

12. *Causality.* The popularity of the banjo was important in perpetuating and preserving many songs that otherwise would have been forgotten.

13. *Correlation.* The tenor banjo was strummed in jazz bands, and the old finger-picking styles were abandoned along with the fifth string.

14. *Genus-species.* Among the many styles of picking and strumming a banjo is the "Lullaby Lick." Three fingers as well as the thumb are used, plucking each string separately, as in the classic guitar. This style is especially useful for slow, quiet songs for which one wants a sustained effect.

15. *Similarity.* The basic principles of the melodic style are pretty simple. All or almost all of the notes played in this style are melody notes. This is unlike standard bluegrass style, in which the minority of the notes played are used as melody notes (most are used as background, fill-in notes).

16. *Possibility.* No sound is more deeply rooted in American history than the thrilling ring of the five-string banjo.

After having generated (or regenerated) ideas of this sort, you may well have a sense of fulfillment. The helpful thing about the topical system is that it often brings to mind information that we don't realize we possess. Such information is especially important in communication situations because we can normally have greater impact upon others when sharing ideas that are uniquely ours. In the language of Chapter 2, commitment to the message is more easily revealed in such circumstances.

Alas, we were not born all-knowing. Although you may have learned a good deal about banjos through your years as a fan, much of your information is probably (1) disjointed, (2) not comprehensive, and in some cases, (3) insufficiently detailed. Your knowledge of bluegrass has come to you as "incidental information," information that is randomly structured and, therefore, not especially trustworthy. While incidental information may stand us in good stead during informal exchanges with others, it normally can't sustain us in formal speaking situations.

Yet another factor makes incidental information less than reliable —it may not be sufficiently *current*. Dr. Lewis Thomas, Head of the Memorial Sloan-Kettering Cancer Center, suggests why currency of information is a special problem in his area of biomedical research:

> *The enterprise of biomedical research in the United States has expanded in scale and scope so greatly in the past 30 years that no one can begin to keep up with the reading of it. It used to be that a working immunologist could keep abreast of his field by covering three or four professional journals, plus Nature and Science for the first accounts of new observations. Now there are ten times that number of journals, each containing papers on immunology that cannot be overlooked, plus any number of monographs, review volumes, national and international symposium reports, and even a few newsletters. The journals are themselves five times their former size, with briefer articles and smaller print.*[3]

In other words, Dr. Thomas is suggesting that it takes a very special sort of arrogance to presume that personal, or incidental, knowledge is sufficient to sustain our attempts to inform others.

Borrowed Knowledge

How, then, is it possible to collect comprehensive and current knowledge in any area? An indispensable tool is the ability to locate, organize, and use library resources efficiently. This ability, however, is significantly enhanced by first consulting the experts and specialists in the area, individuals who are often readily available on college campuses or in the surrounding community. What books and articles do they recommend? What resources have proved to be specially useful to them? Do they know other people who might guide your search for usable information? When contacting such consultants, you might keep the following suggestions in mind:

1. Engage in preliminary research concerning both the person and the subject matter to be discussed.

2. Contact individuals by phone, specifying the nature of the information sought and the amount of their time requested.

[3]L. Thomas, "Hubris in Science?" *Science*, 30:1459 (1978).

3. Plan an opening for the conversation that builds rapport, orients the individual to the topic, and motivates the person to want to help you.

4. Think through potential topics and subtopics, and record them in the form of a brief list, which will be used to ensure that key topics are not missed during your interview.

5. Choose a suitable method of recording information. This may involve taking notes, or tape-recording the conversation, or writing a summary after the event. Whereas tape-recording or taking notes may be preferable for greatest accuracy, in some cases these methods reduce the willingness of individuals to talk freely and openly with you. When taking notes, explain first why you are doing so, work at maintaining eye contact with your interviewee while writing, and take notes evenly through-out the conversation (to avoid signaling the information that you consider most important).

Should you choose to use a tape recorder, ask permission in advance, get to know the machine thoroughly before interview time, and make the machine as unobtrusive as possible (use a small microphone and place the recorder in an inconspicuous place).

Having sought and received the general advice of experts, you should now be ready to fill in missing details by visiting the library. When conducting research in the library, be sure to take advantage of the services of the reference librarian. He or she is well trained to isolate needed information quickly and efficiently. In addition, familiarizing yourself with the information that follows will fortify you as you search for speech materials.

Books. Current textbooks can help you locate reference materials on almost any topic. Those that are in your library will be recorded in the card catalog, which is organized like the telephone directory. The author/title catalog is like the white pages and might be used when, for example, an expert has nominated a good, current book and you, there-fore, already know the name of the author or the title. If you need to locate books on a subject but don't have any authors or titles in mind, use the subject catalog, which is similar to the yellow pages of your phone book. In general, when using the subject catalog, the most recently published book on the subject is the most reliable. Once you have obtained the book, relevant chapters can be scanned. Also, further your search by using the author's index at the end of the book and the extensive bibliographies that appear either at the end of particular chap-ters or at the end of the book as a whole.

Periodicals and pamphlets. A volume entitled *Uhlrich's International Periodicals Directory* lists over 60,000 periodicals throughout the world; these periodicals are grouped by subject headings, arranged alphabetically within subjects, and cross-indexed by subject area. Locating those periodicals especially related to your topic sometimes constitutes a formidable task. For more general help, consult *The Readers' Guide to Periodical Literature*, an up-to-date listing of popular magazines that are largely nontechnical in nature. Here, articles are listed alphabetically by author, title, and subject. This index is published monthly, and the monthly installments are assembled into quarterly and yearly volumes. A variety of more specialized indexes cover scholarly journals and literature not included in *The Readers' Guide.* Some of these indexes are

> *Art Index* (featuring the fine arts, photography, film, architecture, art history, city planning, and interior and landscape design)
>
> *Business Periodicals Index* (economics, marketing, accounting, finance, and management)
>
> *Education Index* (elementary education, secondary education, educational philosophy, special education, philosophy and history of education, and educational administration)
>
> *Humanities Index* (English and American literature, history, philosophy, religion, music, speech, foreign languages and literatures, journalism, and theater)

Social Sciences Index (sociology, communication, psychology, political science, anthropology, geography, and criminal justice)

Most of these latter indexes cover much more than the journal literature on the topic. They also include such items as monographs, dissertations, convention papers, symposia, reviews, research communications, and preliminary reports. Thus, consulting a specialized index for your speech topic is often an extremely efficient way to obtain the most recent literature on one's topic.

Computer searches. A relatively recent addition to the services of most research libraries is the use of the computer to retrieve citations from indexing and abstracting services. The DIALOG Information Retrieval Service (from Lockeed Information Systems), for example, has been serving users since 1972 and currently searches more than 100 data bases containing more than 35 million records. The advantages of such a computerized service are numerous: (1) It's faster and more economical —the computer can search all uses of a key concept (e.g., *bluegrass*) contained in a data base; it can scan a large volume of information without getting tired, and multiple data bases can be searched simultaneously; (2) it's easier—the computer provides a legible and well-formatted printout, thus eliminating the drudgery of writing out citations by hand; and (3) it's current—data bases are more up-to-date than are the printed indexes; also, some data bases are not available in printed formats.

Such computer-based services are not without their pitfalls, however: (1) Often they cover a limited time span and do not go back to the start of an index; (2) when the vocabulary of an area is vague, the

computer will not catch all semantic variations of a key concept; thus, an article entitled "Bluegrass Gaining Popularity in London" would probably not be retrieved by a computer search focused on the key concept *culture;* and (3) citations are not screened for relevance. Thus, a search using the key word *banjo* would probably retrieve an article entitled "Eddie Cantor: Banjo Eyes Stuns Vaudeville Audience." Despite these disadvantages, however, the potential payoff in expanded research capabilities and in saved time makes the computer search often worthwhile. Be sure, therefore, to check with your local reference librarian to see if such services are available to you.

Other resources. The resources of the library are vast, and it is impossible to list all of the useful guides to the wealth of information it contains. Six of the more useful sources of information, however, are (1) encyclopedias that are valuable for their brief, general articles on a wide variety of subjects and for their short reference lists at the end of principal articles; (2) newspaper indexes such as *The New York Times Index,* which twice a month indexes all articles appearing in that newspaper. Indexes are also available for the *Christian Science Monitor,* the *Wall Street Journal,* the *Washington Post,* the *Chicago Tribune,* and others; (3) the *Federal Index,* which indexes monthly the *Congressional Record, Federal Register, Presidential Documents, Commerce Business Daily,* and *Washington Post;* (4) the *Monthly Catalog of United States Government Documents,* which lists all publications of executive branch agencies and congressional committees arranged by subject and title; (5) a large number of sources of biographical information such as *Who's Who, Who's Who in America,* and *Directory of American Scholars;* and (6) collections of noteworthy quotations, the most notable of which is John Bartlett's *Familiar Quotations.*

By using resources such as these, you will surely find more than ample information for your speech on bluegrass music. A list of your primary resources for such a speech might appear as follows:

INTERVIEWS WITH BANJO PICKERS

Eddie Adcock, Second Generation

J. D. Crowe, J. D. Crowe and the New South

Steve Hanson, Bluegrass Crusade

Alan Munde, Country Gazette

BOOKS

Bob Artis, *Bluegrass.* (New York: Hawthorn, 1975).

Steven D. Price, *Old as the Hills: The Story of Bluegrass Music.* (New York: The Viking Press, 1975).

Earl Scruggs, *Earl Scruggs and the 5-String Banjo*. (New York: Peer International Corporation, 1968).

Pete Seeger, *How to Play the 5-String Banjo*, 3rd ed. (New York: published by the author, 1962).

Peter Wernick, *Bluegrass Banjo*. (New York: Oak Publications, 1974).

PERIODICALS

Banjo Newsletter, Box 364, Greensboro, Md. 21639.

Bluegrass Unlimited, Box 111, Broad Run, Va. 22014.

Frets: The Magazine of Acoustic String Instruments, P. O. Box 28836, San Diego, Calif. 92127.

Pickin', not published after 1979.

Muleskinner News, not published after 1976.

Taking Notes

Although generating ideas is important, they must be written down as they surface if they are to be truly useful. This requires discipline, for if one merely resolves to record the idea later, "when I get a chance," the odds are that the idea will not be available when needed. Although workable approaches to recording ideas are numerous, the following guidelines may help you preserve the information you have generated through research:

1. Write your notes on cards or heavy slips of paper. This makes them easier to file and sort while gathering material, flexible when you are organizing them into a speech, and more convenient to use when actually speaking. While the size of the cards employed is a matter of personal preference, most persons settle upon the 3 × 5 size because they find 4 × 6 cards too large to carry and file conveniently.

2. The important rules governing the writing of research notes are be accurate, be complete, write legibly, and *put one unit of information on a card*. When implementing these rules, record the source of the information in complete form, enclosing verbatim quotations in quotation marks (''), and indicating omissions by ellipses (. . .) and interpolations by brackets ([]). An example of a research note that applies these rules is provided in Figure 5-1.

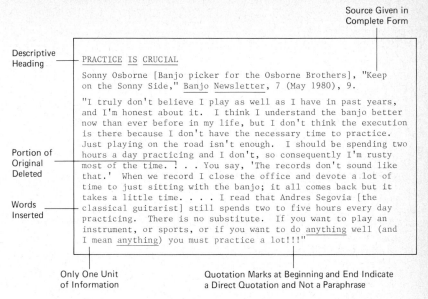

Figure 5-1 Sample Note Card for Informative Speaking

3. When an exact statement is not necessary, use a paraphrased summary. Remember, however, the injunction to summarize fairly. The note must always reflect as accurately as possible the view expressed by the source.

In a sense, researching material for an informative speech is similar to discovering information for use in a term paper. However, unlike the writer of a term paper, the informative speaker must be concerned with how his or her unearthed ideas can be *adapted to a particular set of listeners.* Thus, it becomes paramount for such a speaker to recall the many audience-based suggestions we made in Chapter 4. It will profit you very little to obtain the "complete story" of bluegrass music if you are unable to *intensify* those ideas for ordinary, nonspecialized hearers. Therefore, always "filter" your information by asking yourself which of it will be immediately clear and compelling for listeners and which will demand orientation from you as speaker. Unfortunately, perhaps as much as half of the information you uncover will not meet this latter test. On the other hand, anything that you learn about your topic will repay you dividends in terms of your own increased understanding of the subject matter and your confidence in discussing it with others.

Making Ideas Intense: Clarification and Attention Devices

In this section, we would like to present two major resources a speaker has for making complex ideas understandable to others. The importance of understanding how to use these devices has never been more apparent. As the world grows increasingly convoluted, there seems to be an ever-increasing need to know more and more, and to be able to do more and more. The amount of information generated to meet these needs is staggering. As Louis Martin points out, "If an average reader tried to catch up with one year's output of learned publications in the sciences, it would take him about 50 years of reading at 24 hours a day for seven days a week."[4] As a result of the "information explosion," the communication of new and complex information is an important feature of a modern technological society.

But information, especially technical information, is often hard to comprehend. Our premise here is that information has very little social value until it is "intensified" for listeners—until it is made both *clear* and *compelling* for them. It is only when information becomes intensified that listeners are motivated to act upon it and thereby to use it in some practical way.

Clarifying Devices

Clarity does not simply "exist." It is produced by a combination of what a speaker says and the resources listeners have within them for dealing with such information. The producers of "Sesame Street" can teach a youngster the alphabet because they are aware of certain needs imbedded in their audience.

The list of such needs will not overwhelm (or surprise) you: *Listeners usually prefer the specific to the general, and the concrete to the abstract.* But do not get carried away with this. When your boyfriend asks you why you love him, you should not reply, with all the specificity and concreteness in the world, "I love you because you make a good salami sandwich." Such a refrain might make things clear, but it sure would take the mystery out of life.

Another reason why you should not follow the letter of our "law" blindly is that it is often necessary for a listener to understand the general makeup of the forest before she is able to appreciate the characteristics of the stately maple. Similarly, unless a listener is able to build abstractions from concrete material, he is unlikely to grasp truly the

[4]L. Martin, "Science Is Polluted by Printed Words . . . Billions," *Chicago Tribune,* June 7, 1970.

import of his knowledge. So, clarifying ideas is a process of (1) pointing out to listeners things they have "seen" but not "noticed" and (2) helping them interpret things they may have noticed but not treated as important.

When attempting to clarify a complex idea, several resources are available to us. Suppose, for example, that you are a sociology major and have decided to give a speech on the importance of reference groups. When preparing your remarks, you will have available to you several "complexity reducers." Table 5-3 lists a number of them.

One profitable way of using Table 5-1 might be as a checklist. When you are having difficulty finding a good way of explaining an idea, you could run through these standard clarification devices to see if anything "clicks." It is probably wise to vary the methods of clarification used in a speech in order to provide variety. It is also good to remember that some subjects lend themselves to the use of certain clarification devices more than others. (What physical education professor, for example, could resist comparing and contrasting the motor movements utilized in basketball with those used in football?) The most important thing to remember about these methods of clarification, however, is to keep their functions uppermost in mind: These devices are used to support and clarify ideas—they should not "overtake" the general principle being explained lest the listener remember, say, the interesting story and forget the concept being discussed.

Factors of Attention

When trying to clarify ideas, it is often good to remember that a person cannot learn a thing until he or she first attends to it. Because it is so basic, this proposition is an easy one to forget. Also, because listening is such a complex process, audience members have many "claims" on their attention in any given speech setting—the seats are hard, the guy in the front row is good-looking, meal time is approaching, and—oh, yes—the speaker is up there talking!

A learner's attention is an undulating phenomenon. It rises and falls and changes both in force and direction over time. We are wise to remember that *an audience member is always attending to something;* hence, the speaker's job is one of focusing that person's attention on himself or herself and the topic at hand.

The research on attention is limited, but we know that at least 11 elements command attention rather regularly.[5] Thus, you might use the following list as another prespeech checklist to insure that you have

[5] Adapted from J. Wilson and C. Arnold, *Public Speaking as a Liberal Art*, 2nd ed. (Boston: Allyn and Bacon, 1968), pp. 99–100. Reprinted with permission.

Table 5-1 Clarifying Devices

Type	Functions	Example
Serial Examples	Adds *totality* to a speaker's remarks by presenting, in scattered fashion, numerous instances of the same phenomenon.	"Parents can act as our reference groups, as can friends, political groups, religious organizations, social fraternities, and so on."
Extended Example	Adds *vivacity* to a speaker's remarks by presenting a detailed picture of a single event or concept.	"Let's consider what happened to John Jones, an undergrad who has had trouble 'sorting out' his reference groups. John started school like most people, and soon . . ."
Quantification	Adds a feeling of *substantiveness* to a speaker's remarks by means of concrete enumerations.	"Some experts estimate that 70 percent of our decisions are affected by our reference groups, and that one out of every three people experiences tensions in relation to reference group choice."
Isolated Comparisons	Adds *realism* to a speaker's remarks by drawing analogically upon a listener's past experiences.	"Reference groups are like spouses—you can't live without them, but sometimes it's darn hard to live with them!"
Extended Comparisons	Adds psychological *reference points* to a speaker's remarks by successively structuring his or her perceptions along familiar lines.	"A reference group is similar to a mother—it nurtures our feelings when we are hurt, it disciplines us for violating its norms, it helps us mature by . . ."

Table 5-1 (Continued)

Type	Functions	Example
Testimony	Adds to the *inclusiveness* of a speaker's remarks by quoting appreciatively from known or respected sources or depreciatively from sources of ill-regard.	"Sociologist Carolyn Sherif has said that none of us can really escape the influence of the groups we identify with—our reference groups."
Pictorialization	Adds to the *concreteness* of a speaker's remarks by presenting graphic representations of the speaker's assertions.	
Definition	Adds to the *specificity* of a speaker's remarks by limiting the speech topic in some fashion.	"Let's consider what is not meant by a reference group. It is not just any group we belong to, nor is it always identifiable. Rather it is . . ."
Contrast	Adds a *dramatic* quality to a speaker's remarks by depicting opposed elements.	"Those who identify with many groups have very different attitudes from those who are more individualistic."

built materials into your speech that will help sharpen listeners' perceptions and cause them to focus on the information you're presenting:

1. *Activity:* depicting elements in a state of real or imagined motion

2. *Proximity:* depicting elements as being close in space or time to the listener

3. *Specificity:* depicting detailed aspects of an element

4. *Intensity:* depicting one element (the speaker) as being psychologically immersed in another element (the topic)

5. *Novelty:* depicting new or unusual aspects of an element

6. *Humor:* depicting incongruous, unexpected, juxtaposed, or familiar elements

7. *Realism:* depicting and emphasizing the sensory qualities of an element

8. *Conflict:* depicting two or more elements in opposition

9. *Familiarity:* depicting elements as being psychologically close to the listener's past perceptions

10. *Suspense:* depicting an element with uncertain consequences

11. *Variety:* depicting a large number of apparently unassociated elements

To make this list somewhat more concrete, let us assume that you have chosen to alert your classmates to the dangers of pollution. Following are statements you might make to incorporate the (verbal) factors of attention:

1. *Activity.* No matter where you drive these days—from the wheat fields of Kansas, through the winding Rockies, and then down to the Great Salt Lake—our ecology is going to pot.

2. *Proximity.* Heck, right here at the university we've got problems. Just look out the window and see how the power plant is polluting the air.

3. *Specificity.* I have just returned from a trip to Connersville, where the Mylon Paper Company has been fined for dumping pollutants into the Fairfax River. Some progress is being made.

4. *Intensity.* I have been working my tail off for over three years trying to get this school to offer a curriculum in environmental problems. I've been buffeted and battered by every bureaucrat on campus, and I'm tired of it!

5. *Novelty.* If we keep polluting the atmosphere at the rate we are now, in ten years you won't be able to walk in a city without getting lung cancer.

6. *Humor.* One report I've heard states that our forests are in such bad shape that Smokey the Bear has resigned from the Forest Rangers!

7. *Realism.* Try driving through Gary, Indiana. Your nostrils burn, your breath becomes short, and your head starts to throb because of the noxious gases in the air.

8. *Conflict.* Nature could do her job if people would stop battering the plant life, raping the land, and crushing the topsoil.

9. *Familiarity.* Think about the nature hikes you went on when you were in grade school. The water was fresh, the air clean, the plants resilient. Now look what we've got.

10. *Suspense.* We can continue to overpopulate; we can continue to increase thermal pollution; we can continue to dump our wastes indiscriminately; but if we do, . . .

11. *Variety.* Think about drinking toxic residues. Think about living in glassed-in cities. Think about seeing thousands of dead fish on the beach. Think about pollution.

Several facts are important to note about this matter of attention. Because of the basic biological and psychological nature of people, *attention is easy to get but difficult to maintain.* For example, a psychedelic light show will immediately arrest our attention, but unless the stimulus is changed, the variegated intensities and hues of the lights will soon become boring, and our attention will wander—our senses will have become saturated. Thus, although the tried-and-true, surefire joke in the speech may help the audience attend to the speech initially, the humor alone will not insure the continued adherence of the audience to the speaker's message.

As mentioned before, the speaker's job is not so much one of getting attention, but rather one of *focusing attention* on the speaker and his or her message. A listener's attention has a tendency to scatter when presented with a fixed stimulus (e.g., a speaker standing in front of the room talking). So, the speaker must constantly be on guard to make sure that the attention factors he or she employs are constricting the attentive powers of the audience. Walking a donkey into the room will surely serve to command the attention of the audience, but it is unlikely that such a tactic will focus their attention on matters pertaining to the space program. Like everything else worthwhile, there are no shortcuts to intensifying ideas. Careful forethought and consideration of multiple approaches are still the surest methods of constructing an intense and understandable message.

Making Ideas Coherent: Organizational Devices

Perhaps the most important resource for clarifying ideas is that of *sequencing* information in the simplest and most straightforward manner possible. Why is this the case? Most likely, speech organization is crucial because *people habitually think in patterned ways.* Thus, a speaker must give serious thought to methods of linking ideas together. Having considered some of the elementary aspects of speech organization in Chapter 3, we can now delve into this important matter in greater detail.

To assist us in making these sequencing decisions, some basic facts about human listeners may help: (1) Listeners must have their attention focused on a matter before they can comprehend it; (2) listeners want to know *why* they should listen before they will listen; (3) listeners find it easier to move from the familiar to the unfamiliar than in the reverse direction; (4) listeners need to understand the simple before they can comprehend the complex; and (5) listeners like to move from the concrete to the abstract. Although none of these elementary principles will shock you, it is surprising how often speakers violate such basic tenets of human communication. In their desire to delve into the material, speakers often forget about their listeners' needs for pattern and hence foster confusion and frustration.

While no single method of organizing ideas will be satisfactory in all speaking situations, the system known as Monroe's Motivated Sequence is useful for understanding listeners' psychological demands.[6] Streamlined a bit, Monroe's system looks something like this:

1. *Orientation.* Studies have suggested that appropriate "frames of reference" must be established before a person can grasp unfamiliar material. This search for common ground between the audience's knowledge and the material to be discussed in the speech must be made if the speech is to be effective. By "reminding" the audience of experiences they have had previously, of things they have already learned, or of needs they are desirous of fulfilling, the speaker can "precue" the speaking experience and thus make the subsequently presented material easier to comprehend.

2. *Need.* From what we have said previously about attention and motivation, it should come as no surprise to learn that audiences

[6]For a more complete discussion of this approach, see D. Ehninger, A. Monroe, and B. Gronbeck, *Principles and Types of Speech Communication*, 8th ed. (Glenview, Ill.: Scott, Foresman and Company, 1978), pp. 142–163.

operate best when they perceive that a potentially important topic is being dealt with by the speaker and that, by giving the speaker their attention, they will be able to improve their lives. Dramatizing the "need" to pay attention is not always easy, especially when the material being dealt with seems trite at first glance. Thus, many speakers begin by showing why the audience should pay attention and how the material to be presented will affect their lives.

3. *Satisfaction.* If a listener's curiosity has been piqued by the general problem being dealt with, he or she is likely to "stay around" mentally for the solution. Listeners need "closure"— that is, the completion of the story—and hence, one of the major jobs the speaker has is to "process" or wrap up the speech. Audiences do not appreciate loose ends and become frustrated if a problem has been presented with no means of resolving it. Consequently, the speaker must guard against the mistake that almost every novice speaker makes sooner or later: cramming too much material into too short a time and thus leaving no time to summarize and thereby to satisfy the audience's need for completeness.

Methods of Organization

Armed with just these few casual observations of the audience's condition, the speaker can avoid many of the problems that develop because of poorly sequenced messages. Yet these general remarks about speech organization do not reveal the specific resources available to the speaker.

While any number of reliable methods may give shape to a body of ideas, it is not true that the subject itself will suggest the best method of organizing the message. For example, consider the case of the child development major who is dealing with the general topic of childhood autonomy. At first glance, it might appear that only a chronological presentation of the facts would be advantageous. But after a bit more reflection, it should be apparent that the same material can be structured in many different ways. Consider some of the standard forms of organization shown in Table 5-2, and let us examine the options available to our speaker.

When deciding upon a method of organization, it might be helpful to keep in mind a few criteria: (1) Does the method of organization help to present a comprehensive view of my topic? (2) Is the structure of the speech suited to highlighting the most significant aspects of my topic? And, most importantly, (3) does the method of structuring the speech get my audience to see what I want them to see? Some speakers favor some methods of organization more than others, but experimenting with all of them from time to time may be worthwhile. Although such trial-and-error approaches may not be totally comforting to you, it is still the best procedure we have in communicating effectively.

Table 5-2 Methods of Organization

Type	Description	Example
Chronological	Places time relationships of message topics in the foreground. Maintains a narrative line.	"Even the infant's scream can be seen as his attempt to dramatize his unique needs. By the age of 2, the child is beginning to experience the rewards and costs associated with independence. At around 5 years of age, the child has made a significant number of choices relative to dependence-independence."
Spatial	Shows coherence or differentiation among message topics in terms of space relationships.	"The child soon learns that autonomy is a relative matter—at the dinner table, he is submerged in the family group; at the playground he must fight his siblings for Mommy's attention; but in his own bedroom, he is king!"
Causal	Attempts to show the clear, sufficient, and/or practical implications of cause-to-effect or effect-to-cause relationships.	"By the age of 4, the child can be a fairly independent entity. This can be attributed to three acculturating influences: parents, siblings, and forces from the outside world. Let's consider each of them in order."

Table 5-2   (Continued)

Type	Description	Example
Ascending-Descending	Places message topics in sequence according to their relative importance, familiarity, or complexity.	"Parents undoubtedly exert the most influence on the child's capacity to be independent. Next come his brothers and sisters, who positively or negatively reinforce such parental pressures. Outside forces (such as television) can also affect the young child but generally less so than his immediate family."
Problem-Solution	A standard pattern of organizing speech topics by means of dramatizing an obstacle and then presenting alternative remedies.	"In his early years, the child fights a Herculean battle between dependency and autonomy. He is constantly torn between striking out on his own and bending to the will of the family. Typically, children handle such problems in one of three ways: submission, rejection, or compromise."
Topical	Perhaps the most common method of organization whereby selected but parallel elements of the same subject are focused on successively.	"There are three areas in which the child's struggle for autonomy becomes pronounced: social development, intellectual maturation, and physical development. Let's first consider social development. . . ."

Forms of Emphasis

If the information we present is to have impact, in most cases we would like listeners to remember what we have said. Without looking at the cover of this book, can you remember the names of all three authors? There are probably many reasons for your forgetting our names, not the least of which is that you probably perceived no need to commit them to memory. So how is it that we come to remember? And how may you insure that your listeners will at least retain the information most crucial to your message? Although you may have decided on the *overall* method of organizing your speech, it is also necessary for you to help listeners (1) get from point 1 to point 2 easily, and (2) remember the substance of both points.

Pace and Boren mention three common types of emphasis you can use to help your listeners understand complex information. These include

1. *Proactive emphasis:* accomplished by any method that forecasts, cues, highlights, summarizes in advance, or underscores ideas to be presented and developed later in a message

2. *Coactive emphasis:* accomplished by any method that intensifies the impact of an idea as it is being presented or that stresses the relationship of that idea to some other idea in a message

3. *Reactive emphasis:* accomplished by any method that reviews or summarizes what has passed or that highlights ideas that have already been developed in a message[7]

Sometimes called "previewing," *proactive emphasis* consists of highlighting, in advance, message components that you wish an audience to remember. This highlighting may take the form of an introductory statement of the main points you will cover in your speech, or it may take the form of blatant signposts (e.g., "I want you to remember this") immediately preceding your making an important point. In either form, the function of proactive emphasis is to assist audience members in their "rehearsal" of the information you present and to guide them in following along with your message.

Coactive emphasis serves two functions: It intensifies the impact of your idea as you develop it, and it states the relationship of this idea to the other ideas in your message. By both verbal and nonverbal means, that is, we can use coactive emphasis to highlight the importance of the

---

[7]From *The Human Transaction* by R. W. Pace and R. R. Boren, Copyright © 1973 by Scott, Foresman and Company. Reprinted by permission of the publisher.

point we are making and to show how that idea relates to the overall structure of what we have said. The influence of coactive emphasis on the retention of information is vividly reported by Linkugel and Berg:

> Studies conducted at Atlanta show that when knowledge was imparted to a person by telling alone, the recall three hours later was 70%, and three days later, only 10%. When imparted by showing alone, the knowledge recall three hours later was 72%, and three days later, about 35%. A marked improvement. But does this mean that we should stop speaking and just show pictures? Obviously no. When both telling and showing were the teaching tools . . . the recall three hours later was 85%, and three days later, 65%. This should emphasize that recall increases markedly by using both speech and pictures.[8]

As any confirmed TV viewer knows, advertisers have recognized for many years that our third form of reinforcement, *reactive emphasis* or repetition, is effective in getting listeners to recall products and brand names. Ehrensberger found that directing attention to what has passed and/or pointing to a specific idea that is fundamental to information gain are effective devices.[9] He found that the simple expedient of scattering three repetitions throughout a speech was most effective in promoting retention of the speech material. Even more effective, however, was the use of "concentrated" repetition—state your idea, restate it as you develop the idea, and conclude the development of your idea with a final restatement.

In applying this latter principle to the key ideas of his or her speech, the speaker is wise to remember that just saying something again and again will not enhance clarity significantly. If, for example, you are not familiar with the "linguistic-kinesic analogy," the repetition will not be of much help. Adapted and varied repetition seems to be the key to reducing the complexity of a spoken message.

Making Ideas Coherent: Outlining

Having identified a wide variety of speech materials and some criteria for choosing among them, the time has come for putting the jigsaw puzzle together. Assuming that you have seized upon a particular organizational method, let us now consider some principles of outlining that are equally appropriate to any organizational scheme.

[8]W. Linkugel and D. Berg, *A Time to Speak* (Belmont, Cal.: Wadsworth, 1970), pp. 68–69.

[9]R. Ehrensberger, "An Experimental Study of the Relative Effects of Certain Forms of Emphasis in Public Speaking," *Speech Monographs*, 12:94–111 (1945).

Creating an effective outline involves three principal steps: (1) determining the specific purpose for the speech; (2) deciding which materials are relevant and irrelevant to that purpose; and (3) organizing and patterning the relevant ideas so that both speaker and audience can perceive and remember them easily.

Having discussed the first two steps in Chapter 3, we will focus here on the third. It requires two actions on the part of the speaker: first, identifying those three to five main heads that most directly and effectively support, develop, and explain the specific purpose for the speech and, second, planning and ordering subheads and supporting materials so that they directly develop, clarify, and intensify the main headings. The end result of this process is an outline—a visual, schematic summary of the material to be presented in the speech—showing the order of topics and the general relationship between them. Its chief purpose is to test the organization of the speech and to make its development and delivery both easier and more effective for the speaker.

Basically, there are three types of outlines:

1. *A complete-sentence outline,* which lists each head and subhead in complete-sentence form. Its chief advantage is that of forcing the outliner to think through ideas thoroughly in order to give them complete and elaborate statement. It also makes it easier for the speaker to check organizational choices by giving the outline to others in order to get their reactions to the speech's organizational structure.

2. *A topic outline,* which keeps the form of the sentence outline but reduces the sentences to brief phrases or single words. While it retains most of the advantages of the sentence outline for the speaker, the topic outline makes it difficult for an outsider to check the speaker's organizational choices. For this reason, teachers who require students to submit outlines generally prefer that they be written in complete sentence form.

3. *A speaker's outline* in which only key words and divisions are listed. Such outlines are typically written on file cards and used to trigger the speaker's memory during the speech.

In order to illustrate the three types of outlines and to provide a basis for describing major principles for creating them, it will be helpful to return to our chronicler of the five-string banjo used by bluegrass musicians. Tables 5-3–5-5 depict the alternative methods of outlining for a speech employing the chronological style of organization.

Table 5-3 The Complete-Sentence Outline

I. *The five-string banjo is an adaptation of a much earlier instrument.*
   A. The ancient ancestor of the banjo, an instrument called the rebec, originated in Arabia a thousand years ago and can still be purchased today in the larger markets of the Middle East.
      1. It consists of a skin head stretched over a gourd or hollow body with a neck holding three gut strings.
      2. The rebec was probably carried both east and west with the spread of Islam.
   B. Black slaves brought the banjo to the United States from North and West Africa.
      1. In his "Notes on the State of Virginia," published in 1785, Thomas Jefferson said the "banjar" was the principal musical instrument of the African slave.
      2. The banjo of the slave, although similar to the Arabian rebec, had a fourth string.
   C. The true American Banjo was invented in 1831 when a banjo enthusiast, Joel Sweeney, added a fifth string.
      1. Sweeney, born in Appomattox, Virginia, in 1813, was often billed as the "Banjo King."
         a. At an early age, he organized his own Appomattox band.
         b. During his lifetime, he was the foremost of the blackface minstrels and has been called the "father of American minstrelry."
            (1) He composed many songs based on the melodies of the slaves.
            (2) His company was the first of a long line of minstrel shows, which continued as popular entertainment up until the 1890s.
            (3) He was a hit on the New York stage after a wagon tour through the South, and his fame carried him to England, where he appeared before Queen Victoria at a command performance.
      2. While there were other five-string banjos before the Sweeney invention, his was unique.
         a. He added a fifth string, higher in pitch than any of the others, right next to the lowest pitched string and secured it by mounting a peg halfway up the neck.
         b. The fifth string, plucked solely by the thumb, is the blend in the banjo and creates the familiar ring.
II. *The popularity of the five-string banjo has varied over the years.*
   A. Throughout the nineteenth century, the banjo held its place in Americans' affections.

1. It was an important part of popular entertainment.
2. More importantly, however, it entertained thousands of nameless Americans during long evenings in log cabins, shanties, river steamboats, and gold-mining boom towns.
   a. Banjoists played "old time songs" (now called folk music) and passed on banjo lore from player to player: Old folks taught the young ones, and good players swapped stylistic secrets.
   b. The popularity of the banjo was important in perpetuating and preserving many songs that otherwise would have been forgotten, since little of this music was ever written down.

B. Around the turn of the century, a decline in the popularity of the five-string banjo occurred.
   1. The advent of jazz was one factor in this decline.
      a. The long-necked, five-string banjo was gradually abandoned in favor of the tenor banjo.
         (1) The tenor banjo used four heavier strings and was tuned differently to allow it to produce enough volume to be heard through the loud brass instruments.
         (2) In some cases, the change went even further, and the instrument was reduced to mandolin size and strung with eight strings.
   2. Only a few bands and natives of the more remote parts of the South kept alive the tradition of the five-string banjo.

C. The decades of the 1920s and 1930s produced a continuing decline in the popularity of the instrument.
   1. In the 1920s, however, when commercial recording companies put out their earliest folk discs, some of the remaining old-time banjo players were recorded.
      a. Several recording companies sent teams into the Deep South to record some of the old-timers still playing.
      b. As a result, scraps and fragments of the old playing styles and old songs were preserved on long-playing records.
   2. By 1930, the use of the four-string tenor banjo was fading fast as dance bands replaced ragtime and jazz in popularity.
   3. By 1940, even the country music bands were dropping the five-string banjo.
      a. The banjo players who remained playing on radio were usually billed as a single attraction and were not included in a group of musicians.
      b. By this time, the instrument was no longer being made, except on special order, and demand was very limited.

    D. The 1940s produced renewed interest in the five-string banjo, which continues today.

       1. A few folklorists discovered the five-string banjo and recognized it as one of our most remarkable contributions to the world's music.

       2. It was soon after World War II that a few bands began using the banjo again.

       3. In 1945, Earl Scruggs introduced what is now known as "Scruggs Style Picking" on the Grand Ole Opry.

          a. His style spread rapidly, and within two years the demand for the five-string banjo was so great that the instrument companies began to manufacture them again.

          b. The bands that used a banjo in their group began increasing steadily throughout the United States and foreign countries.

III. *A major style of music that features the five-string banjo is known as "bluegrass music."*

    A. Bluegrass music is traditional mountain music with roots in the ballads and folk dances of Europe.

       1. Instrumentally, it features such acoustic instruments as the banjo, fiddle, guitar, mandolin, and bass.

       2. Vocally, it features higher and more intense singing and harmony—duets, trios, quartets, sometimes even quintets and beyond.

    B. Three of the more prominent styles of banjo playing in bluegrass music are Scruggs Style, Single String Style, and Melodic Style.

       1. Scruggs Style is a three-finger style of picking introduced by Earl Scruggs.

          a. It uses the thumb and two fingers of the right hand to work out various intricate and syncopated patterns of single strings.

          b. Most of the notes played are background, fill-in notes rather than melody notes.

          c. An example of a tune played in this style is Earl Scrugg's "Foggy Mountain Breakdown."

       2. Don Reno introduced single-string banjo playing to bluegrass.

          a. Reno and Eddie Adcock popularized the style in the 1950s and early 1960s.

          b. With this style, all the notes are played as melody notes, with the thumb and index finger alternately playing single notes, imitating the up-and-down motion of a flat pick.

     c. An example of a tune played in this style is Eddie Adcock's "Sunrise."

  3. Bobby Thompson introduced the Melodic Style while playing with Jim and Jesse in the 1950s.

     a. It was popularized by Bill Keith, playing with Bill Monroe in the 1960s, as Keith Style or Chromatic Style.

     b. In this style, all or almost all of the notes are melody notes that are built in as rolls by choosing the strings the right hand plays so that the right hand never plays the same string twice in a row.

     c. An example of a tune played in this style is Bill Monroe's "Sailor's Hornpipe."

Table 5-4   The Topic Outline (Abbreviated)

I. Adaptation of earlier instrument
  A. Arabian rebec
    1. Gourd with three strings
    2. Spread with Islam
  B. To United States with slaves
    1. Jefferson's "banjar"
    2. Four strings
  C. Sweeney's 1831 adaptation
    1. Banjo King, born Appomattox, Virginia, 1813
      a. Early band
      b. Father of minstrelry
        (1) Slave songs
        (2) Minstrel shows popular to 1890s
        (3) Successes in South, New York, England
    2. Sweeney's five-string was unique
      a. Peg halfway up neck meant higher pitch
      b. Plucked by thumb for blend

Table 5-5   The Speaker's Outline (Abbreviated)

Adaptation
  Rebec
  "Banjar"
  Sweeney (1831)
    Banjo King, Appomattox, 1813
    Unique (peg)

Principles of Outlining

While the major conventions of outline form are shown in the examples, four guidelines are worth isolating for additional comment:

1. *Appropriate numbering system.* The most widely used numbering system alternates letters and figures, as shown in the example. That is, roman numeral (I) is used first, followed by capital letter (A), arabic numeral (1), and the lowercase letter (a). When they are necessary, subsequent arabic numerals and lowercase letters are placed in parentheses [( )]. In outline form, then, the numbering system for our example looks like this:

> I.
>> A.
>>> 1.
>>> 2.
>> B.
>>> 1.
>>> 2.
>> C.
>>> 1.
>>>> a.
>>>> b.
>>>>> (1)
>>>>> (2)
>>>>> (3)
>>> 2.
>
> II.
>> A.
>>> 1.
>>> 2.
>>>> a.
>>>> b.

Note that the main heads are flush with the left margin and that the subheads are indented two or three spaces, forming a clearly identifiable column. Heads or subheads that run more than a single line are further indented so that the content portion of the entry is flush with the content above it.

2. *Heads of equal importance.* The main heads (those marked by roman numerals) show the main divisions of the speech and should be of equal importance to the speech topic. Similarly, the first line of subdivision of these heads (capital letters) should designate logical and equally important divisions of one phase of

the subject. The same principle applies to the further subdivisions represented by arabic numerals and lowercase letters.

3. *Consistency in form.* A sentence outline should use complete sentences throughout and shouldn't lapse into topical heads; a topic outline should use topic heads, not sentences. No punctuation is needed at the end of lines in a topic outline. In the sentence outline, the punctuation should follow written conventions.

4. *Balance in form.* Since an idea is not "divided" unless there are at least two parts, an outline should usually have at least two subheads under any main head. That is, for every heading marked "I" there should be *at least* a "II"; for every "A" there should be a "B," and so on. Sometimes, an exception is made for an outstanding illustrative example that may be put in an outline as a single subhead.

Outlines, of course, are not meant for listeners; they are meant for *speakers.* At the risk of sounding rash, it is our feeling that almost all confusion a speaker creates for listeners can be attributed to deficiencies in outlining. Yes, outlining is a hardship. And yes, too, people should probably not have the bad taste to misunderstand us. But a carefully outlined message is a kind of *cognitive insurance,* a way of insuring that ideas make patterned sense, that no unconnected idea finds its way into our remarks. Another thing to think about: When standing on your feet before an audience, you've already got enough to occupy your attention as you try to cope with situational demands. A carefully outlined speech is thus a kind of *psychic insurance* as well, a source of comfort in what can be an uncertain situation. Outline carefully. The premiums aren't steep and the benefits are substantial.

Making Ideas Graphic: Visual Aids

Earlier in this chapter, pictorialization was identified as one of nine methods of clarification. Because of its central importance to the informative speech, it receives additional treatment here.

The primary purpose served by visual aids is that of enhancing concreteness and clarity. Aids do, however, have many additional functions as well: They serve as effective attention-and-interest-gaining devices (the visual often commands more interest than the verbal), and they enhance the listener's memory of especially significant points. They sometimes increase the credibility of the speaker (by demonstrating both knowledge of and commitment to the topic), and they help the speaker control apprehension about speaking (by providing a silent, but familiar, companion in a sometimes threatening situation).

Capitalizing on these many advantages requires one's ability to select appropriate aids and one's skill in using them well. To illustrate the many options available to you, we have compiled a selected list that features possible choices for our five-string banjo expert. This list can, we hope, be useful to you as you think about ways of making your speech ideas graphic for listeners untutored in your subject matter.

1. *Actual objects* (bring my 1927 Gibson Mastertone complete with prewar Gibson flathead tone ring)

2. *Blackboard* (create an outline of significant time periods in the history of the five-string banjo, which can be written on the board as I discuss them)

3. *Cartoons* (bring transparencies of some of my favorite banjo cartoons from *Banjo Newsletter*)

4. *Charts* (use a chart to display personnel changes in the bluegrass group, J. D. Crowe and the New South)

5. *Demonstrations* (start my speech by playing a version of "Feuding Banjos," a well-known bluegrass tune)

6. *Drawings* (bring some tracings of banjo pegheads and fingerboards)

7. *Film strips* (show portions of the film strip on Bill Monroe's Indiana Bean Blossom Festival)

8. *Flannel or felt board* (demonstrate how the parts of a banjo relate to each other)

9. *Flip cards* (sequence tracings of banjo pegheads to show the wide variety of artistry and individuality involved in their construction)

10. *Graphs* (show the appeal of various styles of picking the banjo in graph form)

11. *Maps* (use a map of the United States to show where bluegrass festivals are held annually)

12. *Models* (bring a cutaway of a banjo to show how it is constructed)

13. *Movies* (show the "Dueling Banjo" segment of the movie *Deliverance*)

14. *Paper pad on easel* (use one sheet of paper per decade to outline significant events in the history of the five-string banjo)

15. *People* (bring Bluegrass Crusade or Sandy Creek Pickers to class)

16. *Slides* (show photographs taken at various bluegrass events)

Using aids well requires effort during preparation as well as skill in actual use. Below, we suggest some guidelines that can assist you in both of these phases.

Preparing Visual Aids

Decide whether aids are necessary. Because their primary function is to amplify and clarify meaning, they should only be used in situations where a supplement to the speaker's best effort at verbal presentation is required for clarity. Aids should never be used as a substitute for an original idea. A speaker also needs to consider the possibility that aids can detract from meaning by attracting attention to themselves.

Plan aids that are large enough to be seen. This requires informed guesses about the number of people in the audience and average viewing distances. If possible, pretest visibility from all positions listeners will occupy during the speech. Having aids large enough for everyone to see clearly and easily is every bit as important as your speaking loudly enough to be heard.

Keep aids as simple as possible. This involves working hard at discovering the simplest possible visual stimuli capable of reinforcing and clarifying speech content. Only features and details that are essential to clarity should be retained. Details that can send audience thoughts in unrelated directions should be eliminated. Unnecessary labels and names on a chart or graph should also be avoided because, to be seen, they must be large, and even a small number of large labels produces a cluttered effect.

Create aids that are carefully executed, precise, and accurate. Carelessly prepared material will be taken by the audience as an indication of the speaker's attitude toward them and the speech topic. Diagrams should be drawn to scale and graphs should represent figures or trends without exaggeration. All drawings should faithfully represent their subject matters.

Engage in careful, realistic rehearsal. The speaker needs to test all plans in advance to learn if electric outlets are available, if the audiovisual equipment is working, if tape will hold exhibits on the wall, if sight lines and sound levels are adequate for all positions in which listeners will be seated, if the easel will stand where needed, if a pointer is readily available, if spare chalk or a backup projector bulb is in the room, and so on.

Using Visual Aids

Position aids so that they can be easily seen by everyone. This may take some thought. Generally, classrooms have hooks and clips above the chalkboard on which materials can be hung. If your classroom doesn't have some, you may need to locate an easel. Your goal should be to place the display high enough so that sight blockage is prevented; then, when speaking, stand to one side of it without blocking the view of your listeners.

Highlight the important features of the aid for your audience. Let them know what they are supposed to see, hear, and understand from the visual aid *before* introducing it (leading questions can be helpful for this); then, restate what should have been learned *after* you have used the aid. While talking about the visual aid, use a pointer, pencil, piece of chalk, or finger to locate the specific feature you are discussing at the moment.

Display your aid only when you are using it. Aids should be agents of communication while you talk. If possible, therefore, keep them from being seen until you are ready to use them; similarly, remove them from sight when finished with them. If you fail to do so, your aid will compete with you for the attention of your auditors. To prevent this, practice (during speech rehearsal) setting up and taking down your material quickly and smoothly.

Talk to the audience and not to the aid. Your listeners need your attention and you need to be able to "read" their reactions when you are speaking. It is very important, therefore, to preserve as much eye contact with your audience as you can while referring to your aid and not to allow your eyes to stray from your listeners longer than is absolutely necessary.

Avoid passing aids through the audience while you are speaking. There is no surer way to lose audience attention than to "build in" your own competition. Displays are better passed through the audience *after* you have finished speaking. If handouts are used, do not try to talk until they have been distributed.

Visual aids can be remarkably helpful to you as a speaker because they concretize ideas so well. But don't let the gimmickry of visual aids unwisely attract you. A poorly prepared aid can make you seem foolish, and a well-prepared aid can still set up competition between you and it for your listeners' attention. Thus, visual aids should be used with discretion and should be made subservient to *your* purposes as a speaker. The old maxim "a picture is worth a thousand words" is simply not true in many cases. Visual aids need *your* help in explaining themselves; alone, they are often mute. Feel free, therefore, to use pictorializations when necessary, but don't view them as an elixir. People, not objects, communicate.

Suggestions for Speaking

Making complex ideas simpler and foreign ideas more familiar for listeners are major challenges for the public speaker. We trust that the specific techniques described in this chapter will give you ample confidence that such challenges can be met effectively. Despite its peculiarities, informative speaking is no alien task. You have been explaining things to others since you were old enough to talk. Informing others is thus the most natural of human experiences and should be thought of in this natural, human way—you know something that others don't know and you wish to share your thoughts with them. All of the techniques we have presented here for informative speaking are meant to supplement, not to supplant, your native instincts for explaining things to others. Don't think of public speaking as hocus pocus. Don't think of our strategems as being like the amulets of the witch doctor. There are no magic potions in informative speaking, just sensible, expedient, and very human devices for making things clear. Here are some additional hints:

1. When speaking informatively, think of how you became *interested* in your topic, and build your audience's motivation to listen by recapturing for them your own initial experiences.

2. Oral rehearsal is especially important in an informative speech because you're never really sure that you understand a concept until you *hear* yourself explain it.

3. Don't become overly specific too early in an informative speech because listeners forget foreign details easily; concentrate on explaining one central feature of your concept.

4. Try to recall the specific sequence of events that caused you suddenly to *understand* the topic you'll be discussing; try leading listeners down the same path you took.

5. Dictionary definitions of key terms are rarely very helpful in an informative speech because listeners need more fully amplified and more colorful explanations of a concept.

6. Long quotations from expert sources may be lacking in flair and clarity; oftentimes, you will need to supplement such remarks with your own, better-adapted paraphrases.

7. Each major section of a speech outline should contain a minimum of one extended example and two or more brief examples if a concept is to be truly clarified for others.

8. We strongly advise preparing a sentence outline for every speech you make, although you may choose to use a shorter version of it when actually delivering your speech.

9. Put the burden of proof on the use of visual aids because their "distracting" capacities can outweigh their helpfulness in clarifying ideas.

10. Remember this proposition above all others: If there is any chance that listeners can misunderstand you, they will.

CHAPTER 6

The Resources of Language

When a word was a word and it meant
What it said, and the world was simple and new
A man made his words and he knew what
They meant, and his friends knew their mean-
ing, too,
Living was easy; communication was brief;
Complexity ne'er spoiled one's view
When a word was a word and it meant
What it said, and the world was simple and new.

Now I look at the sky and I say that it's
Blue and you smile and say yes, sky is blue
But I don't know that blue, as I think of
Blue, is the same blue to me as you.
And I scream in disgust and I know
That I must make you see how blue is my blue
But I know it's but nought when I see
All I wrought was a lopsided point of blue.[1]

[1]From L. B. McAnally, "Communication A.D." A publication of the Interpersonal Communication Clearinghouse, Texas Tech University, Lubbock, Tex. Reprinted by permission.

Our poet succeeds in capturing here the tremendous feelings of inadequacy we often have when trying to share our ideas with others. The poet wisely recalls that polite but deceptive smile people give us when they feign understanding. The poet zeros in on the essential problems of communication: the basic differentness of people, their ideas, and their language habits. And the poet nicely summarizes the eternal dilemma of communication: Language creates great gulfs of understanding between people, but only language can create bridges between those same people.

In this chapter, we would like to discuss the nature of spoken language and how the resources of language help us influence listeners. At the outset, however, we would like to dispel two myths about language. One myth—the Myth of Invincibility—holds that there exists in some secluded place a set of words appropriate to each and every occasion, and that all a speaker need do is polish a speech text or massage a speech outline until that magical set of words comes to the fore. When such verbiage suddenly presents itself, the speaker is home free, or so says the myth.

Not true. Language can do much, but it cannot offset the effects of a badly conceived thesis, a poorly structured speech, or an insensitive speaker. To look for some fail-safe verbal formula instead of attending to the hard work of careful speech preparation is foolhardy. But foolish, too, is the Myth of Impotence, which holds that speech is such a natural human process that attention given to the details of language is necessarily wasted. This myth encourages the speaker to "just think about" the topic, scratch out a few notes, and then prepare to be welcomed with thunderous applause.

Also not true. Language is a powerful and delicate creature. The right word at the right time can sometimes win the day. The striking image, the carefully wrought description, and the nicely turned phrase can often succeed in breathing life into otherwise dormant or mundane ideas. It is well worth paying attention to the language we use, but before doing so it is helpful to consider why language is necessary in the first place—because even though people may share physical space with one another, they live in very different worlds indeed. The speaker who acknowledges these differences in world view is the speaker most likely to feel that language is worth whatever attention is paid to it.

Language and Perception

Some day, someone might become rich and famous by authoring a book entitled *The Games Students Play*. The book will deal with such topics as Excuses Students Use, Courtship in the Classroom, and How to Cheat Creatively. But Chapter 1 will have to be devoted to the Ostrich

Game, which takes place when the professor is looking for a response to a very convoluted and long-winded question. He or she looks around the room, searching for a student to call upon, but nobody will establish eye contact. The students are sanctimoniously scanning their notebooks, looking out the window, searching, gazing, staring everywhere and anywhere except at the professor. Should our pedagogue be offended by this mini-form of social isolation? Not at all. He or she should just be reminded that students play the Ostrich Game, that well-entrenched, head-in-the-sand, classroom reaction that asserts, "If I can't see you, you can't see me, and hence you can't call on me because I'm not really here."

Absurd as this statement may seem, you know from your classroom experience that such behavior takes place. Students, like everyone else, are in a very real sense imprisoned in a world of their own creation. They can engage in such ostrichlike delusions because they know, or think they know, that "others" can never really enter their world entirely because it *is* their world—they created it, they sustain it, and they will determine who or what is admitted through its portals. Their worlds, or more accurately their perceptual worlds, are perfectly capable of keeping out intruding professors.

We are taking the position here that each and every listener is "locked into" a unique and sometimes very private perceptual world, that this makes him or her fundamentally different from the speaker, and that only human language can bridge these perceptual gaps. In this section, we would like to discuss some of the relationships between language and perception, and isolate some helpful attitudes a speaker might have toward language usage.

Perceptual Differences and Similarities

We bring up this notion of perceptual worlds for several reasons: (1) Speakers, like all other people, seem to have a "natural arrogance" that others' worlds are but imitations of their own, (2) if a speaker *assumes* that another's unique norms and past experiences are irrelevant to effective listening, he or she will use language egocentrically, (3) alternatively, if a speaker assumes *fundamental* differences between himself and his listeners, he will have no choice but to "look at" the world through another set of perceptual lenses and to select language accordingly. It is painful to have to be so concerned about others. *Our* worlds are always nicely ordered; theirs, disorganized. Our values are beneficial; theirs, questionable. Our norms are correct; theirs, foolish. Thus, *the most natural tendency in the world is to talk to ourselves in the presence of others. But that is pure egocentricity, not communication.*

We all slip into this sort of self-talking from time to time, not bothering to account for the perceptual differences that are always part of using language for communication. For example, perhaps you have had the experience of seeing an exceptionally good film, one that literally makes you burst at the seams to explain the show to someone else and to generate the same excitement in him or her. You rush back to your apartment, "tie" your roommate to the chair, and explode with every memorable detail of the movie. You do not worry about providing orientation at the beginning of your "speech," or placing the details in an understandable sequence, or even monitoring her responses to your talk; you simply tell it the way you feel it, remembering it as you do. When you have "wound down" finally, you slump in your chair with all the satisfaction that speech-for-pleasure can give a person. Now, if your roommate is kind, one who is able to appreciate the richness and uniqueness of your experience, she will not throw a book at you for wasting her time while you "thought out loud." If she is especially kind, she will not even let on that she had not understood a thing you have said; instead, she will ask for a few more details, desperately hoping that after your moment of passion has passed you will be reminded of your fundamental perceptual differences.

What could account for your roommate's extraordinary restraint? One explanation for her forbearance might be that she can see a bit of herself in you—she can see some of her past experiences in yours. Although she has never seen "your" movie, she has had other experiences that have pushed her beyond the usual limits of human excitement. Your experiences and those of your roommate have been different yet similar enough for her to make accommodations for you. Different but alike. Perhaps after all, such rugged approximations of experience are our only real basis for making safe bets in communication.

But similarities, even rough ones, do not simply "exist" between users of language. Unlike kindly roommates, most listeners are not so willing to "extend" themselves in communication—speakers must demonstrate where theirs and their listeners' views converge. Speakers, in all but the friendliest of circumstances, must build the bridges of understanding through language and invite listeners to meet them halfway. Thus, although we feel that *total communication* is impossible, we do feel that experiences can be shared in an approximate way and that complex ideas can be made simpler for others by the judicious choice of language. Let's consider an example.

Being of the Captain Kangaroo era, you are probably unfamiliar with "Mister Rogers' Neighborhood," a delightful show aimed at 3- to 8-year-olds and appearing on the Public Broadcasting Service. This daily excursion into the mysterious worlds of children has a number of important lessons to teach any serious student of language.

Consider the premise. Fred Rogers, an ordained minister and professional musician, in his fifties, attempts for 30 minutes a day to communicate with children whom he can neither see nor hear. An even greater task is his attempt to convey some extremely sophisticated concepts to his audience and to do so without boring them. Any of you who has ever tried to break into the world of the 4-year-old probably has some idea of the linguistic challenge that Rogers continually sets for himself.

What is perhaps most interesting about Fred Rogers' approach is that *he does not assume irreconcilable differences between himself and his audience.* Instead, he concentrates on similarities. Admittedly, as an adult he shaves, pays taxes, drives too fast on occasion, and engages in the numerous other daily routines that are part of the adult world. All such considerations, it is probably safe to say, lie well outside of the perceptual world of the tot, but *Rogers remembers the child within us all.* Different though he and his audience are (and Rogers is careful to acknowledge this on occasion), his intellectual propositions, his analogies and examples, and even his bodily movements and tone of voice are startlingly attractive to the child. Consider the lyrics from one of his songs and see if you can improve on his ability to choose language so carefully as to "crack" the perceptual worlds of children:

It's great for me to remember
As I put away my toys,
That Mothers were all little girls one time
And Fathers were all little boys.

My Daddy seems so big right now
He must have grown a lot.
Imagine how he felt one day
When he was just a tot.

My Mother's not so big as Dad,
But bigger than my sister.
I wonder if she ever had
A little fever blister? . . .

My Daddy didn't even have
A real electric fan.
He had to wait a long time too
'til he became a man.

My mother used an ironing board
And play irons that were colder.
She often wished for big folks' things
But she waited, and got older.

So knives and plugs and hot things
Are OK for Mom and Dad,
'cause when they were a girl and boy
They played with what they had.

And I think I can wait now
And grow the way they do,
And I will use the grown-up things
When I'm a grown-up too. . . .[2]

Even if the poem does not bring a tear to your eye, it surely reveals a rare communicative mind at work, a person who is able to get a reading on the past experiences, norms, and values of his listeners and, most remarkably, find words and images suitable to a somewhat "alien" audience.

Efficient Use of Language

Unless a speaker assumes, initially and fundamentally, that his or her listeners live in very different worlds, he or she will have no need to adapt, no need to choose among alternative phrasings, no need to discover the linguistic habits of others. In fact, if individual differences did not produce so many uncertainties for a speaker, he or she could just grab hold of a random idea, attach it to any language that seemed handy, and "place" meanings directly into the crania of listeners.

Unfortunately, human language does not operate this way. *We do not send or transmit meanings.* Rather, we use a very fragile system of verbal and nonverbal symbols, and thereby *induce* listeners to react to us.

In this section, we would like to discuss this process of induction. To do so, let us first consider a childhood experience you might have had: It's a hot summer's eve and you cannot sleep. You steal out of the house, being careful not to let the door slam, and head for your favorite "thinking spot." You sit on that very special stump at Old Listening Lake and, being the 12-year-old you are, quite naturally proceed to throw a stone into the quiet water.

Because it is the blackest of nights, you cannot see exactly where the stone hit nor can you see the number of ripples it produced. You cannot see how high the water splashed nor can you gauge how quickly your unseen missile dropped to the bottom of the lake. All that your efforts have evoked—that is, induced—is a splash. The only information

[2]F. Rogers, *Let's Be Together Today*. Album produced by Small World Enterprises, Inc. Reprinted by permission of Family Communication Inc.

or feedback you've received from the water is a "kerplunk." But you like the sound of the "kerplunk" and attempt to see if, by controlling as many of the "variables" as possible, you can, with another stone, reproduce this fascinating sound. So you try again. You look for a stone whose dimensions approximate those of your first weapon. You wait for the wind to die down, and as you hurl your next projectile, you are careful to match the velocity of the throw and the amount of wrist-snap to that of your first effort. And what do you get for your trouble? You guessed it, a "kerploosh"!

A "kerploosh" and not a "kerplunk"? What's wrong with that lake? Doesn't it have the good sense to interact intelligently with the very best rock thrower in these parts? It is after all the same lake on both occasions. Or is it? Was Old Listening Lake in the same "mood" in both instances, what with the wind, the floating logs, and the trout to bestir it? And how about your stone "messages"? Were they the same in both cases? Since you could not "see" these little wavelets—the perceptual worlds of dark lakes being just as mysterious as are those of people—you really could not assess the covert feedback the lake was providing. Meanwhile, what has happened to your stone? Is the water "digesting" your message even as you stand there? Is it reconstructing your beautiful stones into some sort of moss-and-sand-covered underwater creature? It is all too frustrating to contemplate, so you trudge on home and, this time, kick the door!

There is not much difference between the frustration our 12-year-old feels and the anguish many of us experience in our daily attempts to share ideas through language. Communication, as we have said, is a

fragile instrument, not very precise, not very predictable, sometimes not even much fun. But communication is extraordinarily complex, and just when you think you have got the process "knocked," it throws you a curve ball.

We define the efficient use of language as a process by which a speaker manipulates symbols within his or her perceptual world and, through a complex process of message exchange with a listener, alters the listener's perceptual world in ways the speaker desires. Let us discuss the constituent elements of this definition one by one.

"Efficient use of language is a process by which a speaker . . . As we have said previously, communication is at best an attempt. It is never a completed "product" as far as the speaker is concerned. Like our 12-year-old with the stones, it is a guess-throw-and-guess-again proposition in which the speaker simply makes bets, some intelligent and some not, as to what effect will be produced by the language he or she selects.

Manipulates symbols within his or her perceptual world, . . . It should go without saying that we do not send "thoughts" to one another. We can't do so because thoughts are locked within our perceptual worlds and cannot "escape" on their own. They need "vehicles," and the only such vehicle humans have been able to produce to date is a very delicate and most imperfect system of language cues. Symbols—those verbal (and nonverbal) "things" that stand for our thoughts—are really all we have to go on in communication. Fortunately, we get pretty adept at manipulating these symbols. Much as it does for our stonethrower, the process of learning teaches us, in approximate fashion at least, the "size, heft, and probable impact" of the language systems available to us in communication.

and through a complex process of message exchange with a listener, . . . A stone is thrown, a "kerplunk" returns. As our 12-year-old soon discovers, communicating with lakes is not simple. Speakers (and stonethrowers) are only a part of the process, because they must interact with other persons (or objects). The trouble is, nobody is ever sure what symbols (and stones) "do" to their recipients or what the returning symbols (or ripples) "mean" in any absolute sense. All that is known is that a stimulus produces a response and, for humans at least, life becomes a process of ferreting out what these returning symbols—this feedback—"mean" for our perceptual worlds.

alters the listener's perceptual world in ways the speaker desires." Attempting to manipulate symbols and exchange messages is only part of the story. Communication scholars often argue that we cannot *not* communicate. Even a person sitting rigidly mute in a chair "says" something about himself or herself to others. While all of this is true, we can fail to communicate efficiently. From a speaker's standpoint, efficient communication occurs when the listener's perceptual world "absorbs" a bit of the speaker's and is changed in ways deemed adequate by the speaker.

Naturally, we have been discussing some highly complex matters here in a very simple way. Perception is an extraordinarily intricate psychological process, not to mention the equally complicated process of using language. As we move on now to consider the nature of language and how the public speaker can master its complexities, it will be helpful to remember the Ostrich Game, Fred Rogers, and Listening Lake. This trio of characters tells a humbling story indeed. They tell us that no ringing phrase or semantic nicety can *alone* produce communication. *It is only when a speaker thinks simultaneously about language and peoples' perceptions that efficient communication is likely to occur.* Of course, when speaking in public we usually demand more from language than simple efficiency. We want grace and liveliness and distinctiveness, too. Let us now consider how such qualities come to be.

Properties of Language

Think about the great speeches that have been given in this century, speeches that were both impressive and thoughtful. What people remember most about such addresses are probably the great phrases, the elegant and inspiring assemblage of words. We remember Winston Churchill's heartfelt offer of "blood, toil, tears, and sweat" to the British people at the start of World War II or John Kennedy's Inaugural Address in which he instructed Americans to "ask not what your country can do for you, ask what you can do for your country." Who can forget Martin Luther King's stirring call of "I have a dream"? The ability to choose words that are exactly appropriate for an audience, to invent a metaphor or stylistic device of freshness and imagination—these are the skills that make speeches memorable, ideas lively, and speakers influential.

The fact that well-turned phrases impress audiences is not the only reason for studying the resources of language. Careful choice of words is also a way to express ideas with clarity. People not only remember the great words spoken by a Churchill, a Kennedy, and a King, but they remember, too, the great ideas for which they stood. We remember Churchill as a savior in a time of sacrifice; we remember Kennedy's vision of public service and King's appreciation of human dignity. And in each case, the ideas and the men become memorable because they used forceful and imaginative language.

Learning how to use words well is as important a part of *strategy* in public speaking as the ability to appeal to an audience's basic beliefs and values. As with other elements in speech, language must be adapted to specific occasions and audiences. One cannot use the same style of language in roasting a friend at a testimonial dinner as one would when eulogizing him at his funeral. Such situations make different demands on the sobriety of our language and on its tone and tenor as well.

Different audiences also call for various styles of language, just as different audiences require unique value appeals and supporting materials. When discussing nuclear power plants before an audience of high school students, for instance, a speaker must necessarily be simple, clear, and conversational. When addressing that same topic before a group of physics professors, on the other hand, one's style must be more scholarly, technical, and perhaps a bit more terse. Let us examine some of the factors that make words clear, interesting, and memorable.

Denotative and Connotative Meanings

Perhaps the most obvious thing that words do is that they contribute to *meaning*. Without meaning, spoken words are mere noise. The shout of "Fire!" is only air passing over the vocal folds unless people understand what it signifies. But how do words mean?

One important part of meaning is the thing or idea that a word *points to*. Part of the meaning of the word *book*, for instance, is this thing you're holding at present. The word *happiness*, on the other hand, points people to a certain idea or feeling they experience when, for example, passing an exam based on this book. Such meanings are called *denotative* because they link an object or event to some specific mental impression.

An alternative way of describing denotative meaning is to call it the *dictionary definition* of a word. Basically, people look up a word in a dictionary when they aren't familiar with the object or event a word points to. Although the dictionary cannot actually take people by the hand and show them the particular thing or happening to which the word refers, it can give the reader other words that also point to that thing or idea in hopes that the reader will be able to "triangulate" an understanding of the word.

Yet another method of describing denotative meaning is to say that it is the meaning of a word that nearly everyone can agree upon. Most people will grant that the meaning of *yawn* is the thing you'll do if you read too much of this book at one sitting. Most people in our "linguistic community" would agree that this movement of your jaw is what *yawn* means. In an ideal world, all words would have clear and sharp denotative meanings, and communication would be simple and direct with errors in understanding one another virtually nonexistent. In such a world, speechmaking would become the simple process of arranging these words in some likely fashion, and listening would be little more than a matter of "sweeping up" the ideas spilling out of the speaker's mouth.

But denotative meanings have a set of notorious rivals. To illustrate that point, let us consider the difference between an active child and a spoiled brat. Are they the same person? Do the words used in each case point to (i.e., mean) the same thing? Even if *active child* and *spoiled brat* were discovered to point to the same person, the "meanings" involved in the two expressions would clearly differ. Why are these meanings different? How can two different phrases single out the same concrete person and yet "editorialize" about that person in very different ways? And how can all of that happen simultaneously?

The differences, as you might have suspected, lie inside people, not inside the words spoken. An active child is *your* little brother or sister, the person toward whom you have a positive attitude. The child's playing and shouting merely make him or her active in your mind. But your neighbor may view such activity much more harshly, especially when that activity involves jumping about in a prize bed of roses. Thus, an important part of what a word means is the *attitude toward* that object, event, or idea implied by the word. We call this implied attitude the *connotative* meaning of the word.

The connotative meaning of a term, or the attitude it conveys, will usually not be found in the dictionary. Also, the attitude conveyed by a word will not be shared by everyone. Rather, people develop their own connotations for a term based on their experiences with the thing that a word refers to. While everyone could agree that *book* denotatively means the thing you are now holding, some people have had good experiences with books, whereas others have only been depressed by them. Thus, the wide range of connotations available for a single word or phrase makes life more than a bit interesting from time to time.

But what does all this have to do with public speaking? Well, for one thing, although speakers refer to things in the world time and time again, they usually want their audiences to have specific attitudes about the objects, events, and ideas to which the speakers refer. For example, it is usually not enough to refer to executions in a speech on capital punishment. A speaker also wants the audience to *feel* one way or the other about such executions. Thus, many of the important choices made during speech preparation center around connotative strategy. Calling an execution "legalized murder," for example, will surely serve to place the whole notion of capital punishment in a very different light, while the phrase "justified vengeance" will refer to this same event in markedly different *attitudinal* ways. Especially in ceremonial speaking, where "new" ideas are often not expressed, it becomes doubly important to use the powers of connotation to charge listeners' emotional batteries.

And it goes without saying that connotative shadings, even *subtle* ones, can make a practical difference in communicative outcome. One of your authors once taught a communication course at a state maximum security prison. The class was composed of both residents of the prison and the guards. Intriguingly, both groups comprising the class had a different way of referring to the permanent residents. The guards called them the "population." Think about the attitudes implied by this term. *Population* is not an actively hostile but a rather cold and uncaring term, a designation of a large, faceless mass of people. Furthermore, *population* has a "mathematical" feel to it, perhaps a function of the guards' responsibility for counting the prisoners to make sure that the total is correct night after night.

The residents themselves referred to each other (in our presence, at any rate) as "inmates." Notice that the connotations here are much friendlier and warmer. The term *inmates* carries images of brotherliness, of "mates" embarking on a joint experience. *Inmates* also carries institutional attitudes with it. The term implies that one is being housed against one's will; one can be an inmate of a psychiatric ward or a sanatorium but not an inmate of a football team.

The interesting thing about such connotations is that they have a way of "clouding out" other aspects of a speaker's message. That is, as listeners we sometimes become fixated by certain words and end up paying undue attention to specific word choices. Thus, it is likely that the antiseptic sounding "population" will be so alien to the "inmates" that the latter will reject other aspects of the guards' messages as well. With few exceptions, words mean things at multiple levels and, oftentimes, at different *emotional* levels.

Levels of Abstraction

Besides containing denotative and connotative meanings, words also operate at some *level of abstraction*. That is, most words refer not to particular objects and events but to groups or categories of objects and events. The word *chair* does not point to a particular chair but to the category of all chairs. The word *run* refers not to one instance of running but to all running events whenever they occur. Some words refer to enormous categories, categories containing a great number of things. *Property* is one such word. Other words refer to very small groupings. *Professor Henry Scheele,* for instance, refers to a very small category, a category of one. Level of abstraction is an indicator of a word's concreteness, its relative ability to "stand for" one thing or many things.

Thus, *your copy of Public Communication* is very concrete; it names but one thing. The term *Public Communication* is more abstract because it names your book plus all the other copies of the book. The term *book* is still more abstract, naming your book, all copies of *Public Communication,* plus every other book of any sort ever published. The term *property* is even more abstract because it subsumes all of the preceding terms as well as stereos, buildings, flower pots, and so on. Perhaps the term *earthly goods* would be the most abstract rung on this ladder we're constructing because it names everything included in *property* as well as nonowned entities such as the air, the ocean, and so on.

An interesting thing happens as we move up this ladder of abstraction (i.e., from highly concrete to highly abstract). Not only does the size of the category named by the term increase, but the connotations or attitudes people share toward that category become stronger and more generally motivating. Thus, although we're sure that you cherish your particular copy of this book, few of your friends are concerned about it. More people care about all copies of *Public Communication;* your authors, for instance, would like to see these copies find pleasant (and numerous) homes. A great many more people are fond of books in general—people who like to read, scholars, librarians, publishers, and so on. Even more people have strong attitudes about *property,* with some of them willing to live or die for that term and the things it names. And *earthly goods* may excite the most intense feelings of all; they may become the object of one's life, passionately praised or bitterly denounced.

As individuals, of course, our feelings about highly concrete phenomena are often emotionally charged. Thus, we would defend to the death our concrete mother. But the *public* speaker would be more likely to discourse about motherhood because more people have stronger feelings about that category of object and event. Naturally, we are simplifying the features of language a good deal when we say that, but it is generally true that when the speaker seeks out motivating ideas, he or she tries to find language to which listeners can "look up"—up the ladder of abstraction, that is. Therefore, the eulogist tells us about the deceased's "essential goodness" while the political orator urges us to revere "the American way." Our speakers could have uttered their thoughts more concretely, but they would be sacrificing some of their *general* impact by so doing.

Ultimate Terms

Words that are extremely abstract are sometimes called "ultimate terms," a phrase introduced by Richard Weaver.[3] Ultimate terms are important to public speakers because these terms often relate quite

---

[3] R. Weaver, *The Ethics of Rhetoric* (Chicago: Henry Regnery, 1953).

closely to *cultural values* and because they also are *consensually shared;* that is, they evoke common feelings in people when uttered. Such properties make ultimate terms—terms like *Americanism, justice, beauty,* and *honor* —quite useful, especially in ceremonial situations. Naturally, not all highly abstract terms become "ultimate." The word *entropy,* for example, is a highly abstract method of referring to the process by which physical properties become random and disordered. But such a phrase will motivate few persons on the Fourth of July because it implies no particular set of shared cultural values.

Ultimate terms are also popular because they are easy to apply. Since very abstract terms refer to so many things, it is difficult to say what they do *not* make reference to. For instance, *racism* is a negative ultimate term and can point to many things. It can be used to characterize a tuition increase, for instance, because minority students tend to be economically disadvantaged in disproportionate ways and therefore would be hurt most by a hike in tuition. One might refer to the game of professional football as racist because so few quarterbacks or coaches, and so many linemen, are black. Many other things might well be referred to as "racist" depending upon a speaker's creative use of ultimate terms. Sometimes, even a *veiled* reference to these powerful and emotionally charged ultimate terms can be beneficial from a speaker's perspective. On the other hand, to use them indiscriminately is to show callous disregard for a society's sacred symbols and to depict oneself as an overly emotional, and hence not particularly trustworthy, speaker.

Typically, ultimate terms carry *absolute* connotations with them— they tend to polarize an issue, to make an event all of one sort and none of another. Thus, ultimate terms often come in pairs—*racism and justice, peace and hatred, duplicity and truth.* Such terms can be intoxicating for listener and speaker alike as they draw us further and further away from the world of "pure denotation" and allow us to revel in a fully abstract and highly connotative jungle of images. Again, however, one should be cautioned to use such resources sparingly, lest one tread foolishly upon an audience's sacred ground or become so abstract in conception and swollen in language that listeners dismiss one as impractical. The properties of language discussed here are more easily abused than they are used wisely.

Achieving Distinctiveness in Language

In the later portions of this chapter, we will discuss some techniques for "polishing" language. Before doing so, however, it seems wise to consider just what makes a person's language unique in the first place. In particular, we would like to encourage you to think a bit about your own habits of language, the sorts of expressions and pet phrases you find yourself using in day-to-day discussions. By introspecting a bit, you may discover that some of your habitual ways of using language are quite appropriate when speaking to a friend over lunch but unsatisfactory when presenting a prepared message in public. Let us consider factors that contribute to distinctiveness in language.

Strength of Style

In many ways, language is a finely tuned instrument. With just a minor adjustment or two, a speaker can provide either a lukewarm or a complete endorsement of some product, idea, or person. For example, I can say "John is a fine candidate for mayor" or, alternatively, "John would probably be many people's choice for office." In this example, a simple modification in the verb form has transformed a potentially vigorous endorsement into a mere sociological observation. Typically, when any form of the *verb "to be"* is used by a speaker (e.g., is, are, will, etc.), he or she speaks with strength. In addition to verb forms, *leveling terms* can signal certainty. Words such as *everyone, all, never,* and the like are used to ignore individual differences and hence reduce everything to the same level. On the other hand, *tentative verb forms* like *could, might, may,* and *would* have the capacity to soften a speaker's statement and to remove the certainty of a speaker's commitments. Similarly, qualifying terms like *almost, nearly,* and *perhaps* can give the speaker some rhetorical elbow room.[4]

More than likely, you already have preferences in regard to this matter of verbal strength. You may feel that it is best to be absolutely honest, regardless of the consequences. Or you may feel that verbal discretion is preferable, and a prudent course is the best approach when speaking to others. Because the relative *strength* of an expression is often going to determine the acceptability of that expression, it may be wise to conduct a short inventory of your preferences in this matter.

For example, does your language tend to "harden" when discussing topics that are emotionally close to you? Do you find it difficult to accept the remarks of a speaker who qualifies his or her thoughts a great deal? Or do you find yourself becoming very rigid about certain matters but rather chameleonlike at other times? Whatever your habits may be, it is probably wise to remember that a golden mean operates here as in other areas of communication—listeners, especially American listeners, detest weak-kneed speakers but, at the same time, normally cannot abide

[4]For further information about linguistic strength, see R. Hart, "Absolutism and Situation: Prolegomena to a Rhetorical Biography of Richard M. Nixon," *Communication Monographs*, 43: 204–228 (1976).

ideologues. Striking a balance seems to be called for in most speaking situations.

Public speakers are particularly wise to monitor the strength of their remarks. Your habitually strong way of phrasing things in informal conversations may turn out to be quite inappropriate when, say, speaking to a local church group. Although hard-and-fast guidelines are difficult to come by in relation to language, public speakers often find the following advice to be helpful:

1. When speaking to a highly educated audience, qualify your language more fully than you normally do.

2. Be careful not to use excessively strong language when discussing particularly emotional topics.

3. Verbal strength should characterize most speech introductions so that listeners become convinced of your competence and trustworthiness.

4. Don't respond to listeners' questions with too much strength lest they accuse you of not appreciating the subtlety of their questions.

5. Friendly listeners normally can tolerate more verbal strength from a speaker than can hostile listeners.

In addition to these bits of advice, keep in mind that verbal strength is a very subtle but very influential communicative force. The strength of our own expressions is often hard for us to monitor (as are most personal habits), but *listeners,* in contrast, have little difficulty in distinguishing between an appropriately qualified statement and a wishy-washy expression or between a foolish overstatement and a judicious call-to-arms. Developing an inner ear for making such discriminations may well become a goal for the public speaker.

Breadth of Style

One interesting aspect of traveling for the student of communication is the possibility it provides for collecting "local language." Even within the United States, for example, we find great variations in the breadth or narrowness of people's vocabulary. By breadth, we are referring to the relative amount of idiosyncratic or unique language a speaker uses. Members of one religious group, for example, may talk about being born again, while those of another sect may talk about shunning their fellow parishioners. Football players talk about red-dogging, basketball players discuss sky hooks, and baseball players seek

to double-up their opponents. All such in-group language or jargon serves to make these various groups special in members' eyes as well as in the eyes of outsiders. Some groups, like teenage rock fans, sometimes seem to talk in a completely foreign language—at least when viewed from the perspective of middle-class, fortyish parents. We sometimes use such restricted codes to keep others from feeling part of our group or from invading our turf. Indeed, the ceremonies used by many groups to induct new members often involve introducing the neophytes to the organizations' "special" languages.

But we need not belong to organized groups to possess "narrow" language. Simply growing up within a particular economic background, or in a particular geographical location, or with persons of a single ethnic identity will provide us with more than enough special language. Such forms of language are often helpful when talking to members of our groups because they allow us to take verbal shortcuts and to get to the meat of communication quickly. Why describe a college class as being comparatively less onerous than the norm when calling it a cake course operates much more efficiently?

The public speaker, however, must always be careful not to narrow his or her language unwisely. After all, *public* speaking often brings us into contact with diverse persons, people who bring their own special languages to the speaking situation. It becomes intrusive, not to mention confusing, then, for a speaker to pepper a speech with alien terms and arcane, even if colorful, images.

When preparing a public speech, therefore, it is often wise to examine the relative "breadth" of one's language. This is often not easy because pet words and phrases are used so frequently by us as to be unnoticeable. One way of conducting a self-inventory is to ask yourself such questions as the following: (1) What terms or phrases are particularly important for my listeners to understand if they are to appreciate this topic? (2) Must I define these terms or will they be self-evident? (3) Are there any odd phrases or words that I use in informal conversation that might sneak into my public speech without my knowing it? (4) Have I heard my listeners use any special words previously that I might refer to in my remarks? (5) Are there any regional, or class-related, or time-bound expressions that may create communicative roadblocks for me in this speech?

Questions such as these will be helpful when conducting your linguistic self-examination, but you should be careful *not* to foolishly resist finding your own "voice" when speaking. Much color, interest, and humanity are revealed when speakers artfully use personal expressions. Search, then, for your verbal distinctiveness, but remember that no word or phrase is so precious that it alone has a right to frustrate mutual understanding.

Complexity of Style

If you have never listened to an audiorecording of your informal conversation before, you have a treat in store—and, perhaps, a bit of embarrassment, too. When listening to yourself talk, you will notice the strong/weak and broad/narrow aspects of language just mentioned. In addition, you are also likely to notice the tremendous amount of "inefficiency" to be found in oral communication. When speaking, we seem to use more words than we have to. We seem to interrupt ourselves constantly and digress aimlessly. When searching for just the right idea during a speech, we often use words to cover up our thinking processes. All of this inefficiency, of course, is most normal and, in fact, useful. After all, unlike readers (who have the permanence of the printed page to guide them), listeners receive their ideas via a set of ephemeral sound waves. Thus, the normal complexity one finds in a spoken message is really designed to give the listener a second chance to capture the meaning the speaker has in mind.

Still, enough is enough. Speakers can accept the fact that oral discourse will never sound as consecutive and as completely packaged as their written remarks, but they need not make their communicative task any harder by adding unnecessary complexity. Typically, a needlessly complex style results when one employs the following factors:

1. *Lack of immediacy:* Examine the sentence you have just read. It would be hard to find a more "textbookish" sentence. The sentence is impersonal. It has no "I" or "me" but refers to the somewhat neutered "one." It is the sort of sentence one writes,

rather than speaks. It is more the sort of sentence one writes to a general audience than to one's lover. Immediacy, then, is a measure of the amount of me-ness in language.

Speakers who speak in the third person or who refrain from giving personal examples will be low in immediacy.[5] More than likely, they will be correspondingly high in complexity. Self-references, on the other hand, allow a speaker to step into his or her message and to show the listener the real-life benefits of understanding that message. Be careful, therefore, not to become too "distanced" when speaking. Even a formal and very public speaking situation will not release you from the personal expectations listeners have of one who has decided to *talk* to them.

2. *Complicated syntax.* Syntax refers to the structure of language. Syntactically speaking, use of the passive voice greatly increases complexity. Long sentences with many dependent clauses also add to complexity. While it is somewhat easy to monitor syntax when writing a term paper, it is much less easy to do so when speaking. Fumbling with note cards and monitoring listeners' reactions often distract us from the finer points of style. A good rule of thumb seems to be that the clearer your subject is to you, the more likely you will be to use a simple syntactical structure. Confused minds produce confused sentences. Listening to an audiorecording of a practice speech, however, also gives you a chance to see if you have been as simple as you could be. Also, total familiarity with your outline will give you the confidence to speak clearly.

3. *Too much embellishment.* In their desire to impress an audience, many speakers "lay it on thick." That is, they depend for effect on a great assemblage of adjectives rather than the sleek power afforded by well-chosen verbs. Generally speaking (and one can only speak generally about matters of language), adjectives are the refuge of the speaker who has a weak case to present. The salesperson who hawks a product as the "most colossal, modern and handy-dandy invention known to society" is a person with a gross of pink bottle-openers to unload. It is best not to depend on adjectives exclusively for communicative impact. Adjectives produce long, languid, tortuous, involved, convoluted, and endless sentences. Verbs act.

---

[5]The classic work on verbal immediacy has been done by M. Wiener and A. Mehrabian, *Language Within Language: Immediacy, A Channel in Verbal Communication* (New York: Appleton, 1968).

A distinctive style, then, emerges from the speaker's ability to combine strength of expression with appropriate breadth and complexity of language. These three forces will combine differently in each of us and will conspire to produce our distinctive "voice." By careful self-analysis, you can find your natural voice and then determine what modifications in that voice might be necessary for situations demanding public speech. There is no particular voice in public speaking that is best for all persons. But you, on the other hand, have a best you.

Achieving Liveliness in Language

One of the most helpful resources of language that a speaker can use is the stylistic device or figure of speech, a colorful way of expressing ideas and an aid to clarity as well. Since the days of ancient Greece, experts on communication have compiled long lists of stylistic devices designed to ornament and strengthen public speeches. Here, we will present only a few of the more common and useful stylistic devices, selecting those that the novice speaker would be particularly likely to use.

Perhaps one of the best ways of witnessing the dramatic impact stylistic devices can have on an audience is to examine a portion of the speech "I Have a Dream," given by Dr. Martin Luther King, Jr., on August 28, 1963. On that day, almost a quarter of a million Americans walked in two columns to the Lincoln Memorial to demonstrate for equality in civil rights. Later that afternoon, they assembled at the Washington Monument, where the high point of the entire day's activities was reached when Martin Luther King, Jr., gave his powerful, inspirational speech. Although somewhat dated now, it is still a superb example of public speaking aimed at drawing people together in a spirit of unity and cohesiveness. A segment of the speech, which demonstrates how stylistic devices can "elevate" the feelings of the group and overcome the more mundane notions of individuals, follows:

> So I say to you, my friends, that even though we must face the difficulties of today and tomorrow, I still have a dream. It is a dream deeply rooted in the American dream that one day this nation will rise up and live out the true meaning of its creed—we hold these truths to be self-evident, that all men are created equal.
>
> I have a dream that one day on the red hills of Georgia, sons of former slaves and sons of former slave-owners will be able to sit down together at the table of brotherhood.
>
> I have a dream that one day, even the state of Mississippi, a state sweltering with the heat of injustice, sweltering with the heat of oppression, will be transformed into an oasis of freedom and justice.

I have a dream my four little children will one day live in a nation where they will not be judged by the color of their skin but by the content of their character. I have a dream today!

I have a dream that one day, down in Alabama, with its vicious racists, with its governor having his lips dripping with the words of interposition and nullification, that one day, right there in Alabama, little black boys and black girls will be able to join hands with little white boys and white girls as sisters and brothers. I have a dream today!

I have a dream that one day every valley shall be exalted, every hill and mountain shall be made low, the rough places shall be made plain, and the crooked places shall be made straight and the glory of the Lord will be revealed and all flesh shall see it together.

This is our hope. This is the faith that I go back to the South with.

With this faith we will be able to hew out of the mountain of despair a stone of hope. With this faith we will be able to transform the jangling discords of our nation into a beautiful symphony of brotherhood.

With this faith we will be able to work together, to pray together, to struggle together, to go to jail together, to stand up for freedom together, knowing that we will be free one day. This will be the day when all of God's children will be able to sing with new meaning—"my country 'tis of thee, sweet land of liberty, of thee I sing; land where my fathers died, land of the pilgrim's pride, from every mountain side, let freedom ring"—and if America is to be a great nation, this must become true.

And so let freedom ring from the prodigious hilltops of New Hampshire.

Let freedom ring from the mighty mountains of New York.

Let freedom ring from the heightening Alleghenies of Pennsylvania.

Let freedom ring from the snow-capped Rockies of Colorado.

Let freedom ring from the curvaceous slopes of California.

But not only that.

Let freedom ring from Stone Mountain of Georgia.

Let freedom ring from Lookout Mountain of Tennessee.

Let freedom ring from every hill and molehill of Mississippi, from every mountainside, let freedom ring.

And when this happens, and when we allow freedom to ring, when we let it ring from every village and hamlet, from every state and city, we will be able to speed up that day when all of God's children—black men and white men, Jews and Gentiles, Catholics and Protestants—will be able to join hands and to sing the words of the old Negro spiritual, "Free at last, free at last; thank God Almighty, we are free at last."[6]

⟩ [6]From R. L. Hill (ed.), *The Rhetoric of Racial Revolt* (Denver: Golden Bell Press, 1964), pp. 373–375. Reprinted by permission of the publisher.

In this, the concluding portion of King's speech, we can see how rather ordinary notions of social and economic progress are given true grandeur by the appropriate use of language. As with many ceremonial speakers, King makes ample use of highly connotative words (e.g., symphony, molehill), richly abstract terms (e.g., heat of oppression, jangling discord), and a good number of ultimate terms (e.g., pride, justice) as well. In addition, however, King employs other devices that are the stock-in-trade of many public speakers. Let us consider two of these devices.

Metaphor and Simile

Everyone is familiar with metaphors and similes, although most people might not be able to identify them as such readily. These two stylistic devices are very much alike. A metaphor equates two things. It says or implies that one thing is another: "My love is a red, red rose," "life is a bed of roses," "all the world's a stage." Sometimes, this equation is implied rather than stated explicitly. When one refers to "the cancer of communism," one implies that communism *is* a cancer. "That professor really torpedoed me" insinuates that the professor *is* a hostile submarine and behaves as an enemy behaves.

A simile is very much like a metaphor except that the two elements comprising the simile are compared rather than equated: "He ran *like* a deer," "that old miner is *as hard as* nails." Similes and metaphors differ primarily in strength of expression, with the latter being more definitive, more sure of their linkages.

It is indeed difficult to get through a paragraph of ordinary prose without using a metaphor or simile. Keep your ears open for the next 24 hours and notice the metaphors and similes bombarding your ears: "That test was a real bear," "he's as happy as a clam at high tide," "I think the senator will win by a landslide."

But if you stop to think about it, a metaphor or simile is really a very odd thing to say. Does a speaker actually mean to say that his or her love *is* a red, red rose? Why don't people content themselves with simple, straightforward explanations rather than invent bizarre comparisons? For one thing, expressions like "she's a fox" or "he's a hunk" *cannot* easily be replaced by a factual, sober explanation of what its user feels. Ordinary phrases like "she's attractive" just don't seem to adequately express the *intensity* of our sentiments. We could, of course, say that "she's very, very, very attractive," but such expressions become cumbersome, not to mention inelegant. Metaphors and similes, on the other hand, are *capable of signaling emotion economically.*

How do metaphors function? Perhaps most obvious is that they equate or compare *essentially different* phenomena. Think, for example, of the many ways in which "my love" differs from a red rose. One is a person; the other, a plant. One has silken locks; the other, brutish thorns. One graces my parlor; the other, my backyard. Such differences are necessary in linguistic constructions because these differences create *freshness* and *surprise*. Rather than use an ordinary expression, therefore, Dr. King describes how one racist's lips "drip" with the venom of interposition and nullification. Such dehumanizing of a governor shocks the listener into reexamining the nature and extent of racist attitudes.

Metaphors and similes also serve to *highlight a particular characteristic;* they emphasize one feature of an element to the exclusion of others. King wants us to appreciate the mutuality of brotherhood as well as its day-to-day demands upon us. Therefore, he sits us down at the "table" of brotherhood. Later, after he has impressed upon us the desirability of viewing brotherhood in this way, King turns to another feature of brotherhood—its promise for the future—by allowing us to think of it as a "symphony." In many ways, then, metaphor allows us to be *more specific* than we could be with literal expressions.

Using Metaphors and Similes

But how does one go about creating such telling images? One thing you might do is to think about some element in your speech that you wish the audience to understand with special clarity. Ask yourself what *particular* characteristic of that element you wish to emphasize. Let's suppose, for example, that you wish to describe American consumers and that you want to emphasize their wasteful attitudes toward energy. What other forces operate at harmfully high rates of consumption? Upon reflection, you may decide that a heroin addict is also unwise when consuming large quantities of a pleasurable, but ultimately deadly, substance. So, you compare the two: "The American consumer of oil is like the heroin addict who needs his shot every day; he is hurting himself and his family because of the habit." Framing your thoughts in such a fresh manner may well cause your listener to become more concerned about modern patterns of consumption. It becomes harder to glory in one's gas guzzler when one looks in the rear-view mirror only to find a sallow-faced addict staring back in return.

When casting about to find such lively expressions, *try not to mix metaphors.* That is, if a metaphor or simile says that "A is (or is like) B," don't go on to add, "and it's like C and D as well." For instance, here is a mixed metaphor: "He's an open book; you can see right through him." Such a statement first equates a person's tendency to disclose thoughts easily with the information available in a book, but then goes on to discuss the transparency of a pane of glass as well. Naturally, either metaphor would be appropriate on its own, but one cannot be both a book and a window at the same point in time.

It is sometimes interesting to *extend a metaphor* throughout a speech in order to give coherence and balance to one's thoughts as well as to show the *many* unsuspected similarities between two different elements. Notice, for example, how King's "bell of freedom" emerges directly from his "symphony of brotherhood," thus giving structural integrity to his remarks and pointing up how necessary it is to be loud about injustice at some moments and soft at other times. This extended musical metaphor therefore encapsulates King's nonviolent philosophy as well.

Michael Osborn has identified what might be termed *families* of metaphors—metaphors that cluster together often enough in public speeches to give them distinctiveness.[7] These *archetypal metaphors* may be particularly convenient to you as a speaker because they are among the images ordinary listeners confront most frequently in daily life. Here are some of the most common metaphorical groupings and some examples from Dr. King's speech:

1. *Water* ("oasis of freedom")

2. *Light and dark* ("glory of the Lord will be revealed")

3. *Human body* ("all flesh shall see it")

4. *War* ("to pray together, to struggle together")

5. *Structures* ("table of brotherhood")

6. *Animals* ("lips dripping")

7. *Family* ("land where my fathers died")

8. *Above and below* ("this nation will rise up")

9. *Forward and backward* ("speed up that day")

10. *Mountains* ("every valley shall be exalted")

Clearly, there are other clusters of metaphors, but these ten could alone be very useful to you when searching for ways to enliven your ideas. You might use these archetypes as a kind of checklist, going through it carefully to see if any images are "triggered off" for you. If you truly open your mind to such possibilities, interesting ways of

[7]M. Osborn, *Orientations to Rhetorical Style* (Palo Alto, Cal.: S.R.A. Publishers, 1976).

phrasing your thoughts should appear. It is important to remember, however, that metaphorical expression can be abused rather easily. One or two carefully chosen and well-crafted images are always superior to a variety of them randomly dispersed throughout your speech. Dr. King, for example, favored "family" images and "above and below" images, and extended them throughout his remarks. Such careful choices kept his language from appearing bloated and formless. Therein lies a graceful style.

Achieving Variety in Language

In this section, we would like to discuss briefly a set of stylistic devices available for helping you vary the pace and intensity of your speech. These devices are among the most commonly utilized speech elements and can really freshen up moldy ideas as well as help to keep your listeners' attention from lagging.

Rhetorical Questions

These are questions that the speaker asks of an audience in such a way that the answer to the question is made obvious—clearly implied by the very phrasing of the question. Why should students have to read these long and tedious textbooks? is a rhetorical question. The answer it implies is obvious: They shouldn't have to. Another rhetorical question might be, Is it wise for the United States to allow its sworn enemies to build up overwhelming numbers of nuclear weapons aimed directly at us? Of course, the implied answer is no.

A rhetorical question is good for *involving the audience* in seeing things from the speaker's perspective. Such questions are hard to ignore. When people are asked questions, they tend to answer them (silently, if not out loud). The rhetorical question capitalizes on this communicative "reflex" of ours and thereby elicits the mental cooperation of the listener.

When using the rhetorical question, the speaker should *not* ask the audience to answer out loud. In other words, if one starts a speech by querying, How many of us actually enjoy paying higher and higher tuition rates that threaten to go through the roof? one should not wait for a show of hands! The audience, by providing the appropriate answer in their own minds, will be more involved in the speech from the speaker's point of view; they will have made a kind of "silent commitment" to the speaker and to the proposition he or she is advocating. The rhetorical question is also a good device for subtly making a point that the stronger, declarative construction would have made seem too stark or bold.

Antithesis

An antithesis is designed to *show the contrast between two ideas*, be that difference large or small. An example of antithesis is President Kennedy's famous quotation from his inaugural address, "Ask not what your country can do for you; ask what you can do for your country." Another example, also from President Kennedy is, "Let us never negotiate out of fear; but let us never fear to negotiate." In each case, Kennedy is trying to distinguish two concepts—selfishness and patriotic service in the first example, bravery and political wisdom in the second.

Antithesis works by expressing its pair of ideas in similar ways, using as much repetition as possible. In each of the Kennedy quotations, notice how many words are duplicated in both halves of the antithesis. The *difference* between the two ideas stands out more sharply because of the *similarity* in the ways that the ideas are worded. Dr. King used an antithesis in his "I Have a Dream" speech when he said that "a Negro in Mississippi cannot vote and a Negro in New York believes he has nothing for which to vote." Mixing such a "poetic" phrase with much more hard-nosed "rhetorical" phrases is what gives a speech a distinctive flavor; it at once *advocates* a particular proposition but also tries to make that proposition a *timeless* truth.

Irony

Irony is useful for involving the audience and for *gently criticizing* some person or idea. The ironic speaker plays with language in such a way that the audience knows that the speaker means quite the opposite of what he or she has said. If a speaker refers to Fidel Castro as "that neat and tidy fashion plate," the audience knows that the speaker means much the opposite (assuming, of course, that they have previously seen pictures of the Cuban leader). Similarly, your roommate would understand you quite well if you said, "No, I don't mind that you leave your clothes and dirty dishes all over the couch; I sort of like sitting on day-old sandwiches." Often, one's *delivery* helps to transform a literal expression into an ironic one.

One does not use irony just to be perverse or because one wishes to avoid being straightforward and honest. Rather, irony establishes a common understanding between speaker and audience because it creates a kind of "in-joke." When using irony, the speaker knows that the audience knows that the speaker means the opposite of what he or she says. And the audience knows that the speaker knows that they know it. As a result of this silent coding device, speaker and audience can become partners in semantic crime. Also, irony is a classier way of criticizing something or someone than taking out a rhetorical bludgeon.

Synecdoche

Synecdoche is an interesting stylistic device that emphasizes the most important *characteristic* of something. It does this by referring to a portion of something when the speaker means the whole thing, or to the *whole* of something when the speaker means only part of it. For instance, when the captain of a ship cries "All hands on deck!" he does not expect to see a gaggle of disembodied hands come flopping up out of the hold and lie quivering on the ship's planks. Obviously, he wishes to see *whole* sailors but uses the image he does to emphasize the *work* he expects of his men, thus defining a particular set of characteristics. In like fashion, when a local politician refers to "Washington," he or she also uses synecdoche to emphasize the great amount of governmental activity concentrated in that city. Perhaps such a speaker uses this image to emphasize the government's isolation from the rest of the country.

Speakers can also refer to the whole of something when they mean only one of its parts. Organizers of blood donation campaigns, for example, often urge donors to "give the gift of life." By referring to the *whole*, such speakers emphasize the most important characteristic of blood—its capacity to sustain life.

Synecdoche, then, is particularly valuable for zeroing in on a specific set of characteristics, for emphasizing them to the exclusion of others. When Dr. King urges that freedom ring from the hilltops of New Hampshire, the heightening Alleghenies of Pennsylvania, and Stone Mountain of Georgia, he clearly doesn't mean to endorse racism-as-usual in the lowlands. Rather, he wants to make his listeners sense the loftiness and majesty of a society based on true equality.

Alliteration, Repetition, and Parallelism

The last set of stylistic devices we have chosen to discuss is alliteration, repetition, and parallelism. Repetition is, of course, the repeating of whole words or phrases. Alliteration, on the other hand, is the repetition of parts of words, vowels, or consonant sounds. These devices are good for showing the audience that certain *ideas are linked together.* Take this quotation (also a rhetorical question) from Hubert Humphrey: "Shall we sit in *c*omplacency, lulled by *c*reature *c*omforts, until we are engulfed in *c*haos?" Not only does Humphrey alliteratively repeat the hard "c" sounds, but he repeats them every time he expresses ideas he wishes to be associated in the mind of the audience. Complacency and creature comforts, he is asserting, lead to chaos.

Dr. King uses a good deal of repetition in his speech as well. "I have a dream" echoes throughout his remarks, often helping him bridge from one set of thoughts to another. "Let freedom ring" is repeated quickly toward the end of his speech, signaling the audience that King is approaching the climax of his speech as well as telling them to discover and remove racism from all parts of the United States.

Another device that King and many other speakers employ is parallelism. Parallelism does not involve the repeating of words or parts of words but the repeating of semantic *structures*. For example, when King begins his refrain, "black men and white men, Jews and Gentiles, Catholics and Protestants," he links these various elements together via their organizational sameness. Like Dr. King, many speakers employ parallel structures toward the ends of their speeches in order to show the unity and symmetry of their ideas.

When you stop to think about it, there are preciously few new ideas, especially in the world of social, political, and ethical issues. John Kennedy, Adlai Stevenson, Winston Churchill, Martin Luther King, and the other great speakers aren't revered because of their startlingly new ideas but because of the beautiful *variations* they wrought on very old themes. It is not coincidental, then, that we find in their speeches many of the stylistic devices discussed in this section. Although justice and human dignity are tired, old conceptions, the skillful use of language can bring them to life yet another time. We urge you to examine your language carefully and to stifle the thought that it has all been said before. It hasn't been. With the resources of language, it can never be.

Suggestions for Speaking

Although we have talked a good deal in this chapter about the attractions of the well-turned phrase or the striking image, we hope that you have caught our emphasis on the *functional* importance of language. Our discussions in this chapter have not been designed to make you a poet. The public speaker is a practical person and ponders over linguistic choices only because they may contribute to his or her effect upon an audience. Although the ceremonial speaker and the poet have much in common with regard to language, for the public speaker language is a tool—a powerful and often dazzling one, but a tool nonetheless. The public speaker uses attractive language only because it casts a rhetorical spotlight on certain *ideas* he or she is peddling. If a favorite verbal image becomes too convoluted, if a popular phrase loses its potency over time, or if a string of rhetorical questions becomes too predictable, the public speaker has no choice but to remove them from public view—*no matter how fond of them he or she may be*. Because the public speaker chooses language with an eye to its social impact, he or she is wise to observe certain practical constraints when polishing a public speech. Among them are the following:

1. *Public language should be personal.* Don't borrow someone else's vocabulary. Use language that *you* can use easily. Never use a word in a speech that you haven't said *out loud* previously. Practice pronouncing a new word until you make it yours.

2. *Public language should be fitting.* Listen carefully to the language patterns of your listeners before you speak to them. Adjust the formality of your language to fit the situation. Resist the temptation to use a pet phrase just because you like it. Don't be flip with a serious topic or melodramatic with a light one.

3. *Public language should be consistent.* Be careful not to create a riotous collection of images for your listeners. Make them feel comfortable by using extended metaphors. Don't switch randomly from the active to the passive voice. Be sure that the referents for your personal pronouns are clear.

4. *Public language should be precise.* If you're talking about bulldozers, don't call them earthmoving vehicles. Avoid jargon that is not necessary for comprehension. Define all technical terms for your listeners. Avoid vague generalities. Use concrete and specific language when providing descriptions.

5. *Public language should be simple.* Use five-syllable words sparingly. Employ simple constructions as often as possible (as opposed to compound or complex constructions). Use your *voice* to emphasize a point rather than repeat an idea several times. Avoid using imbedded clauses.

6. *Public language should be unaffected.* Don't seek to have your listeners remember your language. Don't get carried away with metaphors; a single, simple image is always superior to several complex ones. Don't invent "cute" phrases. Euphemistic language often sounds silly (e.g., calling a concentration camp a "pacification center").

7. *Public language should be strategic.* Ambiguity often has its advantages, especially when you're dealing with touchy topics or especially hostile listeners. Try out several different ways of phrasing a volatile idea. Don't depend on the inspiration of the moment to guide your language choice. Think in advance about what you're going to say and *how* you're going to say it.

8. *Public language should be fresh.* It's doubtful that your listeners will be hearing your proposition for the first time. Examine how other speakers have phrased your proposition and find a new, audience-dependent way of saying it. Let your mind wan-

der freely as you search for apt metaphors and similes. If your audience's eyes look glazed, you'll know they've heard it all before.

9. *Public language should be oral.* Except in certain circumstances, manuscript speeches should probably be avoided. A speech is meant for the ear, not the eye. *Listen* to the words and phrases you intend to use. Put "catch phrases" in your outline rather than long, elaborate sentences. Use your voice and body to signal irony and rhetorical questions.

10. *Public language should be "dickmottaish."* Dick Motta was a coach for the Philadelphia Seventy-Sixers, a professional basketball team. A colorful and exciting coach, he was also verbally adroit. When being interviewed by the press, Motta almost always expressed his thoughts in simple, precise, fitting, and highly oral ways. Because he was a free spirit, Motta's language was always personal and fresh as well, a welcome relief from the often pompous commentators who afflict our ears during sporting events. Motta's most famous phrase was delivered on the eve of certain disaster for his Philadelphia ballclub. When being prodded by sportscasters to throw in the emotional towel, Motta summoned up the very best sort of public language when he replied, "The opera isn't over until the fat lady sings." Now *there* is a listenable thought.

CHAPTER 7

The Resources of Delivery

"Our speaker tonight is Dr. Myron L. Fox, distinguished authority on the application of mathematics to human behavior, who will speak to us on 'Mathematical Game Theory as Applied to Physician Education.'"

An introduction such as this, followed by a one-hour lecture and half-hour discussion period, were part of an experiment by medical educators Donald Naftulin and Frank Donnelly of the University of Southern California and John E. Ware, Jr., of the Southern Illinois University School of Medicine.

A group of 11 psychiatrists, psychologists, and social-worker educators heard the lecture and took part in the discussion. The entire session was videotaped and shown later to two other groups of professionals (44 people in all) with similar backgrounds. The audiences were then asked to fill out, anonymously, a question-naire evaluating the lecture. Reactions were strongly favorable, as were the comments volun-teered by individuals. These included:

"Lively examples. His relaxed manner of presentation was a large factor in holding my interest . . . Extremely articulate. Interesting, wish he dwelled more on background . . . Good analysis of subject that has been personally stud-ied before . . . Very dramatic presentation. He was certainly captivating . . . Somewhat disor-ganized. Frustratingly boring . . . Unorganized and ineffective . . . Articulate. Knowledgeable."

"Dr." Fox was a smashing success . . . and a complete phony. Naftulin, Ware, and Donnelly had hired a professional actor and coached him, in their words, "to present his topic and conduct his question-and-answer period with an exces-sive use of double talk, neologisms, non sequi-turs, and contradictory statements. All this was to be interspersed with parenthetical humor and meaningless references to unrelated topics." Source material for the lecture came from a *Scientific American* article geared to lay readers.

The Dr. Fox experiment, which the re-searchers subtitled "A Paradigm of Educational Seduction," was not done as a joke or a put-down of its professional audience, but as a further test of how much student ratings of teachers depend on personality rather than content.[1]

Ever since scholars have written seriously about public speaking, they have differed on the relative importance of content and delivery in enhancing a speaker's effectiveness. Aristotle, a fourth-century B.C. Greek philosopher, for example, argued that speakers ought to be primarily concerned with the logic of their dis-course. While, for practical reasons, such matters as voice and gesture must be considered, admonished Aristotle, delivery is not an elevated subject of inquiry. Demosthenes (Greek orator, political leader, and contemporary of Aristotle) reached the opposite conclusion in declaring delivery all-important. The three rules of good speaking, he is alleged to have claimed, are first, delivery; second, delivery; third, delivery.

Variations of this argument have continued throughout history to the present day. Currently, many teachers of public speaking put little stress on delivery other than to commend the student for appropriate posture, conversational delivery, and good eye contact. In contrast, the Dr. Fox story provides a vivid demonstration that delivery may be much more important than some suspect, and that it is often not necessary (or enough) to have a well-organized and strongly supported speech. The speaker's use of voice and physical action is needed to transform a lifeless set of ideas entombed on note cards into a living, human reality.

The importance of this fleshing out process is demonstrated by Ralph G. Nichols' experiments at the University of Minnesota, where he tested the retention ability of a large group of students. One of his major findings was that many listeners judged the worth of a lecturer by the quality of delivery: If the lecturer overused notes, had a poor voice, used indistinct speech, or displayed distracting mannerisms, students concluded that the content of the lecture was poor.[2] Paul Hinberg reached similar conclusions in his study of college teachers whom he had listen to tape recordings of two kinds of student speeches: self-introductions and persuasive talks. He found that delivery was almost twice as important as content in determining the general effectiveness of self-introductions and almost three times as influential as content in the persuasive situation.[3] Ray Birdwhistell, a pioneer in the areas of nonverbal communication research, concluded that, in general, less than 35 percent of social meaning is conveyed verbally; the rest, he said, reaches us nonverbally.[4] Albert Mehrabian, another well-known expert, made the even stronger claim that 93 percent of all social meaning is transmitted nonverbally.[5] On the basis of his research, he concluded that social meaning = 7 percent verbal + 37 percent vocal + 55 percent facial. Naturally, these gross estimates cannot be trusted completely, but Mehrabian's basic argument is a plausible one: Delivery cannot be ignored.

This chapter follows up our brief discussion in Chapter 3 by examining some guiding principles that underlie effective delivery. Un-

[2]R. Nichols and L. Stevens, *Are You Listening?* (New York: McGraw-Hill, 1957).

[3]P. Hinberg, "Relationship of Content and Delivery to General Effectiveness," *Speech Monographs*, 30:105–107 (1963).

[4]R. Birdwhistell, "Background to Kinesics," *ETC.*, 13:10–18 (1955).

[5]A. Mehrabian, "Communication Without Words," *Psychology Today*, 2:53, no. 4 (1968).

fortunately, we will not be able to provide you with a set of absolute laws here. Because effective delivery is a product of both the speaker's personal characteristics and the speaking situation itself, universal standards for determining effective delivery are simply unavailable. It is possible, for example, to characterize as effective such diverse speaking styles as those of Muhammad Ali, Johnny Carson, Barbara Jordan, Edward Kennedy, and Ronald Reagan. Thus, in this chapter we attempt to provide *a way of thinking* about delivery, which, we hope, can aid you in self-improvement. Our basic argument is that delivery is best when

1. You become somewhat familiar with theories of delivery, the functions of delivery, the elements that define delivery, and the characteristics of delivery that make for effective communication.

2. You learn to recognize the skills of effective delivery in others.

3. You learn to recognize the benefits and shortcomings of your own delivery.

4. You identify techniques for remedying deficiencies in your delivery.

5. You are provided with abundant opportunities for practicing your new-found skills.

This chapter will elaborate upon each of these assumptions, beginning with a brief discussion of the communicative functions served by delivery.

Functions of Delivery

The general functions of delivery can be reduced to two: using nonverbal communication to (1) focus attention on the speaker's message (rather than draw attention to itself) and (2) aid an audience in understanding and retaining what has been said. Authorities on nonverbal communication have identified at least six ways in which delivery can influence the understanding and retention of a speaker's verbal message.[6] Let us briefly discuss each of them.

[6]The following typology is based on P. Ekman, "Communication Through Nonverbal Behavior: A Source of Information About an Interpersonal Relationship," in *Affect, Cognition and Personality*, eds. S. S. Tomkins and C. E. Izard (New York: Springer, 1965).

Repeating

Delivery can be used to "say" the same thing that has been said verbally. A smile, for example, can be used to repeat the verbal message that a speaker "is pleased to be here today." The speaker's right index finger can be extended to reinforce the fact that "my first point this afternoon will be . . ." In both cases, the nonverbal cue provides redundancy and increases the accuracy of communication.

Substituting

Without our saying a word, we may signal particular meanings through delivery. For example, instead of verbalizing his or her commitment to the message, a speaker may signal genuine involvement through the taut, earnest expression on his or her face or through the rapidity of speech itself. Using delivery as a substitute for verbal messages often provides three advantages: (1) A nonverbal message frequently can be conveyed more rapidly than a verbal one, (2) two or more messages can be delivered simultaneously, and (3) for many members of the audience, nonverbal messages possess greater credibility than do verbal messages. Thus, there are both technical *and social* advantages to nonverbal behavior.

Complementing

Delivery can also be used to supplement or modify what has been said verbally. Rather than repeating or replacing speech, delivery can modify or elaborate upon the verbal message. Thus, when describing an embarrassing moment, for example, you might make the story more vivid and reveal how you felt about the incident by recapturing for your listeners the expression on your face when you discovered the spinach on your front tooth *after* your dream date.

The complementing function of delivery can also signal the speaker's attitudes and intentions toward the audience (e.g., holding your body rigidly may signal that you feel threatened by the audience). This function of delivery, then, capitalizes on what many authorities consider to be among the primary uses of nonverbal behavior: (1) expressing emotions (e.g., happiness), (2) conveying attitudes (e.g., confidence), and (3) presenting one's personality to others (e.g., openness).

Accenting

Delivery can also be used to emphasize or accent what the speaker is saying verbally. Vocal intonations and movements of the head and hands, for example, are often used by speakers to underline a point they wish the audience to remember. While teachers are not always subtle about their intentions ("this will be on the next exam"), students who value doing well on exams quickly learn to master the subtle nonverbal clues teachers use to signal that this is material that ought to be included in classroom notes. One teacher of our acquaintance, for example, has a habit of flashing her eyes when an idea or concept is of particular importance to her. After the first exam, students quickly pick up on the importance of such nonverbal hints.

Contradicting

Another function of delivery, useful both for humor and for more serious purposes, is that of contradicting the verbal message. The sarcastically delivered "Good job, Miriam" is unlikely to be misunderstood by either Miriam or by those around her—the vocal inflection has signaled that the verbal message means much the opposite of what it appears to say. Speakers may also use contradictions for more subtle and serious purposes. Eye behavior or vocal elements can be used to signal a commitment only cautiously projected in words (e.g., a wink that follows an apparent denial). Such contradictions between verbal and nonverbal messages are, of course, not always under the control of the speaker. Many of us have heard, for example, a speaker with trembling hands and beads of perspiration on the brow say, "I'm not nervous." Indeed, comic Don Knotts has built an entire career out of this one nonverbal function.

Regulating

Delivery can also be used to regulate the flow of communication between speaker and audience, to decide who will talk when. While this function is less important for public speaking than it is for informal conversations, the speaker may, for example, use delivery to distinguish questions that are purely rhetorical from those to which the speaker seeks an actual response. Delivery cues can also be used to encourage or prevent audience members from interrupting the speaker and to focus listeners' attention more directly on him or her.

Having a full understanding of these various nonverbal functions is just as important as, say, knowing the uses to which a microwave oven can be put. For some people, a microwave is useful for heating coffee or for warming up leftovers, but for the more adventurous cook, the microwave can be used to prepare an entire meal. By becoming more familiar with the many functions of delivery, you can develop a much more subtle communicative repertoire, making points more gracefully and more fulsomely than the person who feels that the sole function of the body in speechmaking is to prop up the speaker's head. Clearly, much more is possible.

Components of Delivery

As we have seen, there are many aspects of delivery available for focusing attention on the speaker's message and for aiding an audience in understanding and retaining what the speaker has said. Students of communication have also identified numerous factors of nonverbal communication (those elements of communication that are not essentially linguistic in nature) that may influence the sending and receiving of messages. In fact, entire textbooks have been written that discuss these factors in detail. Here, we will examine five factors that are especially relevant to the enterprise of public speaking: setting, physical appearance and dress, body motion (kinesics), vocal cues (paralanguage or vocalics), and space (proxemics).

Setting

The environment for public speaking may be described in both objective and subjective terms. Objectively, it consists of, at minimum, the categories of structure, function, and physical setting. Structurally, for example, it matters whether the speaker is addressing an audience of fellow students or a group of employees. The function served by the public speech also conditions communicative effectiveness. As we shall see in Chapter 12, audience expectations for an impromptu speech differ considerably from those surrounding a technical, informative presentation. In addition, elements within the physical environment, including room size, temperature, color, furniture, lighting conditions, and sound, all influence the speaker's attempts to communicate. While many objective elements of the setting are beyond the speaker's control, others are not. Wise speakers, therefore, learn to modify the changeable elements of the setting to aid them in achieving their purpose and to plan appropriate adaptations to the elements over which they have no control. If, for example, it is possible to anticipate and eliminate noise caused by outside traffic, it is clearly intelligent to do so. If this is not possible, however, the speaker needs to plan verbal and nonverbal strategies for reducing the negative impact of such external noise (e.g., by speaking more distinctly or by increasing redundancy).

The possible combinations of structure, function, and physical environment are almost infinite. To reduce some of this complexity, it is helpful to reflect upon how audiences subjectively experience physical settings. Mark Knapp has hypothesized six such dimensions[7] for classifying our reactions to communicative environments, to each of which we have added an appropriate example:

Perceptions of formality: a classroom speech to an audience of peers versus a televised presidential address

Perceptions of warmth: remarks made to an audience of friends versus those made to strangers

Perceptions of privacy: a speech in a classroom versus one delivered on the campus mall

Perceptions of familiarity: We feel more at home during the third speech of a semester than during the first.

Perceptions of constraint: Smaller rooms are likely to produce greater feelings of closeness than larger rooms.

Perception of distance: The number of persons per square foot in the audience is likely to influence the intra-audience effects generated.

As Knapp suggests, the foregoing represent only some of the ways we react to communication settings. They are, nevertheless, helpful for revealing needed adaptations. For example, if you were presenting a speech on the charitable works of Nobel Prize winner Mother Theresa,

[7]M. Knapp, *Nonverbal Communication in Human Interaction*, 2nd ed. (New York: Holt, Rinehart and Winston, 1978).

you would probably want to do all you could to arrange classroom furniture so that feelings of closeness and warmth would predominate. Speaking more softly and more slowly than normal might also add the human touch so necessary in such a sterile environment. In short, the six sets of perceptions mentioned above must be reckoned with seriously by the public speaker.

Physical Appearance and Dress

Physical appearance, including both natural elements (e.g., physique or body shape, general attractiveness, height, weight, hair, and skin color or tone) and adornments (clothing, accessories, and cosmetics) can convey a wide variety of messages about the public speaker. Since these elements are among the first things noticed by listeners, they can have quite an impact on the speaker's ability to influence an audience. It is wise, therefore, to analyze all dimensions of physical appearance in terms of how these will be perceived by the particular audience as well as the purpose of the speech itself. Naturally, it is sometimes hard to be objective about such personal matters, but skillful use of a simple mirror can suggest whether your nonverbal cues are working for or against the message you are about to deliver. A speech on dieting given by a rotund person *can* be a most effective one if the speaker has the wit, polish, and sense of irony needed for making the appropriate verbal adaptations in such a circumstance.

Body Motion

The complexity of the meanings contained in bodily movements is illustrated by the following estimates and observations reported by Burgoon and Saine:

—*Pei estimates that communicating man can produce 700,000 different physical signs.*
—*Birdwhistell estimates that the face alone is capable of producing 250,000 expressions.*
—*Physiologists estimate that the musculature of the face permits over 20,000 different expressions.*
—*In a study of classroom behavior, Krout observed 7,777 distinct gestures.*
—*In therapeutic situations, Krout identified 5,000 distinct hand gestures alone that he believed to have verbal equivalents.*
—*Hewes has cataloged 1,000 different postures and their accompanying gestures.*[8]

[8]J. Burgoon and T. Saine, *The Unspoken Dialogue: An Introduction to Nonverbal Communication* (Boston: Houghton Mifflin, 1978).

Because of this seemingly infinite inventory of potential body motion cues, Paul Ekman and Wallace Friesen attempted to subsume them under a more manageable set of five functions that they appear to serve:[9]

1. *Emblems* are intentional behaviors that can substitute for a verbal message with little change in meaning occurring. As examples of emblems, consider how you might communicate the following concepts without using words: (1) "Shame on you!" (2) "She's crazy!" (3) "Up yours, buddy!" and (4) "May I have a ride in your car?"

2. *Illustrators* are used to complement, contradict, emphasize, or repeat the verbal message. Such illustrators can accentuate words and phrases (e.g., putting the heel of the hand to the forehead and saying, "My God!"), point to objects, places, or events (e.g., using the thumb to say "get lost!"), or repeat or substitute for words (e.g., the football player's "high five" eliminates the need for saying "congratulations").

3. *Affect displays,* whether intentional or unintentional, reveal the speaker's emotions. While the face is the primary source for communicating affect (e.g., the grimace of pain), body demeanor can also be read for global judgments of emotion (e.g., the body "slumps" when we feel dejected).

[9]P. Ekman and W. Friesen, "The Repertoire of Nonverbal Behavior: Categories, Origins, Usage, and Coding," *Semiotica*, 1:49–98 (1969).

4. *Regulators* are nonverbal behaviors used to control the flow and content of communication. Head nods and eye movements, for example, can serve to either encourage or discourage further communication.

5. *Adaptors* are developed in childhood and seemed designed to satisfy physical or emotional needs. Because they are normally used to satisfy personal needs (e.g., providing needed functions such as scratching, pinching, or picking), they are usually performed in private. When they occur in public, therefore, it is usually because the individual is experiencing some form of distress or discomfort.

As we have seen, the number of potential emblems, illustrators, affect displays, regulators, and adaptors is large and has tremendous potential to both increase and decrease effectiveness. Because of this, it is helpful to do a personal inventory and assessment of those cues you most commonly employ in both formal and informal communication settings. One of the major problems some neophyte public speakers seem to have is a tendency to forget this public and private distinction. For some reason, bodily motions that seem normal and natural in private conversations (e.g., fidgeting or squirming) draw attention to themselves when used by a speaker, who has suddenly become an object of attention for an entire audience. Because listeners in *public* settings normally do not share the conversational burden, they have more time to "study" their fellow interactant. Thus, the inventory we suggest (perhaps conducted with the aid of a friend or through videotaping a sample speech) can be highly revealing and can genuinely contribute both to self-understanding and to practical success as a public speaker.

Vocal Cues

This category of delivery variables includes all stimuli, other than the words themselves, produced by the human voice. A standard way of classifying such vocal features is to group them into two large classes of variables:

1. *Voice qualities*, or general, distinguishable elements of the voice such as pitch range, rate of speaking, thickness of tone quality, precision and forcefulness in pronunciation, smoothness of phraseology, and smoothness of transition in pitch

2. *Vocalizations*, or three subcategories of very specific sounds or aspects of sounds: (1) vocal characterizers—ways in which the "meaning" of a speaking voice can be subtly "refined" (e.g.,

whispering, whining, yelling); (2) vocal qualifiers—the specific acoustic characteristics of intensity (energy expended to make a sound), pitch height (perceived highness or lowness of the voice), and extent (duration of a sound); and (3) vocal segregates—vocalized pauses such as "uh-huh," "uh," and "ah"

Taken together, both types of vocal cues provide much potential information about the speaker, and they influence his or her effectiveness both directly and indirectly. Directly, variations in volume, pitch, and rate, for example, aid the audience in following and retaining information from the speech. Indirectly, vocal cues play an important role in determining speaker credibility (e.g., would you believe a witness in court who used many "ums" or "ers" when testifying?).

Space

A public speaker's perceptions and use of space are a final nonverbal element that can affect the outcome of communication. The seating arrangement of the audience will, for example, influence how loudly the speaker must project his or her voice or how taxing the establishment of eye contact will be. In addition, both distance and barriers (e.g., a desk or a podium) between the speaker and the audience can create various moods and can condition the intimacy of dialogue possible. The speaker who wishes to reduce the formality of a speaking situation, for example, may do so by moving out from behind a lectern and toward the audience.

Characteristics of Good Delivery

To this point, we have examined five categories of nonverbal variables that the speaker must control in order to achieve the two goals of effective delivery: (1) focusing attention on the message rather than the speaker and (2) helping an audience retain the content of the speech. Before moving to practical suggestions for using this knowledge to improve delivery skills, let us first consider briefly four characteristics of effective delivery. At minimum, successful delivery can be characterized as conversational, direct, unobtrusive, and intelligible.

Conversational

By carefully observing ordinary conversations, we can get some useful hints about effective delivery. In informal dialogue, participants talk loudly enough to be heard, with much variation in the pitch and volume of their voices. Points are reinforced with gestures and physical movement; posture and eye contact indicate their mutual concern for one another. In all of this, variations in voice and physical action *unconsciously* focus attention on and reinforce the content of the interaction. Public speakers could not hope for a better model. Their goal ought to be to incorporate the principles of conversation into their speech delivery as they talk *with* rather than at their listeners. Good delivery, in other words, always demonstrates commitment to the audience.

Direct

In addition to being conversational, good delivery is direct. It signals to the audience a desire to communicate with them. For most individuals in western culture, directness is primarily a function of eye contact; when one attains direct eye contact, variations in voice and other physical actions normally and naturally follow. Achieving the benefits of directness requires eye contact with all segments of the audience. One practical suggestion may be to pick out one or two people in a particular area of the room and talk with them as you develop one idea. When moving to the next idea, establish direct contact with one or two individuals in a different part of the audience. As far as possible, move your eyes back and forth around the room as you proceed through the speech.

Unobtrusive

Good delivery is also unobtrusive; it does not focus attention on itself. Violations of this principle usually involve the unconscious display of distracting mannerisms: rocking back and forth while standing in one place, playing with one's hands, excessive vocalized pauses, lack of appropriate eye contact. In most cases, such mannerisms are manifestations of tension, which will disappear with greater experience as a speaker. Thus, consciously trying to monitor and control distracting mannerisms is best not attempted for your first few speeches. If such behaviors persist, however, a conscious attempt should be made to eliminate them. Oftentimes, bringing them to a level of awareness is enough. If that doesn't help, they can sometimes be eliminated by what clinical psychologists have labeled *negative practice*—consciously overemphasizing the distracting mannerism while practicing delivery of the speech.

Intelligible

A final minimum requirement of effective delivery is that it be intelligible. This involves not only adequate volume and appropriate rate, but attention to articulation and pronunciation as well. Words need to be clearly articulated and properly pronounced so that they are easily recognizable. Not only will mispronunciation contribute to a lack of clarity, it will reduce the credibility of the speaker as well. Thus, whenever there is the slightest doubt about a word, the public speaker should consult the dictionary. Tape-recording your speech during rehearsal can often be quite helpful for gauging your intelligibility.

The most important characteristic of good delivery is perhaps more important than all four of the preceding suggestions. Above all, delivery should be *functional.* That is, it should do what *you* want it to do. And you ought to be blatantly honest about this. You ought to decide what effective delivery is worth to you and what price you're willing to pay to attain it. That is, if you're one of those who feel that if your verbal message is OK, the rest doesn't matter, then you should be prepared to accept the negative reactions of more picky listeners. *Delivery that gets in the way of your goals should be eliminated.* If you set relatively low goals for yourself, then virtually any sort of weird body motion or strange vocal inflection will do. On the other hand, if you become incensed at the thought that something as simple as an inappropriate gesture or a tendency to stammer or "lazy eyes" can distract your listeners from what you have to say, then you may very well seek to improve such a state of affairs.

Improving Delivery

From the beginning, teachers of public speaking have differed more on how to improve delivery than on any other phase of speechmaking. Before presenting our thoughts on this particular subject, let us briefly review three approaches that have attracted wide followings in the past. Samuel Silas Curry, one of the first to discuss them in print, labeled the three schools of thought on delivery as *imitative, mechanical,* and *impulsive.* [10] Let us briefly consider each.

Approaches to Delivery

Teachers committed to the *imitative school of delivery* argue that delivery is a complex art that is best learned from a model—that is, by imitating or copying the delivery of another person such as a teacher, a famous speaker, a classmate, or a hypothetical or idealized person. The earliest written statement advocating this school of thought is probably that of the Greek teacher Isocrates who in 390 B.C. wrote that the teacher must not only expound the principles of the art but "must in himself set such an example of oratory that the students who have taken form

[10]S. S. Curry, *The Province of Expression* (Boston: Expression Co., 1927).

under his instruction and are able to pattern after him will, from the outset, show in their speaking a degree of grace and charm which is not found in others."[11] While lively debates ensued on such topics as who should be imitated, whether the student should imitate one model or many, and which of the imitative exercises (e.g., paraphrase, translation, learning by heart) were most valuable, a belief in the value of imitation for learning the art of speaking was undeviating in Greco-Roman education from Isocrates through St. Augustine (c. 400 A.D.). Imitation of the classics received even greater emphasis in the Renaissance, and the method is occasionally employed today by many teachers of speech.

The *mechanical school of delivery* had its roots in the English elocutionists of the eighteenth and nineteenth centuries. By the mid-1800s, it had been firmly transported to nineteenth-century American colleges where it first became the vogue, and then the standard pattern, for providing speech training. The mechanical school resulted from a number of forces acting together to inspire an intensive study of delivery: criticism of the delivery of the Anglican clergy, philological and linguistic investigations into pronunciation and inflectional patterns, perceptions that power in oral presentation was an important instrument of public persuasion, emergence of a new style of stage delivery for the theater, and acknowledgment of the importance of competence in speaking as a part of general education. The resulting school of delivery was given its broadest definition by one of its founders, drama coach Thomas Sheridan:

> *A just delivery consists in a distinct articulation of words, pronounced in proper tones, suitably varied to the sense, and the emotions of the mind; with due observation of accent; of emphasis, in its several gradations; of rests or pauses of the voice, in proper place and well measured degrees of time; and the whole accompanied with expressive looks, and significant gesture.*[12]

As it developed, the mechanical or elocutionary view of teaching delivery started with a careful analysis of the vocal and visual elements of presentation. From such empirical study, elocutionists derived and taught rules for the correct or "natural" expression of thought and emotion. At its extreme, all action was rigidly prescribed so that the student could follow directions much in the way a musician reads a note. Thus, a fixed gesture or body pose was prescribed for portraying virtually every idea or emotion. To illustrate the extreme to which this movement went, consider the following exercises in facial expression contained in an early twentieth-century elocution book:

---

[11]Isocrates, *Against the Sophists*, vol. 2 (London: Loeb, 1929), pp. 17–18.
[12]T. Sheridan, *A Course of Lectures on Elocution* (London: W. Strahan, 1762), p. 10.

Courage, Determination: Look straight forward.
Joy, Hope, Delight: Raise the eyes slightly upward.
Shame, Modesty, Humility: Look downward.
Disgust, Aversion: Turn the eyes to either side.
Madness: A steady glare, seeing nothing.
Sudden Anger: Let the eyes flash.
Consternation: Open the eyes wide with a fixed stare.
Rage: Roll the eyes well open.
Despair: A vacant stare.
Laughing: Eyes partially closed.
Supplication: Eyes elevated.
Flirt: To the side with a twinkle.[13]

There were, to be sure, many similar (and even more elaborate) exercises for all aspects of the vocal and visual elements of delivery. In fact, most of the speaker's handbooks of the early twentieth century contained descriptions of such exercises complete with photographs demonstrating their proper enactment.

Partly as a revolt against excesses of the mechanical approach, a "think-the-thought" or *impulsive school of delivery* emerged. First advocated by Richard Whately, the approach was based on the belief that delivery is a matter of impulse and, therefore, that natural inclinations are the most reliable guides to how the speaker should behave. Thus, rather than consciously think about the vocal and physical elements of delivery, the speaker is advised to concentrate on the content of the message. Doing so, it was believed, would lead the speaker to gesture and move when speech content seems to demand such action. Thus, a teacher of public speaking within this particular tradition is likely to advise the student to move and gesture when he or she has the urge to do so.

It is this school of thought that dominates current thinking about delivery. While it has much to recommend it, it is wise not to neglect the potential contributions of the other two schools of thought. Thus, in detailing our guidelines for improving delivery, we will attempt to incorporate the best from all three approaches while minimizing their liabilities. We begin our discussion with a focus on the essentials of good delivery and then present our thoughts on fine tuning delivery skills.

Getting Started

As with any skill, improvement in delivery requires frequent practice. Because delivery involves such a large number of independent

---

[13]I. H. Brown, *Brown's Standard Elocution and Speaker* (Land and Lee, 1911), pp. 45–47.

components, it is best that the speaker focus initial attention during practice on the message and the audience. Excessive concentration on delivery should be avoided because it often leads to awkwardness and artificiality (both vocally and physically) when speaking.

To be useful, practice should feature the greatest amount of realism possible. Thus, while you may wish to try out portions of your speech silently in the privacy of your room, eventually you will want to rehearse in the room where you will actually be speaking. When doing so, practice walking to the front of the room, standing as you will for the speech, and pretending that you are talking with members of the audience. If possible, get a friend or friends to go with you so that they can listen and share their impressions with you. After you have practiced the speech a number of times, you may wish to audio- or videotape the speech to listen to yourself. This is probably most helpful, however, *after* you have given a couple of speeches in class because by then you should have a better grasp of the characteristics of your delivery that require examination.

Admittedly, speech rehearsal is a time-consuming task. It is well worth the effort, however, in that it not only leads to improved delivery, but it also provides a test of speech structure, lays the basis for revising thoughts, allows for perfecting language, fixes the speech in the speaker's mind, and aids the speaker in becoming comfortable with the speaking situation.

As you plan and rehearse your initial speeches, you may wish to consider our brief responses to six questions often asked by beginning public speakers:

1. *May I use notes?* Sure, if their use is not obtrusive. Notes on stiff 3×5 cards probably work best in that they are easily handled without distracting either the speaker or the audience.

2. *Should I use a speaker's stand?* Only if it is necessary to hold a manuscript, notes, or a visual aid. For beginning speakers, it is too easy to fall into the trap of playing with the lectern or leaning on it. Thus, you are well advised to learn how to speak without a speaker's stand unless it is absolutely necessary and, even then, it should be used only for those times during the speech when it is truly needed.

3. *What should I wear?* Clothing that makes you feel comfortable and that doesn't distract from the purpose of your speech. Some individuals find that they get a slight psychological edge by dressing up a bit more for a speech than they normally would for class.

4. *Where should I stand?* In a location that allows you the closest possible rapport with your audience. This is usually the center portion of the front of the room. To the extent possible, eliminate obstructions between yourself and your audience by standing in front of or to the side of such barriers as desks, tables, or lecterns.

5. *What should I do with my hands?* Whatever you normally do with them when talking with others. Concentrate on talking with your audience, and your hands and gestures will take care of themselves.

6. *Should I stand in one place?* The speaker needs to be physically comfortable, which involves both comfortable posture and freedom of movement. Movement creates variety, which, in turn, focuses audience attention; thus, emphasizing a point is often possible through natural and graceful movements.

As with any skill (e.g., playing piano, golf, tennis, or banjo), improving delivery skills is a never-ending process. Knowledge to be mastered is constantly accumulating; old skills need to be polished and new skills learned. In this section, therefore, we elaborate on the remaining three of our five assumptions stated at the beginning of this chapter. Competence in delivery is best achieved if

1. You learn to recognize the skills of effective delivery in others.

2. You learn to recognize proficiencies and shortcomings in your own delivery.

3. You learn to identify remedies for such deficiencies.

Recognizing Good Delivery

We hope our description of effective delivery has been suggestive. Naturally, such a description needs to be enlarged by both observation and guided practice. The speech classroom provides an ideal environment for doing so. Not only will you receive feedback from the teacher and fellow students on your performances, but the classroom also provides an opportunity to observe a variety of delivery styles and to observe the reactions of teacher, peers, and self to them. When doing so, it is especially helpful to be looking constantly for useful generalizations about effective delivery.

Equally important is directly observing the speeches of individuals who model effective delivery. The viewing of films or videotapes is an especially effective way to develop such an awareness of delivery standards because of the opportunity it affords for repeated viewing. In picking models, it is usually best not to start with individuals whose delivery is flawless—they may start you out feeling defeated. Instead, select individuals who seem to have skills slightly in advance of your own. Over time, seek out models who progressively demonstrate greater skill. Also, search for a wide variety of models so that you don't set idiosyncratic goals for yourself. Using models in such a way will help you to learn new skills, learn to use existing skills in more appropriate ways (and at more appropriate times), and, finally, to use skills that were previously avoided because of fear or anxiety.

Recognizing Personal Shortcomings

To improve delivery skills, it is helpful to learn to recognize certain problems—via self-monitoring or feedback from others. A good place to begin this process is with the creation of a personal inventory for analyzing your characteristic nonverbal activity in informal settings. While the questions to be included on the inventory should be self-generated, you may wish to include such items as follows:

1. *Physical appearance*
   a. Natural elements: How would others describe your body shape, weight, height, general attractiveness, and so on? What are they likely to conclude about you on the basis of this assessment? Can such personal elements be used to reinforce certain aspects of your message?
   b. Adornments: How would others describe your normal approach to dress? What judgments are they likely to form? Are you able to easily discover standards of appropriate dress?

2. *Body motion*
   a. Emblems: Which emblems do you use most frquently? Which do you avoid?
   b. Illustrators: How actively do you use illustrators? Do you use some types more frequently than others?
   c. Affect displays: How easy is it for others to read your emotions? Do your face and body communicate what you want them to?
   d. Regulators: How do you signal when you want to change a topic? Does your body help you to make smooth transitions?
   e. Adaptors: Do you have difficulty suppressing adaptors in public settings? Which adaptors are most common in your behavior? Do they affect intelligibility?

3. *Vocal cues*
   a. Voice quality: Do you speak with a great deal of vocal variety? Do people ever complain about your rate of speaking?
   b. Vocalizations: Do you fill your conversational silence with vocalized pauses? How would individuals characterize your speaking voice?

4. *Space:* Do you like to have lots of people around you? At what distance do you feel most comfortable talking with a teacher?

5. *In your informal interactions, how do you most typically use nonverbal behavior:* to repeat? to substitute? to complement? to accent? to contradict? to regulate?

6. *Would others describe your delivery as* conversational? direct? unobtrusive? intelligible? Why or why not?

7. *What are the general characteristics of your nonverbal behavior?* Are you very active, active, not very active? Do you use large gestures, medium-sized ones, or little or no gestures? Do you use many or few personalized motions? Do you tend to be more of a verbal than a nonverbal person? Do your nonverbal behaviors generally communicate what you wish them to?

A personal inventory, if honestly and objectively conducted, will tell you a great deal about your nonverbal assets and liabilities. Because individuals are seldom able to see themselves as others see them, however, you will need to supplement the inventory with the views of friendly others. By combining self-monitoring with feedback from others, you should be able to obtain a realistic assessment of any roadblocks to effectiveness in delivery.

Coping with Delivery Problems

In order to truly improve delivery skills, one must learn not only to recognize delivery problems but also to identify their probable causes. Lack of appropriate eye contact with an audience, for example, is a problem that may be caused by (1) a carefully conceived decision to reduce involvement in the situation, (2) fear or anxiety, (3) physical disability, (4) habitual tendencies, or (5) faulty perception of what the situation requires. Our assumption here is that knowing *why* a problem exists is the first step on the road to solving that problem.

Conscious choice. A person who is subject-centered, uses no gestures, and believes there is no need for gestures is a prime example of delivery problems attributable to personal choice. A quick rereading of the first portion of this chapter should convince one that such a choice-routine is unwise.

Fear or anxiety. Probably 80 percent or more of all students feel that their greatest initial problem in public speaking is fear or anxiety. The student who uses distracting mannerisms, whose voice quivers, or who fails to gesture smoothly because of this anxiety is not at all unusual.

For the majority of students, this fear is reduced to manageable proportions by the experience of giving two or three speeches. If this does not happen for you, however, be sure to talk to your teacher. There are a variety of effective techniques (including systematic desensitization and cognitive restructuring) for reducing excessive anxiety, and your teacher is likely to be able to direct you to such remedies.

Physical disability. The student with articulatory or voice disorders obviously will have some problems with delivery. Defects of articulation include some combination of (1) omission of sounds, (2) distortion of sounds, and/or (3) substitution of one sound for another. Usually, such defects result from faulty training or learning. Some defects, however, result from organic conditions such as abnormal structures in the mouth, tongue, lips, teeth, or palate. If the defect of articulation is not easily corrected, therefore, it is best to see a specialist who will recommend any needed treatment and will probably teach you compensatory movements for producing sounds.

Defects of the voice involve the primary attributes of voice, which include (1) *quality*, with problems of harshness, nasality, hoarseness, and breathiness; (2) *pitch*, including levels that are too high, too low, or monotonous; (3) *loudness or intensity*, which may indicate a voice that is too loud, too soft, or no voice at all; and (4) *time*, which includes problems such as rate and duration. As with articulation defects, if voice disorders resist change, you should see a specialist for diagnosis and remediation.

Habitual tendencies. As mentioned earlier, the early speaking experiences of the class are likely to produce all sorts of distracting mannerisms. Waldo W. Braden has compiled a list of 25 such habits, to which many more could be added:

1. *Wringing hands*
2. *Rolling or playing with notes*
3. *Jingling money or keys*
4. *Buttoning and unbuttoning coat*
5. *Pulling an ear or a nose*
6. *Fumbling with a pencil*

7. *Standing with hands on hips*
8. *Putting thumbs under belt*
9. *Scratching*
10. *Fussing with ring, watch, or beads*
11. *Fixing tie or pin*
12. *Clutching or straightening clothing*
13. *Cracking knuckles*
14. *Looking at the ceiling or out the window*
15. *Shifting eyes constantly from place to place*
16. *Folding and unfolding arms*
17. *Giving nervous or silly laugh*
18. *Standing with feet too wide apart or too close together*
19. *Rocking backward and forward from one foot to another*
20. *Standing cross-legged*
21. *Shifting constantly from one foot to the other foot*
22. *Placing foot on a chair or table*
23. *Leaning heavily on a lecture or reading stand*
24. *Wetting lips frequently*
25. *Smoothing repeatedly or replacing stray wisps of hair*[14]

In many cases, these mannerisms are simply adaptors-gone-public because of simple nervousness and lack of familiarity with the speaking situation. They are, thus, best ignored for the first speech or two. In many cases, such mannerisms will simply disappear once you focus your attention on them. If that does not happen, however, you might try overemphasizing the mannerism while practicing your speech, as we suggested earlier. If, for example, you overuse vocal pauses, make a conscious attempt to fill every silence in your speech with a variant of "er" or "uh." If the mannerism still persists, ask your instructor for help in overcoming the problem.

Faulty understanding. The person who is misinformed about the situational requirements of good delivery (e.g., the debater who addresses the class in the rapid-fire fashion of a first affirmative speaker) exemplifies the hazards of faulty understanding. The best remedy for such failures lies in repeated exposure to good models and plenty of guided practice in a variety of speaking situations. Developing your powers as a kind of sociological observer of delivery styles will also help you find what lies within, and outside of, the range of appropriate nonverbal behaviors. Of one thing we would like you to be most convinced: Improper delivery is not a genetic problem. It can be fixed.

[14]W. W. Braden, *Speech Methods and Resources* (New York: Harper & Row, 1972).

Suggestions for Speaking

We want to end this chapter with the most important thought of all about delivery, a thought that we mentioned explicitly in Chapter 3 but that bears repeating here. *Public speaking is not a performance, and a public speaker is not an actor.* Though many factors of voice and gesture are subject to conscious control, the successful speaker usually cannot simultaneously attend to delivery and to other goals at the same time without losing some degree of control over material and audience. To the extent that you try to mimic the behaviors of others, you will become increasingly detached from *your* ideas and from the listeners wishing to communicate with *you.* How your voice and body perform is, ultimately, a function of how your mind works. If you think of speaking as being akin to acting, as if your body's only function is to impress rather than express, you will produce a dehumanized sort of talk indeed. *By remembering the necessity of balancing message and audience commitment, however, you can rarely go astray in delivery.* Your authors are mightily tempted to give you a money-back guarantee on that proposition. We would also like to leave you with some additional thoughts about delivery:

1. When preparing a speech, practice out loud because some ideas have a tendency to look fine on an outline but sound preposterous when spoken as written.

2. Use your delivery to focus attention on your message (rather than draw attention to your delivery).

3. Do *not* practice your speech in front of a mirror lest you be tempted to pay excessive attention to your bodily activity when speaking.

4. For each speech, identify the total arsenal of delivery elements available to you, especially the seldom-noticed factors of setting and space.

5. Try not to be "overresponsive" to feedback and thus give your listeners the impression that you are seeking to curry their favor.

6. When thinking about delivery, always remember that the same function can be performed by different elements and that the same element can perform different functions.

7. While speaking, your posture should suggest readiness without stiffness, flexibility without lack of conviction.

8. If possible, look at every person in the group at some time during the speech; if you can't do so, look at every section of the room at least once.

9. Strive for a conversational voice that underscores your earnestness and social awareness through animation and variety.

10. The greatest boon to the public speaker in the twentieth century is the cheap cassette tape recorder. Use it.

UNIT III

The Persuasive Challenge in Public Communication

CHAPTER 8

Techniques for Building Credibility

My fellow citizens, it is an honor and a pleasure to be here today. My opponent has openly admitted he feels an affinity toward your city, but I happen to like this area. It might be a salubrious place to him, but to me it is one of the nation's most delightful garden spots.

When I embarked upon this political campaign I hoped that it could be conducted on a high level and that my opponent would be willing to stick to the issues. Unfortunately, he has decided to be tractable instead—to indulge in unequivocal language, to eschew the use of outright lies in his speeches, and even to make repeated veracious statements about me.

At first I tried to ignore these scrupulous, unvarnished fidelities. Now I will do so no longer. If my opponent wants a fight, he's going to get one! . . .

My opponent's second cousin is a Mormon.

His uncle was a flagrant heterosexual.

His sister, who has always been obsessed by sects, once worked as a proselyte outside a church.

His father was secretly chagrined at least a dozen times by matters of a pecuniary nature.

His youngest brother wrote an essay extolling the virtues of being a Homo sapiens.

His great-aunt expired from a degenerative disease.

His nephew subscribed to a phonographic magazine.

His wife was a thespian before their marriage and even performed the act in front of paying customers.

And his own mother had to resign from a woman's organization in her later years because she was an admitted sexagenarian.

Now what shall we say of the man himself?

I can tell you in solemn truth that he is the very antithesis of political radicalism, economic irresponsibility, and personal depravity. His own record proves that he has frequently discountenanced treasonable, un-American philosophies and has perpetrated many overt acts as well.

He perambulated his infant son on the street.

He practiced nepotism with his uncle and first cousin.

He attempted to interest a 13-year-old girl in philately.

He participated in a seance at a private residence where, among other odd goings-on, there was incense.

He has declared himself in favor of more homogeneity on college campuses.

He has advocated social intercourse in mixed company—and has taken part in such gatherings himself.

He has been deliberately averse to crime in our streets.

He has urged our Protestant and Jewish citizens to develop more catholic tastes.

Last summer he committed a piscatorial act on a boat that was flying the American flag.

Finally, at a time when we must be on our guard against all foreign isms, he has coolly announced his belief in altruism—and his fervent hope that some day this entire nation will be altruistic!

I beg you, my friends, to oppose this man whose life and work and ideas are so openly, avowedly compatible with our American way of life. A vote for him would be a vote for the perpetuation of everything we hold dear.

The facts are clear; the record speaks for itself.

Do your duty.[1]

To an inattentive listener, this passage may seem like a devastating attack on the good name of another person. The speaker's vehemence can be felt in the parallel structure of his language. His command of the "facts" in the case is also impressive as is his righteous indignation at having been attacked himself. There is a smoothness and assuredness to this speech, and, unless a listener is a student of vocabulary, it is likely that the speaker will be able to build his image convincingly while he destroys that of his opponent. Our speaker's speech is thus another salvo fired in the endless battle of credibility.

[1]B. Garvin, "*Mad's* Guaranteed Effective All-Occasion Nonslanderous Political Smear Speech," *Mad*, December, 1970. Reprinted by permission. 1970 by E. C. Publications, Inc.

In our society, the effectiveness of what is said depends to some extent on who says it. The young child's "Oh, yeah? Who says so?" and the adult's somewhat more subtle "Where did you hear that?" illustrate that credibility plays an important role in communication. Perhaps nowhere is this belief demonstrated more clearly (and more frequently) than in advertising. In the marketing business, it helps to be sponsored by an indisputable source—someone held in esteem by the general public. Whether the reasons for this person's fame are related to the product being sold is irrelevant; it is assumed that the general public will make the transition necessary for, say, an Olympic swimmer to sell Timex watches. Thus, we have been treated to political shootouts between film stars John Wayne and Jane Fonda and a presidential race in which the voices of entertainers Sammy Davis, Jr., Bill Cosby, Martha Raye, and Nancy Sinatra carried much weight.

Ordinarily, people will confidently purchase coffee from Robert Young, cleaning products from Paul Harvey, and antacid tablets from Roger Staubach. And who really knows household cleaning problems like Jonathan Winters? Who can dispute the woman in nurse's clothing who tells how nutritious a particular chocolate drink can be? Or the 55 hospitals in the nation (only 55?) who would not clean their toilet bowls with anything else? Or the mother-in-law's personal endorsement for the see-yourself shine attained by a certain dishwashing liquid?

No doubt you can think of many additional examples of the importance of a speaker's credibility to the communication experience.

However, we should not be totally facetious about this matter of credibility. After all, people were exterminated in World War II by persons who claimed at the Nuremburg trials, "The Führer told us to do it." Similarly, during the initial stages of the Watergate affair, Richard Nixon repeatedly asserted that he was guilty only of having believed the wrong people about the burglary and cover-up. Equally disturbing is the study reported by Milgram in which he discovered that people were quite willing to administer severe electrical shocks to others as long as such actions were "legitimized" by an authority figure (i.e., the experimenter).[2] Credibility is a matter to be reckoned with.

In this chapter, we shall discuss what is currently known about building credibility. A good deal of research has been done on this topic, and the fruits of this research can be quite helpful to you as a speaker. It is our hope that you will find ample help here for making yourself and your ideas socially influential.

---

[2]S. Milgram, "Behavioral Study of Obedience," *Journal of Abnormal and Social Psychology*, 67:371–378 (1963).

Nature of Source Credibility

Let us begin with a formal definition. Source credibility consists of an audience's perceptions of the speaker (independent of the speaker's intent or purpose), which vary over time and which lead the audience to accept or reject what the speaker proposes. Under a multitude of rubrics (ethos, prestige, expertise, charisma, leadership, image, status, reputation, ethical proof, personal persuasiveness, personality effects, impressions, etc.), theorists and experimenters in communication from classical to contemporary times have devoted considerable effort to the study of credibility. These studies largely support our common-sense observation that source credibility is an important factor in communication.

For example, in an early study, Kelman and Hovland prepared a speech favoring extreme leniency in the treatment of juvenile delinquents.[3] Students doing senior work in a summer high school were requested to listen in class to a recording of an educational radio program—ostensibly to judge its educational value. In the course of the program, three different introductions to the speech dealing with leniency were used in different classes. In one introduction, the speaker was identified as a judge in a juvenile court—a highly trained, well-informed, and experienced authority on criminology and delinquency. In another (ostensibly "neutral") introduction, the speaker was said to be someone picked out of the studio audience. The third "speaker," also just chosen from the audience, revealed during the interview that he had a criminal record and had been a juvenile delinquent.

After the speech, the students were asked how they felt about it. Although the speech was the same in all cases, reactions to the total communicative experience—*message plus speaker*—varied. The audience felt that the judge's speech was much more "fair" than that of the former delinquent. The judgments for the neutral speaker lay somewhere in between.

This makes effective persuasion sound simple: All you must do is find an authoritative figure who will deliver your message. Not so. In order to demonstrate why this clear and meaningful description of source credibility is deceptive in its simplicity, the remainder of this chapter focuses on two questions: What is source credibility? What can a speaker do to enhance it?

We would like to issue one caution to you before answering these questions, however: Credibility is *not a thing*. It is not some sort of overcoat that we put on and take off at will. Rather, it is a *perception* of us that lies inside of the people to whom we talk. In part, an audience accepts or rejects what you say on the basis of personal characteristics they perceive in you. Obviously, if they do not know that you help handicapped people across the street and open car doors for the infirm, they cannot use such data when forming their opinions of you. Even if they do possess this information, members of your audience are likely to act on such data differently—some will see you as courteous, whereas others will label you a busybody. Members of an audience judge your credibility as a speaker on the basis of information they have about you, and how, in turn, they feel about people who possess such qualities. Credibility lies within listeners' minds and is changeful. There is nothing inherent or genetic about it. It is not something we can be assured

[3]H. Kelman and C. Hovland, "Reinstatement of the Communicator in Delayed Measurement of Opinion Change," *Journal of Abnormal and Social Psychology*, 48:327–335 (1953).

of keeping once gotten. Credibility can only be earned by paying the price of effective communication.

Credibility and Time

Communication is a process. Sometimes it is useful to stop the process in midstream to examine the component parts—bearing in mind that we may distort reality by so doing. For source credibility, it is sometimes profitable to examine how it matures or declines at three stages in the process: before, during, and after a communicative act.

Initial source credibility. It is all but impossible for a speaker to begin a speech with a clean slate. Somewhere along the line, members of the audience have formed judgments as to his or her personal credibility or to that of "people like him or her." Some of these perceptions—those constituting initial source credibility—could have been identified 24 hours before the speech, a week before, or even a month before. What concern us most at this point are the ways listeners view a speaker when he or she *begins* speaking.

While the feelings that exist in hearers during this initial phase originate from a variety of sources, Andersen identifies four factors that most frequently contribute to initial credibility: (1) experiences with the speaker either direct or vicarious (e.g., we were in the army together); (2) facts known about the speaker, particularly those that provide indication of reference group membership (e.g., he always hung around with the officers); (3) endorsements offered by others (e.g., Captain Ellis always liked him); and (4) immediate *clues* leading to the actual communication (e.g., his tone of voice on the phone seemed like he's going to hit me up for a loan).[4]

By the time you deliver your first speech in class, you will have interacted with most of your classmates. As a result, they will have formed impressions of you, much as you have of them. This is one of many public speaking settings that do not provide the first exposure of the speaker. Even if one had not actually interacted with a speaker in person, one may have had—probably has had—*vicarious experiences* with her or him. Thus, the mass media, for example, provides much information about newsworthy people before they are seen by local audiences. In addition, friends and acquaintances relate information about the speaker—again, helping us relate vicariously to the speaker or to people similar to him or her. Thus, it is rare to find listeners who have formed no opinion of the speaker prior to the speaking event.

The second category of information about the speaker concerns

[4]K. Anderson, *Persuasion: Theory and Practice* (Boston: Allyn and Bacon, 1971).

reference group membership. What we know about a speaker causes us to associate him or her with a variety of stereotypes or attitudes. We may know little about that girl in class other than that she is president of her sorority, but we are imbued with numerous associations with the category "sorority president"; in the absence of other information, we utilize these associations to make judgments. To hear that one is an athlete, a veteran, a businessperson, or a nurse instantly conjures up sets of associations in many of us. Audience judgments of the label may vary, but the labels provide the audience with a means of associating the speaker with a class or category of people and, most significantly, applying the attitudes they hold toward that class to the speaker.

The third source of information about the speaker is provided by *endorsements.* At some public speaking events, we have little prior knowledge about a speaker aside from who sponsored or endorsed him or her. On this basis, we may decide to hear the official Democratic speaker rather than listen to the candidate endorsed by the Republican party. Evidence also indicates that the introduction of a speaker will provide a source of sponsorship and hence influence his or her credibility rating.[5] A speaker who receives a favorable introduction from a well-regarded individual will be perceived as more credible than a person who receives a positive introduction from a negatively evaluated source. Credibility can be infectious, in other words.

The final source of information about the speaker consists of the speaker's *personal appearance and actions.* The dress of the speaker, the posture, physique, manner, and responses to things happening in the room may all contribute strongly to his or her initial source credibility.

At this point it would be nice if we could offer a formula: A speaker's initial credibility is a function of two parts prior experience multiplied by sponsor and divided by waist size. Unfortunately, it is impossible to say which of the four categories contributes most to initial source credibility in which situation. What we *can* say is that, based on a variety of sources, audiences make judgments about the credibility of speakers before they ever begin to speak. The practical implication? Be as aware as you can of what "categories" the audience has used to judge you, and prepare speech materials that emphasize or correct these "categorical" impressions.

Process credibility. By identifying a second stage of source credibility, we are suggesting that there are shifts in credibility that occur when you actually speak. One interesting research study done by Brooks and

[5]For an extended discussion of credibility effects, see W. Thompson, *The Process of Persuasion: Principles and Readings* (New York: Harper & Row, 1975), pp. 57–90.

Scheidel shows how these phaselike changes occur.[6] Using a tape-recorded speech by Malcolm X (the late spokesperson for black radicals) to a predominantly white college audience, Brooks and Scheidel spliced seven 30-second silent periods into the tape at what seemed to be "natural" divisions of the speech. The speech supported the proposition that American blacks should separate themselves from white society. White undergraduate students in introductory public speaking classes were asked to provide ten evaluations of the speaker—one after each of the seven silent periods plus the silent period at the end of the tape, in addition to a pre- and postmessage evaluation. On a 1–7 scale from negative to positive, the results were as follows:

Pretest	2.53	Time 5	4.39
Time 1	4.54	Time 6	4.97
Time 3	4.06	Time 8	3.93
Time 4	4.30	Posttest	3.82

Because Brooks and Scheidel used a tape-recorded message, the changes in credibility we see across time were probably due primarily to verbal and vocalic factors. In a live public speaking setting, many other cues arising from the speaker, the occasion, and the audience will also lead to changes in credibility. In all cases, however, it seems safe to assume that process credibility is an undulating, changeful phenomenon—something that you as a speaker can never take for granted.

But what are the factors that cause credibility to fluctuate during a speech? Listed below are some of the many factors that may affect your image when you speak. Research studies have shown each of these factors to be influential in *some* situations with *some* speakers, although we do not yet know how each operates or exactly how they might be controlled in all situations:

1. *Source characteristics:* attractiveness of speaker, neatness of dress, mode of dress, height, sex, race, fluency of delivery, extroverted/introverted styles of delivery, use of dialect

2. *Message characteristics:* self-reference, prestige reference, evidence, organization, fear appeals, opinionatedness, language intensity, audience adaptation, metaphors, analogies, obscenity

[6]R. Brooks and T. Scheidel, "Speech as Process: A Case Study," *Speech Monographs,* 35:1–7 (1968).

3. *Channel characteristics:* visual materials; oral delivery and combination of media

4. *Audience characteristics:* credibility proneness, ego involvement, source-receiver identification, stress, observed audience response

5. *Occasion characteristics:* attractiveness of setting, temperature, color, space

We present this list not to depress you but simply to emphasize how complex this matter of credibility can be. It would be foolhardy to assume that you could, when preparing a speech, latch onto a surefire set of "image polishers." *No matter what you do with your message,* there will be a host of other factors that will affect your credibility as well.

Terminal source credibility. The interaction of initial credibility and process credibility results in terminal source credibility. The image a speaker has after speaking probably depends a great deal on the intensity of our initial feelings about him or her. In other words, the more prior knowledge you have about the speaker, the more important is initial credibility to our "summed up" impressions of the speaker. For instance, because the students in Brooks and Scheidel's study did not know a great deal about Malcolm X ahead of time, process credibility (the image he created while speaking) was probably a primary determinant of his final credibility standing.

From a practical standpoint, it is probably wise for you to assume that your final "standing" with your audience is ultimately a matter for them to decide—*you* cannot determine their impressions completely, and in some cases (as research has shown) they may decide to accept your message even though they may not hold *you* in particularly high regard. In any event, *it is probably best not to give your attention exclusively to matters of credibility.* Concentrate on what you *can* control (the content of your speech).

Dimensions of Source Credibility

Thus far, we have talked as if a speaker's credibility falls at some point on a continuum ranging from complete credibility to complete incredibility. A number of studies have shown this idea not to be correct. Apparently, people use a number of independent dimensions when making judgments of a speaker's credibility. To our way of thinking, credibility is composed of seven major factors:

1. *Power.* The speaker is perceived as one who can provide significant rewards and punishments for listeners. ("Well, Kay, if read-

ing *Playboy* makes me so immature, maybe I shouldn't be taking you to the movie tonight.")

2. *Competence.* The speaker is perceived as having knowledge and experience about a topic that others do not have. ("Just look at all the well-known people who support my position and who read *Playboy*—politicians, authors, artists, doctors, and lots of other professionals.")

3. *Trustworthiness.* The speaker's present behaviors are seen as being consistent with his or her past behaviors. ("Have you noticed me treat you or other women with any less respect because I read *Playboy?*")

4. *Good will.* The speaker is perceived as having his or her audience's best interest in mind. ("You've always said you're proud of the way I treat you, and *Playboy* is where I learned how to be suave.")

5. *Idealism.* The speaker is perceived as possessing qualities and values the audience esteems and to which it aspires. ("You've always admired the fact that I know more about current events than you do. Where do you think I get such knowledge? From *Playboy*, of course.")

6. *Similarity.* The speaker is judged to resemble the audience in significant ways. ("Now, Kay, you know that both of us have always said that it is important to be well informed on current social issues. That's why I read *Playboy.*")

7. *Dynamism.* The speaker is perceived to be aggressive, emphatic, and forceful. ("Face it! It's great! Best mag on the rack!")

These seven dimensions appear to be independent: The audience's perception of a speaker on any one dimension may have little to do with their views on the other six. Thus, a speaker who is judged to be powerful (e.g., your favorite senator) can range from highly competent to totally incompetent on another dimension. Or a powerful, competent speaker can be seen as being totally untrustworthy. A salesperson may know the product (is competent), but he or she cannot punish you for not buying it. A teacher is competent but has power as well.

In some instances, trustworthiness may become the crucial communicative issue (e.g., President Nixon after John Dean's revelations about Watergate). At other points in time (e.g., gasoline or food shortages), the battle will be waged between "competent" sources (consumerists versus the Secretary of Agriculture) who are competing for public belief. All of this has been documented by Applbaum and Anatol, who discovered, among other things, that while expertness may be the most crucial dimension of credibility in a classroom speech, in other situations (e.g., sermonizing in church) trustworthiness may be the more relevant aspect of a speaker's image.[7]

Gauging Source Credibility

The first step in discovering the credibility choices open to you as a speaker is to find out what the audience currently thinks of you. This process of developing self-awareness or sensitivity to your own social image is difficult. As numerous authors have pointed out, when a speaker addresses an audience, there are at least three "speakers" present:

1. *The speaker's speaker:* what he believes he is and what he believes he is not (e.g., "Ain't I dynamic!").

2. *The audience's speaker:* what the audience believes the speaker is, what they believe he is not, and the value they attach to these beliefs. This is the image we have labeled source credibility (e.g., "what a piece of deadwood this guy is").

3. *The speaker's view of the audience's speaker:* what the speaker believes the audience believes about her or him. This is the speaker's perception of his or her source credibility ("it's obvious from their closed eyes that my dynamism has put them in a trance").

A difficult but necessary prelude to making choices that enhance our credibility is that of adjusting Speakers 1 and 3 to Speaker 2. Only when speakers have accurately gauged their assets and liabilities, and only when they have carefully evaluated audiences' perceptions will they be in a position to make wise, informed choices among strategies for enhancing source credibility.

Such an assessment might begin with a list of your assets and liabilities—as you see them—in relation to the seven dimensions of source credibility. To this end, a form similar to the following credibility checklist may be useful. Let us assume, for example, that you've decided to give a classroom speech on drug addiction. When assessing your personal resources as a speaker for such a chore, try to use the form as illustrated in Table 8-1.

Even if you are honest with yourself when filling out such a form, you will only be recording your perceptions of your speaker (Speaker 1) and your impression of the audience's speaker (Speaker 3). Such

[7]R. Applbaum and K. Anatol, "The Factor Structure of Source Credibility as a Function of the Speaking Situation," *Speech Monographs*, 39:216–222 (1972).

Table 8-1   Credibility Checklist

Factors	Assets	Liabilities	Suggestions
Power	Not much. I might be able to show them that my speech could save their lives.	They see me as just another person in class, with no special power to reward and punish.	Dramatize the horrors of drug addiction; back it up with plenty of painful examples.
Competence	They know from Bob's comment in class that I made the dean's list last semester.	I've never told them about my interest in drug addiction. Could be starting from scratch with most of them.	Mention early in speech about my work with the Crisis Center. Get that *Time* article.
Trustworthiness	Some of them know I really followed through on the group assignment. They shouldn't feel that I'd trick them.	This will be a new topic for me. Most unlike my last speech on the campus election scandal.	Don't have much to worry about here. Might remind them that I stuck with them when the professor tried to spring a quiz on us!
Good Will	My strong suit. By now the group knows that I'm majoring in social work—who could hate a social worker?	No problem as long as I stay with hard drugs. Can't come down hard on pot.	Many of them smoke, so I'd better steer clear of the marijuana issue or they'll see me as caring more about preaching than about them.

Table 8-1 (Continued)

Factors	Assets	Liabilities	Suggestions
Idealism	They know that I'm always up in the clouds and generally aspire to the same things they do.	Got to be careful not to get too carried away with the moral stuff. Stick to the "fully functioning human being" idea.	Should probably stress our common goals early in the speech before I mention drugs.
Similarity	I've been in class with them all semester. They know I dress and talk like most of them.	Could be a problem if I come on like a know-it-all. Have to steer clear of my religious views on the subject with these heathens!	Better tie this in with Claire's speech on legalizing pot. This should build more common ground between me and them.
Dynamism	My biggie! They know that they can't shut me up when I get committed to a topic.	No problem! (As long as I remember not to talk too fast!)	Pace yourself—pace yourself!

estimates might change, of course, when you speak, when moment-to-moment "credibility adaptations" become necessary. Whenever you do your assessing, however, it is good to remember that the audience's speaker constitutes the acid measure of your credibility. While you cannot climb into the minds of your auditors to check out your social image, you might try duplicating a form such as ours and administering it to your classmates. By comparing their actual responses to your predictions of their responses, you may get some insight into your own native ability to read an audience's view of you. Also, such a procedure may point out those dimensions of credibility of which you are unaware.

Strategies for Building Credibility

Up to this point, our discussion of strategies for enhancing source credibility has been somewhat abstract. Assuming, for example, that you have decided that your best strategy is to build competence, what can you do? What follows is our attempt to catalog the specific strategies a speaker might use to enhance his or her "credibilities." Our list does not pretend to be exhaustive—merely suggestive. It is based, in part, upon our condensations of research summaries.

Power

Use an overt power strategy sparingly and subtly. If you have the ability to reward and punish the audience, you will not need to mention this fact. They will be aware of it. It is not necessary, for example, for your teacher to remind you that his or her ability to grade you serves as a source of power. When he or she overtly reminds you of such power in an attempt to get you to feel, believe, or do as he or she suggests, you —like most people—are likely to resent it and to rebel in some fashion. There is evidence to suggest that more attitude change will occur when an audience does not feel itself forced to comply with the speaker's suggestions. On the other hand, it is often helpful to show how you as a speaker can exert influence on behalf of an audience.

Indicate that the "power balance" between speaker and audience will be maintained. By this we mean that a speaker who indicates that both speaker and audience will profit equally from the interaction is well advised to do so. As mentioned in Chapter 1, a speaker who presumes to address a public audience has, by that very action, implied that he or she seeks something. Thus, in most situations, a speaker is wise to acknowledge what he or she expects to derive from the interaction and what "power" the audience itself is likely to garner as well.

Competence

Associate yourself with other highly credible individuals. For example, evidence suggests that a speaker who receives a favorable introduction from a well-regarded individual will be perceived as more credible than he or she would be without such a psychological link.

Demonstrate personal acquaintance with the topic. If the topic is something with which you are personally involved (you've done it, it's part of your job, it's your hobby, etc.), an audience is apt to believe what you say about the topic. It is important, therefore, to let the audience know why you chose to speak on this topic—how you got involved and why you care.

Demonstrate familiarity with the topic's special vocabulary. An additional way to demonstrate competence is through the correct use of terminology related to your topic. However, don't use jargon for the sake of jargon.

Demonstrate familiarity with persons who are expert in the field. Citing such authorities in support of a point is especially important if the audience perceives you as a moderate or low credible source. When quoting experts, the more credible the source, the more it will do for your own believability. Therefore, it is wise to analyze your audience carefully to discover their indisputable sources. You may perceive Dr. Denton Cooley to be competent and trustworthy, but if your audience does not, citing him in support of your point will hinder rather than help your credibility. If you already possess high competence credibility, quoting experts will not add to it appreciably, or so says the research.

Be sure that your speech is well organized. While a well-organized message may not increase credibility, a disorganized speech will usually decrease it. Thus, it pays to spend time organizing your speech in a fashion that your audience will be able to follow.

Trustworthiness

If at all possible, establish verbal interaction with the audience. This is difficult at times, but speakers who open themselves up to ongoing public scrutiny give the impression that they are sure of themselves and their positions. As we saw in Chapter 2, a spin-off benefit of this approach is that the audience feels complimented when a speaker relinquishes "control" of the flow of discourse. Listeners reason, in such instances, that a speaker who accepts such a challenge is one who will maintain his or her views in other communicative situations.

Demonstrate that your present behavior is consistent with your past behavior. It is often good to "remind" the audience of what you have done in the past on their behalf or on behalf of the proposition you advocate. This is especially important when trustworthiness is at issue. Being the comparers they are, listeners like to see a certain amount of consistency (or excusable inconsistency) in people who speak to them.

Show that you can be trusted by being as explicit as possible and by entertaining alternative points of view. There are times, of course, when explicitness is not very desirable in speaking situations (e.g., when treating a point that can damage you in the minds of your auditors). Still, most listeners appreciate someone who does not waste their time. Also, it is often wise to treat both sides of an issue in order to build an image of fair-mindedness. Such an approach is almost mandated when listeners are highly resistant to the speaker's proposal.

Make sure that your verbal and nonverbal behaviors are consistent. Thousands of subtle, nonverbal cues can suggest that you do not really believe what you are saying. Because people believe that nonverbal cues are harder to fake, we tend to believe the nonverbal more than the verbal.

Good Will

Demonstrate that your proposal will benefit the audience. Show how the audience will gain important rewards by accepting your position or, at least, that they will not lose by doing so.

Show that other groups of similar individuals have accepted your proposal. If other groups have perceived your good will, this one should, too. With such an approach you might make your image contagious.

Communicate genuine expressions of interest and affection. The key word here is *genuine*. False expressions of interest and affection often are easily detected by listeners who have a reason to be wary.

Similarity

Provide an overt statement of agreement with audience on, at least, peripheral issues. If you cannot agree with the audience on major issues, at least take a positive, agreeing position on a minor point. No matter what the audience, you should be able to find some minor issue to agree on.

Learn to control your nonverbal behavior. Personal appearance and demeanor, such as nuances of posture, body position, physical distance, eye contact, dress, grooming, and the like, all provide the audience with cues for seeing the speaker as similar or dissimilar to themselves. Many of these cues are hard to control, but others are not. For example, most of us know how to dress and groom appropriately for various social situations. The challenge for a speaker is to discover those nonverbal cues that communicate similarity for the particular audience in question.

Demonstrate that you represent the "greatest common denominator" of the audience's beliefs and values. In public communication situations, a speaker must be especially careful not to alienate a sizable portion of the audience. Because a group of listeners usually harbors diverse and sometimes opposing viewpoints, a speaker is wise to emphasize those aspects of himself or herself that are likely to meet with the greatest amount of collective agreement.

Disassociate yourself from ideas and institutions that are disliked by the audience. This is the obverse of the previous proposition. For example, during the 1972 presidential race, George McGovern felt it necessary to separate himself from the radical fringe that had brought him to a position of popularity. The need for him to do so became especially pronounced after he was designated as the official representative of the Democratic party, a group that contained a good number of labor unionists and old-time politicos who passionately disliked McGovern's leftist followers. Obviously, he did not succeed in making this disassociation stick in the minds of most.

Idealism

Depict yourself as being both similar to and different from your audience. This is but one of the many dilemmas associated with building credibility. Obviously, listeners admire those who share the values, attitudes, and goals to which they aspire. On the other hand, unless you are somehow different from them, your listeners would have little reason to look up to you. Thus, by demonstrating that you have certain knowledge that the audience needs or that you embody certain of their aspirations in rather dramatic ways, you may be able to build an alike-but-different image for yourself.

Indicate what you have risked (or are willing to risk) on behalf of your proposal. Most of us, it seems, tend to believe those who have taken a stand on behalf of something they strongly believe in. Martyrs, after all, take on an idealized image because they have given themselves totally to some particular group or ideology. While most speakers cannot depict themselves as martyrs in the true sense of the word, they can show that they are ideal representatives of a particular position in that they have placed themselves on the line for their beliefs.

Dynamism

Indicate exactly what behavioral commitments you have made to your position. If you can show what you have done on behalf of your proposal, you might be perceived as being aggressive, emphatic, and forceful. For example, one of the reasons that Jane Fonda was able to rise to a position of influence in the women's movement may be due to the energetic manner in which she demonstrated her commitment to the women's cause. One author claims that a highly intense and strongly opinionated message will be perceived as dynamic and hence build a speaker's credibility.[8]

Learn to control delivery variables. Some research indicates that non-fluencies (e.g., speech errors like "uh" and "er") can call into question a speaker's dynamism.[9] In interpreting such findings, however, we must be cautious. Delivery variables, as we saw in Chapter 7, are difficult to control, and excessive concentration on our bodies may distract us from the more important job of watching for and adapting to listeners' feedback.

As you can see, source credibility is a complex and dilemma-ridden phenomenon. Contradictions abound. For example, when attempting to be dynamic, a speaker can get so carried away that he or she fails to demonstrate good will toward the audience. There is no easy resolution to such a quandary, but perhaps by being aware of the options for building credibility, you can pick and choose among them and hence find techniques appropriate to your individual tastes and needs.

An Example of Credibility in Action

Some people do build credibility, however! Consider the classic case of Senator Edward Kennedy who, in July of 1969, faced one of the most frightening communication situations he has ever experienced. As you may remember, Senator Kennedy was driving Miss Mary Jo Kopechne along a dimly lit road on Chappaquiddick Island, off the coast of Massachusetts. Kennedy's car went off the road and into a pond, and Miss Kopechne drowned. Kennedy was held legally (and more important for our purposes) morally responsible for her death.

Seven days after the incident, Kennedy appeared on television to

[8]C. Larson, *Persuasion: Reception and Responsibility* (Belmont, Cal.: Wadsworth, 1979), pp. 200–201.
[9]J. McCroskey and S. Mehrley, "The Effects of Disorganization and Nonfluency on Attitude Change and Source Credibility," *Speech Monographs*, 36:13–21 (1969).

explain his plight to the people of Massachusetts (his home state) and to ask for their continued support. Because commentary in the press had been mixed, and because many throughout the country doubted Kennedy's veracity, he found himself in a speaking situation that centered around his credibility as a source of information.

Because credibility was distinctively at issue in this situation, we felt that it would be profitable to analyze Kennedy's speech with the tools made available by our discussion of the methods for enhancing credibility. As you read the following remarks by Kennedy, note especially how he attempts to salvage a sagging image of trustworthiness and good will; how he implies that he is still "ideal" in some ways; and how he demonstrates that his power, competence, and similarity to the people of Massachusetts have not been diluted by the events of the preceding week. While some of his language may help you see the dynamism he attempted to muster, only a videotaped version of the speech would show you the emphasis and force connoted by his nonverbal cues. Consider, then, our example of credibility in crisis as analyzed in Table 8-2, remembering that the speech was so successful that Kennedy was almost able to unseat an incumbent president just 11 years later.

Naturally, most of us need not attempt to pull out all of the credibility stops in everyday speaking. We feel, however, that Kennedy's speech indicates that many of the credibility principles we have discussed in this chapter can be put into practice in efficient and meaningful ways. That Kennedy's speech encouraged an outpouring of affection and support from his Massachusetts' constituents does indicate that public speaking can be a highly effective vehicle for extracting oneself from very undesirable circumstances. Still, the fact that many others in the country remain unconvinced of Kennedy's virtue indicates that one person's credibility is another person's foolishness.

Suggestions for Speaking

Although we have talked a good deal about building credibility in this chapter, you should remember that credibility is a *means to an end*, never an end in itself. One builds credibility in order to make certain ideas compelling and to remove any hurtful, personal biases that would make those ideas appear unattractive. Thus, unless one is an egomaniac, one studies techniques for building credibility in order to further some cause, to make some concept clearer, or to awaken in others a set of important values. All of the techniques we have discussed here will turn to dust in your hands if you use them for self-centered and short-term gains. Credibility has a way of shunning those who curry its favor most avidly. Thus, we especially want to call your attention to the following propositions:

Table 8-2 Analysis of Senator Kennedy's Speech

Commentary	Sample Message
Demonstrates personal acquaintance with topic through self-references	My fellow citizens:

I have requested this opportunity to talk to the people of Massachusetts about the tragedy which happened last Friday evening.

This morning I entered a plea of guilty to the charge of leaving the scene of an accident. Prior to my appearance in court it would have been improper for me to comment on these matters.

But tonight I am free to tell you what happened and to say what it means to me. |
| Shows that an explicit discussion of events is possible and desired by this speaker | On the weekend of July 18 I was on Martha's Vineyard Island participating with my nephew, Joe Kennedy—as for 30 years my family has participated—in the annual Edgartown Sailing Regatta.

Only reasons of health prevented my wife from accompanying me.

On Chappaquiddick Island, off Martha's Vineyard, I attended on Friday evening, July 18, a cook-out I had encouraged and helped sponsor for a devoted group of Kennedy campaign secretaries.

When I left the party, around 11:15 P.M., I was accompanied by one of these girls, Miss Mary Jo Kopechne. Mary Jo was one of the most devoted members of the staff of Senator Robert Kennedy. She worked for him for four years and was broken up over his death. For this reason, and because she was such a gentle, kind and idealistic person, all of us tried to help her feel that she still had a home with the Kennedy family. |

Table 8-2   (Continued)

Commentary	Sample Message
Carefully chooses language that indicates an awareness of audience's sense of morality	There is no truth, no truth whatever, to the widely circulated suspicions of immoral conduct that have been leveled at my behavior and hers regarding that evening. There has never been a private relationship between us of any kind.
Disassociates himself from ideas and actions disliked by the audience.	I know of nothing of Mary Jo's conduct on that or any other occasion—the same is true of the other girls at that party—that would lend any substance to such ugly speculation about their character. Nor was I driving under the influence of liquor. Little over one mile away, the car that I was driving on an unlit road went off a narrow bridge which had no guard rails and was built on a left angle to the road.
Gives a dynamic (vivid) presentation of the events	The car overturned in a deep pond and immediately filled with water. I remember thinking as the cold water rushed in around my head that I was for certain drowning. Then water entered my lungs and I actually felt the sensation of drowning. But somehow I struggled to the surface alive. I made immediate and repeated efforts to save Mary Jo by diving into the strong and murky current but succeeded only in increasing my state of utter exhaustion and alarm. My conduct and conversations during the next several hours, to the extent that I can remember them, make no sense to me at all.

Commentary	Sample Message
Indicates that he is willing to entertain alternative points of view	Although my doctors informed me that I suffered a cerebral concussion as well as shock, I do not seek to escape responsibility for my actions by placing the blame either on the physical, emotional trauma brought on by the accident or on anyone else. I regard as indefensible the fact that I did not report the accident to the police immediately.
Uses chronological pattern of development so that listeners can follow along easily. This depicts him as being methodical and well organized.	Instead of looking directly for a telephone after lying exhausted in the grass for an undetermined time, I walked to the cottage where the party was being held and requested the help of two friends, my cousin, Joseph Gargan, and Phil Markham, and directed them to return immediately to the scene with me —this was some time after midnight— in order to undertake a new effort to dive down and locate Miss Kopechne. Their strenuous efforts, undertaken at some risks to their own lives, also proved futile.
Asserts that present behaviors are excusably inconsistent with past behaviors	All kinds of scrambled thoughts—all of them confused, some of them irrational, many of them which I cannot recall and some of which I would not have seriously entertained under normal circumstances—went through my mind during this period.

Table 8-2   (Continued)

Commentary	Sample Message
Associates himself with other highly credible individuals	They were reflected in the various inexplicable, inconsistent and inconclusive things I said and did, including such questions as whether the girl might still be alive somewhere out of that immediate area, whether some awful curse did actually hang over all the Kennedys, whether there was some justifiable reason for me to doubt what had happened and to delay my report, whether somehow the awful weight of this incredible incident might in some way pass from my shoulders.
Attempts to show that his feelings (verbalizations) and (nonverbal) behaviors coincide and are mutually reinforcing	I was overcome, I'm frank to say, by a jumble of emotions, grief, fear, doubt, exhaustion, panic, confusion, and shock.
	Instructing Gargan and Markham not to alarm Mary Jo's friends that night, I had them take me to the ferry crossing. The ferry having shut down for the night, I suddenly jumped into the water and impulsively swam across, nearly drowning once again in the effort, and returned to my hotel about 2 A.M., and collapsed in my room.
	I remember going out at one point and saying something to the room clerk.
	In the morning, with my mind somewhat more lucid, I made an effort to call a family legal adviser, Burk Marshall, from a public telephone on the Chappaquiddick side of the ferry and belatedly reported the accident to the Martha's Vineyard police.

Commentary	Sample Message
Depicts himself as having certain idealized attitudes toward religion and morality	Today, as I mentioned, I felt morally obligated to plead guilty to the charge of leaving the scene of an accident. No words on my part can possibly express the terrible pain and suffering I feel over this tragic incident. This last week has been an agonizing one for me and the members of my family and the grief we feel over the loss of a wonderful friend will remain with us the rest of our lives.
Subtly and self-effacingly reminds audience of his own position of political power	These events, the publicity, innuendo and whispers which have surrounded them and my admission of guilt this morning—raises the question in my mind of whether my standing among the people of my state has been so impaired that I should resign my seat in the United States Senate. If at any time the citizens of Massachusetts should lack confidence in their Senator's character or his ability, with or without justification, he could not in my opinion adequately perform his duty and should not continue in office.
Demonstrates familiarity with persons who are "expert" in the field	The people of this state, the state which sent John Quincy Adams and Daniel Webster and Charles Sumner and Henry Cabot Lodge and John Kennedy to the United States Senate, are entitled to representation in that body by men who inspire their utmost confidence.

Table 8-2   (Continued)

Commentary	Sample Message
Shows agreement with audience's sense of right and wrong	For this reason, I would understand full well why some might think it right for me to resign. For me this will be a difficult decision to make.
Reminds the audience of favorable past ties they have shared	It has been seven years since my first election to the Senate. You and I share many memories—some of them have been glorious, some have been very sad. The opportunity to work with you and serve Massachusetts has made my life worthwhile.
Suggests that speaker-audience interaction on this issue is possible and desirable	And so I ask you tonight, people of Massachusetts, to think this through with me. In facing this decision, I seek your prayers. For this is a decision that I will have finally to make on my own. It has been written a man does what he must in spite of personal consequences, in spite of obstacles and dangers and pressures, and that is the basis of all human morality.
Indicates what he can potentially risk on behalf of his proposal	Whatever may be the sacrifices he faces, if he follows his conscience—the loss of his friends, his fortune, his contentment, even the esteem of his fellow man—each man must decide for himself the course he will follow. The stories of the past courage cannot supply courage itself. For this, each man must look into his own soul.

Commentary	Sample Message
Holds out the hope that both speaker and audience can profit from the interaction	I pray that I can have the courage to make the right decision. Whatever is decided and whatever the future holds for me, I hope that I shall be able to put this most recent tragedy behind me and make some further contribution to our state and mankind, whether it be in public or private life.
	Thank you and good night.[10]

1. When assessing your credibility, always do so in light of the *particular topic* you are addressing.

2. Don't appear to be self-consciously building your credibility; listeners appreciate "effortless authority."

3. Subtlety should be the byword in building credibility; implied self-confidence normally is superior to frantic bombast.

4. Mention endorsements of your ideas without being a name-dropper, and align yourself with favored reference groups without being intrusive.

5. Adopt the attitude that your audience's acceptance of your message is of ultimate importance; "credibility" will then take care of itself.

6. "Reluctant competence" is especially impressive, and thus you should save a bit of your best material for the informal interchange of the question-and-answer session.

7. If you know that the audience particularly doubts one aspect of your credibility, try discussing that matter with candor early in your speech.

8. Resist the temptation of trying to build *all* dimensions of credibility at the same time during the same speech.

[10]E. Kennedy, "Address on the Mary Jo Kopechne Incident," July 25, 1969.

9. Before speaking, you can make plans to reinforce your competence, similarity, and, to some extent, your good will; trustworthiness is a matter that should never be brought up initially by the speaker.

10. It is best *not* to lay extensive plans ahead of time to be dynamic, ideal, or powerful; except in especially difficult situations, these dimensions of credibility should emerge spontaneously.

CHAPTER 9

Techniques for Changing Beliefs

Meeting a new girl is like meeting a new anyone. You don't plunge right in and begin discussing the most sensational or gory details of your or their sex life. You sort of edge in. When you first meet a new girl, the object is to casually warm her up. Start off with something general, something that won't frighten her or put her on guard. Then, as the conversations heat up, try edging her further and further into a corner so that she begins revealing important things about herself. Once you get her to do this, she's made sort of an emotional commitment to you. She'll feel you understand her. She'll feel close to you. And she'll want to feel even closer.

A large part of picking up girls is hanging on to them once you've made initial contact. Just because you've been successful at flagging some broad's attention doesn't mean she's going to come with you right then and there, or accept a date, or even give you her phone number.

If you commute to work or school by bus or train, keep your eyes open for girls you like. Chances are you're going to see them at least two or three mornings a week. Pick out one and try to get a seat near her. After a few mornings you'll sort of automatically become old friends— without even speaking. Before long you should feel quite free to say something to her like, "If this train is late one more time I'm going to personally murder the engineer." Or, "Where do you work?"

When you approach a woman with an intense, serious expression on your puss, you frighten her. She doesn't know whether you're going to ask directions to the nearest deli or snatch her purse.

Conversely, a good smile automatically melts a woman. Girls want to feel loved and appreciated. And when you smile at them, it makes them feel you love and appreciate them. It makes them feel secure.

Here's a great little technique to use once you've made contact. As soon as you can, find out the girl's name. Then, as soon as you do, use it. Plenty. Carol and Jane and Claire and Bernice her to death. She'll love it . . .

Women feel the same way you do. Their name is literally music to their ears. When you say a woman's name with warmth and feeling, it makes her feel warm. It flatters her. It makes her like you.

The moral of this little story is that one of the best ways to compliment a woman is to tell her you dig something about her she had no idea was particularly digable. Pick out some insignificant little feature she's probably overlooked. Tell her she's got fantastic eyebrows or beautiful slender fingers. Tell her anything as long as its nice. And don't be afraid to really lay it on thick.

Because when it comes to discussing their looks, women are insatiable. They can't get enough![1]

These remarks, made by Eric Weber in a book entitled *How to Pick Up Girls!*, can be dismissed on numerous fronts. Many would react negatively to his objectification of women—the crass way in which he suggests that females are but things to be dangled on the end of a great persuasive yo-yo. Equally passionate objections could be made about his arrogant male chauvinism. Your authors are distressed with his comments, for these and for one other reason—these comments are dumb.

Essentially, Weber is trying to suggest that his years of experience in singles bars have qualified him to wax knowingly on the art of influencing others. In his book, he argues that there are certain surefire, never-fail "rules" according to which any red-blooded American male can ply his seductive wares. But your own experience with meeting people discounts such a claim. You are aware that the minute you attempt to apply Weber's type of persuasion to the people in your life, you probably will fall flat on your face. You know that to posit incontrovertible "rules" about human communication is at best shortsighted and, at worst, just plain ignorant. Most importantly, you undoubtedly have found that when it comes down to basic people interactions, all the canned lines, the detailed seduction strategies, and the standard one-liners seem to escape you just when you open your mouth.

Although we will talk a good deal about persuasion in this chapter, we will not offer you unfailing techniques for dealing with recalcitrant audiences. Rather, we will try to present you with some of the findings, theories, and (when all else fails) hunches that researchers in persuasion have generated. In addition, we will describe what some apparently successful speakers have done when confronting difficult audiences. In all cases, our attempt will be to present you with options for handling communicative situations. We will not lay out a series of laws about human persuasion. When it comes to law-generating in communication, the individual speaker is his or her own legislature.

Resistance to Persuasion

Even Pollyanna would admit that people disagree with one another. Exactly why they do, when they do, and about what issues they

---

disagree are queries not easily answered. Recent theorists on conflict have argued that disagreements, even violent ones, are part and parcel of the human condition.[2] Others have argued that conflict and confrontation are among the healthiest signs of being human. In this chapter, we are concerned with speaking situations in which speaker and audience have significant disagreements with one another. Thus, it is especially important that we discuss some of the basic sources of human discord. As we discuss these matters, we urge you to keep in mind the persuasive speaking situations that have presented themselves in your life and to compare the advice we offer to your own experiences.

General Sources of Resistance

In his book *Future Shock*, Alvin Toffler says that the possibility of change is one of the most frightening prospects confronting modern people.[3] According to Toffler, it is not so much the specific changes that concern us, but it is the overall aura of change that worries us (sometimes literally) to death. If this is true, then it seems to follow that any persuasive proposal to alter one's attitudes would meet with resistance —so disconcerting is the prospect of still more change.

Naturally, we cannot get carried away with such doomsday thoughts. All of us change our attitudes, jobs, tastes in liquor, sometimes even our life-styles. But before we do so, many of us take the "show me" approach of the Missouri farmer. In a very real sense, *persuasion is a way of showing*—showing that current beliefs will reap fewer dividends than alternative beliefs; that listeners' present behaviors run contrary to values they hold, or should hold; and that, if change must come, the listeners might as well engage in it on the persuader's terms.

Research has suggested, however, that some of us are more resistant to change than are others. Simons has suggested that the following types of persons are likely to be particularly resistant to persuasion[4]:

1. *Those who are highly ego-involved in the issue under consideration.* Researchers have discovered that when a person has much psychological and behavioral investment in a particular issue, he or she will be especially resistant to changing positions on the issue (e.g., the fraternity president who, in defending Greek life, is also affirming his own life-style).

[2]R. Doolittle, *Orientations to Communication and Conflict* (Palo Alto, Cal.: S.R.A. Publishers, 1976).

[3]A. Toffler (New York: Random House, 1970).

[4]H. Simons, "Persuasion and Attitude Change," in *Speech Communication Behavior*, eds. L. Barker and R. Kibler (Englewood Cliffs, N.J.: Prentice-Hall, 1971).

2. *Those who have already taken an extreme position on the matter under consideration.* By taking a polar position on an issue, we necessarily cut down severely on the range of attitudinal options open to us. The father who states that his son will absolutely not have the car for that weekend date would probably find it most difficult to save face and to relent from his position after listening to his son's woeful pleas.

3. *Those who have a well-ordered, highly consistent system of attitudes.* The key here is the word *system.* Some of us, for one reason or another, tend to lock all propositions into a well-integrated matrix of attitudes. The Ku Klux Klanner, for example, is typically quite resistant to persuasion on issues that run counter to his system of beliefs. Thus, he embraces rigid law and order, rigid religion, rigid Americanism, and rigid ethnocentrism—not because of the issues themselves but because of his passion for rigidity.

4. *Those who have certain highly specialized personality traits.* Research has demonstrated that dogmatic persons, those low in self-esteem, and those who have authoritarian tendencies seem to resist persuasion in wholesale fashion. Especially when the issue is highly ego-involving for such individuals, their very personality structures do not permit them to change their ideas.

5. *Those who have certain demographic characteristics.* While the research is not totally in agreement on such matters, it often appears that males, older persons, intelligent individuals, and those who avoid anxiety are generally hard to persuade. These findings must be interpreted with caution. All of us know, for example, that intelligent males are often persuadable. As a group, however, they may present special problems for the public speaker.

Specific Sources of Resistance

Let us now consider more detailed explanations for the persuasive resistances that exist in some public audiences. Such an excursion is not unjustified. If the public speaker is to achieve success, it is best that he or she be aware of the reasons underlying an audience's recalcitrance.

In *Conflict Among Humans,* by Robert Nye, several explanations for the existence of conflict are offered.[5] A liberal interpretation of Nye's postulates suggests that persuasion becomes difficult when

[5]R. Nye, *Conflict Among Humans* (New York: Springer, 1973).

1. Both the speaker and listeners are authoritarian.

2. There is a clash between speaker and listeners over basic needs and values.

3. Listeners have been previously rewarded for their present opinions.

4. Listeners have received too little information (or too much "wrong" information) about the speaker's position.

5. There has been minimal previous contact (of any sort) between speaker and listeners.

6. Speaker and listeners hold differing orientations toward authority (i.e., one is highly respectful and one isn't).

7. Speaker and listeners have competing identifications (i.e., they admire different groups).

These sources of conflict seem to imply their own solutions. Speakers who face such conditions are wise to (1) avoid making "authority" an issue in the persuasive situation, (2) minimize the effects of contrasting values and identification, (3) maximize the availability of information favorable to the speaker's position, and (4) devise some sort of persuasive "punishment" for the listeners' current beliefs and behaviors. While there is value in having these general persuasive goals in mind, actually carrying out such techniques in pragmatic ways is much more difficult. As we shall see later in this chapter, there are specific methods available for changing listeners' ideas, but there is no such thing as a recipe for Instant Persuasion. Nevertheless, these four approaches to persuasion might provide you with some of the ingredients.

When preparing a persuasive message, it would be quite helpful to go through our list of seven "danger signals" and to use them as a type of audience and topical analysis. Be candid with yourself when conducting such analyses, for if these seven factors are not seriously reckoned with, they will undermine even the most polished speech outline.

Beliefs and Resistance

Still another view of why persuasion sometimes becomes difficult is afforded by considering the structures of listeners' belief systems. As you will remember from our discussions in Chapter 4, there are a number of different types of beliefs within us, and these beliefs vary in their vulnerability to persuasion. Thus, we might profitably think of an individual's belief system as constituting a set of "building blocks." Figure 9-1 depicts this idea.

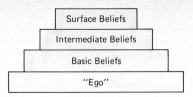

Figure 9-1 The Building Blocks of Beliefs

The most obvious conclusion that we can draw from our model is that the beliefs are hierarchically related. That is, surface beliefs are less ego-involving than are intermediate or basic beliefs and hence are more easily altered through persuasion. Consistent with our building block metaphor, changes in basic beliefs (e.g., I believe in God) will in many cases mandate changes in our intermediate beliefs (e.g., I should follow God's law) and surface beliefs (e.g., I should go to church on Sundays) —a sort of "earthquake" effect.

The reverse relationship does not necessarily hold. A person may fail to attend church regularly, but this does not necessarily imply that he or she will compromise more basic beliefs or give the ghost up entirely. There can, of course, be "avalanche effects" in a person's belief system. Usually, however, such changes would be the result of a long series of persuasive communications.

As we move down our model, it is probably safe to say that the need for social reinforcement of our beliefs decreases because our personal involvement with the beliefs is increasingly higher. It also seems to follow that we are generally more protective of our basic beliefs than we are of the beliefs at the upper levels. Thus, it is not difficult to imagine that if basic beliefs are changed, severe alterations in attitudes, opinions, behaviors, and sometimes even in personality itself may follow.

The practical implications should be clear. It is undeniably important for a persuader to know "where" he or she is attempting to operate in a listener's hierarchy of beliefs. For a speaker to operate in casual fashion when, for instance, attempting to effect changes in a listener's basic beliefs is to commit persuasive suicide. On the other hand, for a speaker to "bring in the big guns" to effect changes in surface beliefs is not only foolhardy but, most likely, is insulting to listeners.

Thus, using gauche humor when speaking about nuclear destruction is just as ill-advised as being pompously serious when addressing the topic of clothing fashions. When preparing to speak, you should also be careful to estimate where in the belief hierarchy the target belief resides for *all* listeners. Some of your hearers, for example, may see abortion as just another surgical procedure, whereas others may regard it as the most basic of basic issues.

The general point we have been trying to make in this section is that it is extremely hard to change someone's beliefs unless you know *why* that person is opposed to your position in the first place. You can, of course, prepare your persuasive message with only instinct to guide you. A better option, we feel, is to consider the sources of resistance mentioned here. Effective persuasion, we feel, is more good detective work than it is unguided inspiration.

Logic of Persuasion

Still another view of resistance to persuasion is available. Consider the hypothetical case of Erle Stanley Gardner's Perry Mason, the famous lawyer of novel and television fame. Fresh from law school, Perry knew all of the precedents, all of the legal and logical intricacies, all of the arguments and counterarguments. It was now time for his very first courtroom appearance. Armed with weighty legal tomes and a three-month supply of yellow legal pads, he sashayed into court ready to do battle. He built his case carefully, intricately. He produced documents, tapes, affidavits, previous legal decisions, photostats, statistics, note cards, testimony from the great figures of jurisprudence, more facts, more figures—until he finally collapsed with the satisfaction that only a young attorney can have in knowing that he has built a perfectly logical case.

The jurors sat in amazement—impressed with Mason's verbal adroitness, his clever twists of logic, his dazzling array of data. They could hardly turn their attention to the bumbling, stumbling country lawyer who called but one witness. Mason smugly watched the proceedings, sat back, mentally rending the logical fabric of his adversary, amazed at the verbal ineptitude of his opponent. Then Mason walked out of court—a loser.

Later, after his sixth martini, Mason looked woefully at his resourceful secretary, Della Street. "What happened?" he queried. It was all Della could do to recount the tearful, homespun plea of Mason's opponent—a plea replete with folksy stories and gingham prose. "How dare he," retorted Mason as he ordered his seventh martini, "doesn't he know that a courtroom is run on the basis of cold, hard logic?" Apparently not.

It really was not Mason's fault. For many years now, the logic of persuasion has not been very well understood. In the past, it was common to assume that communication could best be understood by knowing the logical fallacies, the rules of scientific reasoning, and the dictates of formal logic (syllogisms, Venn diagrams, etc.). What Mason did not know was that human listeners reason differently from logic books;

people can be influenced by considerations such as, "Oh, how could she have killed him? She looks just like my sister."

Aspects of Persuasive Logic

In order to get some understanding of how human persuasion works, we probably should revise our conceptions of what is reasonable in communication. Today, researchers argue that in persuasion we must be less concerned with how scientific or formal logic works and concentrate more on how ordinary human beings reason.[6] That is, we should adopt a "psycho-logic" approach; we should think less of what constitutes inherent reasonableness and more about what listeners do to a message when processing it. Although we know very little at present about the psycho-logic of persuasion, the following propositions seem central to the way listeners reason:

1. *In persuasion, logic is created jointly by speaker and listeners.* Listeners do not sit listening with empty heads. They have experiences, feelings, and prejudices, which they add to a speaker's message as they filter and complete the remarks. In a very real way, listeners *make* sense through an active process of matching their feelings with those of the speaker. Because communication is transactive—involving joint contributions from both speakers and listeners—speakers cannot be inherently logical unless, of course, they are talking to themselves.

2. *In persuasion, the psycho-logical connections that a listener makes determine the reasonableness of a speech.* To understand the logic of persuasion, we must develop a new lexicon. Instead of talking about proof, we must speak of the sufficiency of a speaker's remarks—has he or she tapped enough of his or her listener's potentials? Rather than speaking of the validity of an argument, we must look to the associations listeners are likely to make as they match what a speaker has said with what they already know or feel. When your classmates fall asleep as you drone on in your 3- to 5-minute persuasive speech, they probably do so not because of any inherent fallacy in your remarks but because you did not deal with enough of their potentials.

3. *In persuasion, logic is measured not by what is but by what seems to be.* This is a bitter pill to swallow for the scientists in the crowd. After all, many of us cling desperately to facts—cold, hard expla-

[6]For a more complete discussion of the perspective, see H. Kahane, *Logic and Contemporary Rhetoric* (Belmont, Cal.: Wadsworth, 1971).

nations of how the world is. Unfortunately, there are few real facts in the world of human interactions. After all, there are people who believe that the world is flat. Call them foolish, or illogical, as you will; they do exist, and only some force of *persuasion* will encourage them to see the geometry of the world as you do. We live in a world of probabilities, and it is the most persuasively probable assertions that win the day in human communication.

The way you think about communication will determine how you approach others. If you believe that your message can be inherently logical, that it need not measure up to the petty biases and strange experiences of your listeners, then you will proceed differently than if you believe that *you as the speaker contribute at best one-half of the logic-making in persuasion*. While, in the eyes of the Campus Crusader, the Bible may contain all of the truth and pure logic worth knowing, it is not until a human contact is made that the nonbeliever is intrigued enough to open the book.

Logic as Decision Making

When approaching obstinate listeners, it might be useful to remember that listening is a process of decision making. That is, a speaker is seen as psycho-logically credible by a listener only if that listener can render favorable judgments at a set of crucial decision points. Consider, for example, the logic of the following message created by an undergraduate philosophy student for an audience of history majors:

I would like you to give generously to the Campus Hunger Drive for the following reasons: (1) Your great grandchildren will appreciate it; (2) apples, pears, and bananas; (3) when I miss my daily caviar, I know what it means to be hungry; (4) 99 out of every 100 people starve to death; (5) hunger, when it progresses to the stage of malnutrition, inhibits numerous enzymatic reactions, and, over the long period of time, can lead to terminal illness; and (6) the Catholic Church urges us to help starving people. Thank you for your kind attention.

Quite illogical, is it? No. It is nonpsycho-logical! We could, of course, look at the speech and find some undistributed middles, some unscientific premise-connecting, and the like; but such a procedure would miss the basic foolishness of the message.

Perhaps the best way to view this attempt at persuasion would be to consider the types of decisions listeners would be likely to make during and after the speech. In response to statement 1, a listener might ask, "Who cares?" To statement 2, he or she might say, "Huh?" Statement 3 would hardly bring a tear to the eye, and 4 would be labeled as blatant foolishness. Unless the listener understood biochemistry, he or she would not know what to think about statement 5, and if the listener were a Protestant he or she would be walking out of the room by the time the speaker got halfway through the last statement. Rather than help the situation, our philosopher's speech would inhibit favorable decisions from being rendered by the audience.

Listeners probably meet countless and complex decision points when matching a speaker's remarks with their own preferences. Figure 9-2 presents six of the most common.

Credibility decision. Our model is based upon what seem to be common psycho-logical needs that listeners bring to a persuasive situation. As we mentioned in Chapter 1, it is almost impossible for a listener to divorce his or her perception of a speaker from perceptions of the speaker's message. Because of this, and because credibility is always at issue in *public speaking,* our model implies that a listener never strays very far from considering the person standing behind the persuasive message. At other moments in time, a speaker's own remarks (e.g., statement 3 in the previous example) force decisions to be made about the speaker's credibility. In addition, the credibility decision colors all other decisions and, in turn, is affected by the judgments listeners render at all points during the communicative experience. If this were not true, how could we explain the common reaction, "I don't know what he said, but didn't he say it well?"

Clarity decision. When deciding whether or not a speaker is reasonable, a listener must also know what he or she is being asked to do or to believe. "Apples, pears, and bananas" does not come across as a clear invitation. The clarity decision was placed first in our model because if listeners are unable to determine what is being asked of them, they are unlikely to stay around mentally for further remarks from the speaker.

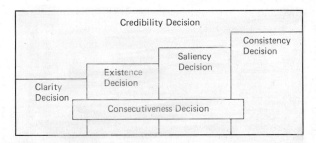

Figure 9-2   Listeners' Decisions and the Logic of Persuasion

Existence decision. Assuming that listeners understand what they are being asked to "give" in persuasion, they must then determine whether they have what it takes. Unless listeners are scientific whizzes, they are unlikely to respond favorably to statement 5 in our previous example. The psycho-logical potential for "enzymatic reations" probably does not reside in the intellectual repertoire of the average history major. While the statement might be factually true and scientifically logical, it has, in our example, run up against a stone wall.

Saliency decision. One of the really important factors to most of us is the matter of saliency. In everyday terms, saliency is a measure of the immediacy and importance of an issue. Statement 1 in our example loses on both accounts. The speaker who demonstrates that a proposal can bring immediate and important benefits to listeners has overcome one of the most serious hurdles to the reasonableness of a persuasive message.

Consistency decision. If we view listeners as comparers—people who compare a speaker's remarks to what they know to be fact, to what they believe to be right, or to what the speaker has said on a previous occasion —we can see why the consistency decision is central to the logic of persuasion. As hearers make intellectual connections while listening to a speaker, they do so in the presence of a storehouse of beliefs and recollections, all of which potentially can be brought to bear on the speech in question. Should a speaker's remarks contradict what a listener values dearly or with what the listener believes to be true, then the speaker might very well lose the psycho-logical battle.

Consecutiveness decision. A final decision listeners make might be called a consecutiveness decision, and it involves listeners' need to perceive some sort of discernible pattern in the world about them. As we saw in Chapter 5, there are many sorts of patterns (e.g., chronology, cause-effect, etc.) with which listeners find it especially easy to work. When looking at the above remarks in our example, we notice an almost random set of claims being made, a total lack of any "signposting" or bridging between thoughts, and no attempts on the part of the speaker to precue or postcue the listener. Such a potpourri of assertions (i.e., enzymes, Catholics, great grandchildren, etc.) made in such a short period of time would hardly help one work through this cacophony of data. People in such a situation would probably want to know how the individual assertions "connect"; they would want to discover if they were being presented with a package of statements or with a series of unconnected pieces and parts; finally, they would want to know if all of the assertions add up to anything in particular. Because the speaker in our example has failed to take listeners' needs for pattern into consideration when generating discourse, he or she is likely to be viewed as being misguided, foolish, or both.

The details of our discussion here are not as important as the state of mind that underlies our remarks. If we view persuasion as a psychological process whereby listeners continually render decisions by comparing the speaker's assertions with their own values, beliefs, and sources of information, then we will remember that communication is not a push-pull process whereby information travels on some mythical railroad car from speaker to listener. The speaker who fully acknowledges that listeners "do things" when listening, that they have the capacity to tune out at any moment, and that their adherence is a prized, yet fragile entity does much to increase his or her chances of meaningful dialogue.

General Suggestions for Persuasion

In this section, we would like to discuss in a general way some ideas that may prove helpful to you in persuasive situations. The first set of suggestions derives from experimental studies in communication. Researchers have conducted a number of interesting studies and have some practical advice to offer. Research summaries suggest that the persuader keep the following ideas in mind when preparing a persuasive message:

1. Material acceptable to the audience should be presented first in a persuasive speech in order to short-circuit mental "counterarguing" on the parts of listeners.

2. Speakers addressing hostile audiences must exhibit speaker-audience commonality even though that commonality may be irrelevant to the topic at hand.

3. An explicit proposal for change should not be stated initially by a speaker if a hostile audience is being addressed.

4. A speaker should at least mention the opposition's point of view when listeners are initially opposed to his or her proposal.

5. Factual evidence is especially effective when the speaker's credibility is low.

6. When listeners are minimally involved in the issue the speaker is addressing, especially strong arguments should be placed in the beginning of the speech.

7. Speakers are often advised to invite audience participation in order to overcome their listeners' resistance to persuasion.

8. Speakers who explain why a given audience might be opposed to them and to their proposal are often advised to offer such an explanation.

9. Fear appeals are best used when the audience views the issue under consideration as being important.

10. For a number of reasons, speakers should be aware that fear appeals reach a point of diminishing returns when used excessively.

11. Speakers facing hostile audiences are advised not to attempt total conversion but rather to change specific beliefs gradually.

12. Strange as it may seem, the more attitude change asked for in a persuasive message, the more actual change one is likely to get.[7]

As stated, these 12 principles are relatively general, abstract, and certainly not lawlike. As usual, the hard part of persuasion lies in actually putting such advice into practice. Some people are capable of doing so:

> . . . Let me start this speech off by saying that I am very, very grateful and deeply moved to be addressing my own university after five years of speaking at colleges all over the country. I am very grateful for the opportunity afforded me by the academic community. It is the last (as far as I'm concerned), it is the last vestige of free speech left in the country. Sorry to say it is usually accorded me by liberals. Conservatives are usually too chicken to let me speak. And I want to again say how grateful I am to be invited here regardless of the politics of [the sponsoring organization]. I am most grateful to them for the fight they have put up to see there's also free speech for anticommunists. . . .
>
> I am not here to agitate. You see no uniforms. There are no party buttons. There will be no attempt in any way to agitate. I am here to present, to the best of my ability, facts and ideas which changed me from an ordinary student at Brown University—as many of you are—to the point where I am proud to stand before you as a National Socialist. . . .
>
> And I am going to try to give you some insight tonight into the facts which came to my attention which I believe you have been denied and which caused me to make that change. All I can do, ladies and gentlemen, is to present

[7]For more specific information, see M. Karlins and H. Abelson, *Persuasion: How Opinions and Attitudes Are Changed* (New York: Springer, 1970), Simons, op. cit., and J. McCroskey, "A Summary of Experimental Research on the Effects of Evidence in Persuasive Communication," *Speech Monographs*, 36:169–176 (1969).

to you a few, a very few, samples of what I consider to be shocking facts. And ask you to do what I had to do after I found out these things and go check 'em out for yourselves. . . .[8]

Well, how would you start a speech if you were George Lincoln Rockwell, late head of the American Nazi Party, telling a liberal university audience (and a goodly number of riot-control police) that they should be sympathetic to the neo-Nazi movement in America?! Rockwell's approach seems to point up a canny, shirt-sleeved awareness of some of the 12 persuasive principles we have just discussed. Rockwell starts his speech in a complimentary fashion, reminds his audience of certain bonds they already share with him, withholds any specific proposal for change from his introduction, promises to present factual evidence, acknowledges that there is an opposing point of view, and, although he goes on in the speech to ask for at least tacit sympathy for the National Socialist movement, he is probably aware that the best he can expect is open-mindedness from his audience.

While it is highly doubtful that Rockwell was aware of our list of research findings when making his speech, his remarks should indicate that our list is a practical one. As we move on in this chapter to consider various approaches to persuasion, you might want to consider, from time to time, what other options for response were open to Rockwell when attempting to peddle his racism. Two general approaches he could have taken are the common premise and detachment strategies.

The Common Premise Approach

Let us start with a kind of a self-quiz. Read the following remarks and see if you can guess who the speaker is, when the speech was given, and under what circumstances.

Three hundred years ago a man who gave his name to this state, William Penn, a Quaker, was prevented by an Act of Parliament from speaking in his church, from giving a sermon. So he went out and he gave his sermon in the streets of London, on Gray Street. He was arrested and charged . . . with inciting to riot . . . and he was brought before a magistrate at the Old Bailey in London.

And the magistrate said, "Mr. Penn, you've been charged with crime. How do you plead?" And Penn said, "What is the charge against me?" And the magistrate said, "That's no consequence to you. How do you plead?" And William Penn (and I brought his remarks in here tonight), William Penn

[8]G. L. Rockwell, "Speech at Brown University, 1966". Reprinted by permission of the National Socialist White People's Party, Arlington, Va.; previously the American Nazi Party, headed by George Lincoln Rockwell.

said, "Shall I plead to an indictment that hath no foundation in law? Tell me, please, what is the nature of the indictment, so that I may determine whether I am innocent or guilty." The judge said, "You are a saucy fellow. Speak to the indictment." And Penn said, ". . . I say, unless you show me and the people the law you ground your indictment upon, I shall take it for granted your proceedings are merely arbitrary."

The judge said, "The question is whether you are guilty of the indictment." And Penn said, "Where there is no law, there is no transgression, and that law which is not in being is so far from being common that it is no law at all." And the judge said, "You are an impertinent fellow. Will you teach this court what law is?" . . . And Penn said, "You tell me what the law is, I mean no affront, and I shall answer with my plea." And the judge said, "Sir, you are a troublesome fellow, and it is not for the honor of the court to suffer you to go on." And Penn answered, "I have asked but one question and you have not answered me, though the rights and privileges of every Englishman be concerned in it." And the judge said, "If I should suffer you to ask questions til tomorrow morning you would be never the wiser." And Penn said, "That depends on the answers."

And the judge said, "We must not stand to hear you talk all night." And then Penn said, . . . "I design no affront to the court but to be heard in my just plea, and I must plainly tell you that, if you will deny me knowledge of that law which you suggest I have broken, you do at once deny me an acknowledged right and evidence to the whole world your resolution to sacrifice and arbitrary designs." And the judge said, "Bind and gag him." And that's what happened to William Penn.[9]

This speech, given in the early 1970s at Pennsylvania State University, was part of an introduction to a speech dealing with the Chicago Eight conspiracy trial, a highly charged contest between a scruffy and boisterous group of antiwar protestors and an arch-conservative, rather tyrannical trial judge by the name of Julius Hoffman. The speaker was William Kunstler, lawyer for the Chicago Eight and an unofficial patriarch of the New Left movement, and the audience he was addressing was largely composed of middle-of-the-roaders.

You may find this a rather strange way to begin a speech. However, Kunstler probably knew that he was not facing a group of hard-core radicals, but a group of middle-class Penn State students who were confused and upset about the turmoil that was sweeping college campuses in the late 1960s and early 1970s. Yet, what seems most incredible about the speech is the amount of time that Kunstler spent on his William Penn story. Why?

[9]From a tape recording of Kunstler's May 1970 speech at Pennsylvania State University. Reprinted by permission of William Kunstler.

For want of a better term, we might label Kunstler's approach the *common premise strategy*—one of the oldest and most viable methods available to persuaders who expect significant resistance from their audiences. Essentially, the common premise approach operates in an analogical fashion by comparing two apparently disparate elements and then using the one to reinforce the other. By beginning with the Penn story, Kunstler apparently reasoned that he was on safe ground—that most students of Pennsylvania would be able to identify and admire a personage of Penn's stature. By building this common premise as carefully as he did, Kunstler was then in a position to apply the clincher: If we respect and admire Penn's stand against improper conduct by a judge, how then can we condemn the Chicago Eight for giving Judge Hoffman such a rough time in court? In essence, the common premise strategy is a technique for inhibiting listeners from thinking up counterarguments *when listening*.

The common premise strategy takes advantage of two of the findings of persuasion research we discussed previously—the proposal should be withheld initially, and speaker-audience agreement on some issue must be established early in the speech. As with all human behavior, there is nothing certain about this approach. Still, it seems to work reasonably well on many occasions and generally proceeds in somewhat the following fashion:

1. *Identify* a belief or opinion that is already held by a listener or by a group of listeners.

2. *Build* the saliency of that belief or opinion so that it becomes operational in the communicative situation.

3. *Demonstrate* that you, the speaker, also share that belief or opinion. (This makes it a common premise.)

4. *Connect* the common premise to the proposal that you are advocating as a speaker.

Naturally, the procedure is not as easy as it seems. You might, for example, select a belief or attitude that is not held strongly by your audience. You might fail to make it really salient for your listeners. Your hearers might distrust your own commitment to the proposal, or they might fail to see any important connection between the common premise and the proposal. If he were not especially careful, Kunstler could have failed to persuade because of any or all of these four factors. Indeed, on that evening in 1970, Kunstler probably succeeded in winning no wild-eyed converts. But he did, perhaps, encourage some open-mindedness on the issue, and that's not a bad night's work.

The Detachment Approach

Again operating at a rather global level, we can envision another approach whereby a speaker attempts to "detach" certain of the listeners' beliefs that anchor another belief the persuader wants to alter. For instance, in an antipollution campaign, ecologists oftentimes reason that John Q. Citizen will not take his refuse to the recycling center because of certain ingrained, habitual feelings he has toward disposing trash. Instead of arguing, "It's your moral obligation to recycle," ecologists sometimes attempt to "cut loose" the more basic attitudes holding the no-recycling belief in place. By assuming that the underlying reasons for resisting modern ecological practices might be due to a penchant for tidiness, the advent of mechanical means such as compactors, or simple human laziness, recyclers attempt to detach such values from the individual's belief system so that the target belief (recycling) will be loosened from the underlying or anchoring beliefs (tidiness, compactors, and laziness). Consider the following examples, which also illustrate this approach.

When attempting to rise to power in post-World War I Germany, Adolph Hitler knew that several forces militated against his establishing a fascist regime. Chief among these "retarding forces" were the press, organized religion, and the government then in power. In rather systematic fashion, Hitler attempted to neutralize the persuasive effects of such powerful determiners of German attitudes (i.e., the religious and political anchoring beliefs) and then later set out to destroy the

German people's allegiance to the target belief (i.e., a non-Nazi government). Had he not opted for such an indirect approach and instead attempted to change the target belief by means of more frontal techniques, he very well might have failed, so powerful were the countervailing forces of persuasion.

To use such an approach effectively, the persuader obviously must know which underlying attitudes are holding the target belief in place. Sometimes, such knowledge is difficult to obtain. In fact, at times, listeners themselves are unaware of the feelings that anchor a given target belief. In such a situation, by simply pointing out these anchoring beliefs and then arguing against them, a persuader has relatively little trouble in subsequently cutting loose the target belief.

For example, an advertisement that once appeared in many campus newspapers asked for contributions to the East Pakistani Relief Fund. Instead of beginning with the help-an-orphan approach, the ad asserted and developed the following points: "We can well understand why you might refuse our plea. After all, giving has become impersonal and involuntary; we've lost the ability to be shocked by man's inhumanity to man; and we've all got our own problems." By thus reckoning directly with the "opposition's" point of view, the creators of the appeal were in a position to alter anchoring beliefs. Later on in the ad, of course, they presented more positive reasons for supporting the East Pakistani fund (i.e., the new belief they wished to instill).

The detachment approach and the common premise strategy have much in common. Both acknowledge that when resistance to the speaker's proposal is expected to be high, a frontal attack on listeners' basic beliefs is oftentimes unwise. With the common premise approach, the speaker refrains from dealing with potentially dangerous material until sufficient speaker-audience agreement (on some issue) has been developed. The detachment technique operates a bit more directly by dealing immediately with the attitudinal forces that threaten to withhold acceptance of the speaker's proposal. Still, there is much overlap between the two strategies. The important thing to note about both strategies, however, is that each is peculiarly useful for speakers facing significant resistance to their ideas.

Specific Strategies for Persuasion

In the final section of this chapter, we would like to present a number of concrete strategies that should prove very helpful to you when fashioning persuasive messages. Before we do so, however, we would like to make a brief digression to talk about the ethics of persuasion.

We are talking in this chapter about strategies. We are talking about methods of influencing. We are talking about persuasion. Without getting into a detailed discussion of morality, your authors would like to make one simple point: No matter how "evil" these terms may sound, we as people in a complex society have little choice but to understand persuasion and to use it effectively. For every persuader of the ilk of George Lincoln Rockwell or Adolph Hitler, there are mass mobilizers like Mahatma Gandhi and Jesus Christ. For every radical like William Kunstler, there is a John Bircher such as Robert Welch. It is our very simple belief that if you do not choose to influence, if the word *strategy* gets stuck in your throat as you attempt to utter it, or if you believe that human beings are capable of *not* influencing one another (either intentionally or unintentionally), you should retreat from human society. To forsake persuasion and the techniques for making it effective might be to forsake some of your deep-seated beliefs and to insure that the world will progress without the benefits of *your* views, *your* concerns, and *your* ideals.

On the pages that follow, we have listed and explained a number of specific persuasive strategies that may be of considerable help to you in preparing persuasive messages. These are offered as communicative options. They are not 16 infallible steps to health and happiness through persuasion. By being aware of these options for responses, however, we hope that you will be able to add to your communicative repertoire, which is, of course, the purpose of this entire book. Thus, we invite you to consider the possibilities for influence presented in Table 9-1.

It probably need not be said that several problems abound in our categorization of appeals: (1) The strategy types we have listed here are not mutually exclusive nor, perhaps, are they at the same level of abstraction in all cases. (2) Furthermore, most persuasive messages will be composed of a veritable network of such persuasive approaches. (3) Research has also not yet delineated the exact conditions under which these individual strategies will be effective in helping a speaker overcome resistance to his or her proposal. (4) Undoubtedly, certain of the strategies listed here are appropriate for use only by certain persuaders with certain audiences under certain conditions.

But we will apologize no further for our listing. As with most aspects of communication, it is the *thinking* about the persuasive situation that separates the dynamos from the ne'er-do-wells. Strategies, attention factors, methods of reinforcement, forms of clarification, and so forth, cannot alone do the job of effective communication. Such devices are, of course, helpful. But devices are forgotten and attitudes toward communication remain. In this chapter, and for that matter throughout this book, we hope to leave you with one major impression: Effective communication (or persuasion) is not something that is done

Table 9-1 Strategies for Persuasion

Type	Definition	Example	Commentary
1. Inclusion	The process of connecting the immediate audience's attitudes, values, and goals to those of a prized reference group.	"All the folks on the block are buying these battery-operated can openers."	Particularly useful with listeners who possess a high need for social affiliation.
2. Maximization	The attempt to demonstrate graphically the superiority of the speaker's proposal over that of competing propositions.	"The Dale Carnegie course will bring you untold amounts of health, wealth, and happiness."	Particularly useful after alternatives to the speaker's proposal have been dealt with and dismissed.
3. Minimization	The process of deprecating the views of those opposing the speaker and/or of slighting apparently detrimental aspects of the speaker's proposal.	"If you want high gas bills, buy a Chrysler. Despite its initial cost, a Cadillac is your best buy in the long run."	A very necessary approach when there are obvious disadvantages to the speaker's proposal or when the listeners have been recently made aware of proposals opposed to that of the speaker.

Table 9-1 (Continued)

Type	Definition	Example	Commentary
4. Association	The method whereby the speaker shows relationships between himself or his proposal and beliefs that are positively valued by the listener.	"If you like plump, fresh-roasted peanuts as I do, you'll love Skippy peanut butter."	One of the most fundamental aspects of persuasion. Particularly valuable when an audience has a well-defined, highly contiguous value system.
5. Disassociation	The process by which the speaker depicts the lack of relationship between herself (or her proposal) and beliefs that are negatively valued by the listener	"Like you good folk, I don't want any Big-Brother-creeping-federal-bureaucracy here in the good old U.S. of A."	An obvious reversal of the association approach. Particularly helpful after a speaker has "reminded" an audience of the things they dislike.

| 6. Simplification | The method whereby a speaker reduces the positive aspects of his proposal (or the negative aspects of his opponent's proposal) to its lowest common denominator. | "When all is said and done, you can't beat Joe's Bar for having fun." | Simplicity should, of course, characterize any attempt to communicate efficiently. Simplification is particularly useful when a speaker desires to treat complex or detailed arguments in a skeletal fashion or when a detailed examination of an issue would raise too many issues to be resolved easily during the speech. |
| 7. Unification | An attempt to demonstrate graphically the underlying similarity among a series of otherwise unconnected elements. | "If you start to think about who's raising taxes, starting wars, and spreading immorality, you'll know for whom to vote." | Especially helpful in campaign or movement persuasion when the issues, arguments, and evidence are numerous and complex. |

Table 9-1 (Continued)

Type	Definition	Example	Commentary
8. Involvement	The actual or simulated attempt to engage the audience directly in dialogue.	"Could I have a volunteer from the audience come up here and sample Dr. Ewbank's Magic Elixir?"	While a difficult strategy to employ in many public communication situations, involvement of an audience (or members of an audience) can do much to generate a sense of interaction between a speaker and her listeners.
9. Gradualism	A technique whereby the speaker argues that the acceptance of his or her proposal does not necessitate radical restructuring of an audience's belief system.	"Look, Barbara, you've been going to school for 16 years now. What's another two years for a Master's degree?"	Research has suggested that interpersonal conflict can be lowered by a gradual process of concession-making.[10] When dealing with a hostile audience, a speaker who asks for a series of moderate changes will probably avoid frightening an audience to death!

[10]C. Osgood, *An Alternative to War or Surrender* (Urbana, Ill.: University of Illinois Press, 1962).

| 10. Overkill | The oftentimes subtle procedure by which a speaker asks for far more attitude change than he or she can hope to get in order to at least obtain some concession from an audience. | "Mommy, can I have a lollipop, some ice cream, a jawbreaker, and some bubble gum … well … at least give me a lollipop." | The reverse of gradualism, the overkill strategy takes advantage of the research findings that show that, in some cases, the more change you ask for, the more you are likely to get.[11] Particularly useful in the beginning of a persuasive movement since such a blatant approach tends to call attention to that movement (e.g., "nonnegotiable demands"). |
| 11. Projection | A common device whereby a speaker hypothesizes the outcomes of the audience's wrongly following the course of action he or she opposes and/or rightly embracing the proposal the speaker endorses. | "Just picture it—your own little retirement bungalow, away from the noise, the pollution, and the hustle and bustle of the city." | A particularly safe device to use when speaking before a hostile audience, where a detailed discussion could raise more issues than it could resolve. Takes advantage of many of the attention factors discussed in Chapter 5. |

[11]See Karlins and Abelson, op. cit., p. 126.

Table 9-1 (Continued)

Type	Definition	Example	Commentary
12. Elimination	The process by which a speaker successively sets aside alternative approaches to the solution he or she supports (often accompanied by minimizing strategies).	"Jones is too far left, Smith is too far right. How about a nice middle-of-the-roader like your candidate and mine, Mark Lane?"	Takes advantage of persuasion research that indicates that a two-sided approach is quite necessary when a hostile or intelligent audience is being addressed.
13. Idealization	A kind of abstracting technique by which the speaker suggests that certain superordinate goals are more important than any disagreements the speaker and his or her listeners might harbor.	"Of course, you and I are of different religions. But that doesn't mean that we can't engage in ecumenical dialogue in order to better do our Christian duty."	Research by Sherif has indicated that agreement on general ends can often obviate serious disagreements between persons of opposing viewpoints.[12] Especially useful when a discussion of ends, not means, is relevant to the persuasive situation.

[12]M. Sherif, "Superordinate Goals in the Reduction of Intergroup Conflict," *American Journal of Sociology*, 63:349–356 (1958).

14. Legitimization	The tangible counterpart to the idealization strategy whereby a speaker argues that some person, document, or institution demands the acceptance of the speaker's proposal.	"OK, so we disagree about busing. But if I read the Constitution right, it guarantees all students, regardless of color, the right to a good education."	Nye indicates that allegiance to a common institution or ideology can sometimes help to settle differences between conflicting factions.[13] By appealing to a "sponsoring" force external to the interaction, a speaker can sometimes make the dispute at hand seem quite petty by comparison.
15. Self-deprecation	A frequently used persuasive strategy in which the speaker admits to certain inadequacies in order to build reciprocity between himself or herself and the listeners.	"Let's talk frankly. Of course I haven't always voted in the ways you would have liked me to. But I have followed my conscience, and that's my job as your congressional reprensentative."	An especially effective device for use in hostile situations because the speaker can take the initiative by temporarily directing the audience's attention to aspects of self that are irrelevant to the acceptance of the proposal but that will depict him or her as fair-minded.

[13]Nye, op. cit.

Table 9-1 (Continued)

Type	Definition	Example	Commentary
16. Apprehension	Better known as the fear-appeal approach, apprehension is a device whereby a speaker graphically illustrates a threatening set of events or depicts the deleterious consequences of an audience's not following the speaker's advice.	"Our environment has become so polluted that medical researchers are now finding that some industrial pollutants are capable of producing skin cancers."	As mentioned previously, research has shown that fear appeals are effective only up to a point, after which listeners regard the appeal as incredible or insulting. A modicum of apprehension is helpful in dramatizing a speaker's proposal, but listeners are unable to assimilate information under conditions of high anxiety.

to people but is an outgrowth of a complex process of exchange in which both speakers and listeners pool their intellectual and emotional resources and, on occasion, achieve some measure of human accord. If we are not able to come to grips with such an intellectual realization, then we will follow the Dale Carnegie road of life—desperately searching for, but never finding, the ten magic rules for effective existence.

Suggestions for Speaking

Persuasion is a fascinating topic. To many people, it appears to be a mysterious art; to others, a scientific process. We suspect it is neither. In this chapter, we have argued that effective communication is the product of intelligent guesswork, so variable are the people we talk to and so complex is the medium of symbolic exchange. We have tried to suggest that resistance to persuasion can be overcome if one fully understands the peculiar logic of persuasion and appreciates some of the basic options available to the would-be persuader. Thus, in studying persuasion, we are doing little more than studying the essential nature of people. If anthropology tells us what societies do, and if sociology tells us what groups of people do, then persuasion tells us what pairs of people do. And because people engage in persuasion so frequently, it behooves us to know as much about it as we can. To advance your understanding of this enterprise, we offer you the following suggestions for speaking:

1. Especially in classroom speaking situations, it is possible to conduct a prespeech poll of your audience's attitudes and thereby determine your persuasive problems.

2. If your speech generates dogmatic resistance in some listeners, don't respond by being equally dogmatic; moderation is impressive.

3. When trying to explain to listeners why they disagree with you, attribute their attitudes to possible lack of information.

4. It is often possible to disarm listeners' opposition to your ideas by humorously discussing the strained nature of your relationship with them.

5. Never assume that an avalanche of facts will win the day; the interconnecting *reasons* you supply will cause an audience to open its mind.

6. In many ways, extended examples (i.e., "vignettes") make ideas clear and salient; no persuasive speech should be devoid of them.

7. Don't attempt to trick listeners by filling your introduction with material irrelevant to your topic; such a technique will make your listeners doubly resentful when you finally discuss your proposal.

8. Don't try to be all things to all people by associating yourself with every value cherished by the listeners; be selective.

9. Resist the temptation to use the all-or-nothing approach whereby you force the listener to accept your position totally or not at all.

10. Don't mimic the clever tricks of star debaters and famous defense attorneys when speaking; in persuasion, your greatest asset is *you* and the ideas *you* stand for.

CHAPTER 10

The Persuasive Speech

You asked me how I feel about whiskey. All right, here is just how I stand on this question:

If, when you say whiskey, you mean the devil's brew, the poison scourge, the bloody monster that defiles innocence, yea, literally takes the bread from the mouths of little children; if you mean the evil drink that topples the Christian man and woman from the pinnacles of righteous and gracious living into the bottomless pit of degradation and despair, shame and helplessness and hopelessness, then certainly I am against it with all of my power.

But, if when you say whiskey, you mean the oil of conversation, the philosophic wine, the stuff that is consumed when good fellows get together, that puts a song in their hearts and laughter on their lips and the warm glow of contentment in their eyes; if you mean Christmas cheer; if you mean the stimulating drink that puts the spring in the old gentlemen's step on a frosty morning; if you mean the drink that enables a man to magnify his joy, and his happiness, and to forget, if only for a little while, life's great tragedies and heartbreaks and sorrow, if you mean that drink, the sale of which pours into our treasuries untold millions of dollars, which are used to provide tender care for our little crippled children, our blind, our deaf, our dumb, our pitiful aged and infirm, to build highways, hospitals, and schools, then certainly I am in favor of it.

This is my stand. I will not retreat from it; I will not compromise.[1]

Now *there's* a persuasive message for you! In a sense, persuasive artistry involves just this sort of human creativity—the ability to examine an idea from multiple perspectives and to find language capable of breathing life into shopworn or outmoded ideas. This is not to say, of course, that the persuader necessarily produces the sort of double-talk our artful politician has produced above. Good, honest persuasion takes a stand and makes that stand one that listeners come to envy. Therein lies persuasive genius.

In this chapter, we would like to offer you some practical ideas for dealing with the persuasive speaking situation. We are hoping, of course, that our preceding discussions have already prepared you, in part, for making a persuasive speech. In particular, Chapter 5 should have given you a good notion of how ideas can be made weighty and appealing, while Chapter 9 should have caused you to begin thinking seriously about the options available to you as a persuasive speaker. Here, we would like to "polish" you up a bit as we consider some issues native to the persuasive speech itself.

Thinking Strategically

We use the word *strategy* quite often in our everyday lives. We refer to a football coach's strategy against a running game or his technique for defensing a passing team. We refer to a political leader's campaign blitz as constituting a good or bad strategy for winning the next elec-

---

[1]From the Associated Press.

tion. We even speak of strategy in relationship to our dealings with other people—one might have a strategy for getting a date, another for coaxing a grade raise out of a teacher or a strategy for making the landlord fix the plumbing. What do we mean when we use the word *strategy* in these many different ways?

To put it simply, a strategy is *a way of doing things so that people can reach their goals.* A strategy is also a way of doing things that one has freely *chosen* from among several options. By and large, nobody chooses how to fall down the stairs, so we don't speak of a "strategy" for tripping. But there may be many ways of inducing a professor to raise a grade, and so we contemplate the best strategy for reaching that exalted goal. In this chapter, we are concerned with using strategies in our interactions with other people so that we are able to provide "good reasons" for them to believe and behave as we do.

Strategic communication involves talking to other people in careful, well-chosen ways designed to achieve certain goals. These goals require the cooperation and agreement of other people. When a politician runs for office, he or she uses speech to secure the cooperation of the voters; when one sits at a dinner table and feels "saltless," one also engages in strategic thinking. "Please pass the salt" is strategic speaking in the purest sense of that phrase. It is speech generated by a persuasive problem, formulated in an option-rich environment, and delivered to a consciously chosen audience.

From the standpoint of persuasion, strategic thinking requires that we understand how the cooperation of others can be secured. But what makes such cooperation possible? What makes people accept a new idea? For one thing, people accept new ideas if they believe that those ideas are *consistent* with or required by ideas that they already possess. If the new idea seems to be consistent with ideas, values, principles, or needs that the audience now holds, then the audience will feel that they have good reasons for accepting the new idea as well.

Suppose, for example, that your teacher were to ask you during class to leap from the fifth-floor window. You probably wouldn't accept such an invitation because it starkly contrasts with certain of the survival needs we mentioned in Chapter 4! There seem to be no good reasons for jumping from the window, no satisfactory way of reconciling what you now believe with what your teacher has requested of you. On the other hand, suppose your teacher asked you to read the next chapter because doing so would help you pass your final test. Acquiescence here is more likely because you have long held to the notion that passing tests is a good reason for doing just about anything. So, when we say that the teacher gave you a good reason for reading the chapter, we mean that the teacher proved that reading the chapter was consistent with your established attitudes and present goals. Sometimes, passing tests is a good reason for you to go to the library. Sometimes, it's a good reason for you to go to bed early.

Besides passing tests, we have many other ideas or values that can serve as good reasons for doing things. The value of having a rewarding career is a good reason for doing or thinking new things. This may be why you're in school, for instance. The belief that one should help one's neighbors is also a good reason for doing things. It may be your reason for returning a lost wallet or for lending someone a copy of your lecture notes. From a practical standpoint, *if a person does something, he or she has done it for good reasons,* for maintenance-of-consistency reasons.

In this chapter, we will try to discover how a speaker's strategic thinking can result in "good reasons" for listeners to cooperate with the speaker's call for action. But these good reasons don't materialize out of thin air. In fact, listeners present a host of problems to a speaker when he or she seeks out good reasons. For example, few listeners have exactly the same sets of ideas and values, or, if they do, don't hold them with equal strength. The idea of curbing government expenditures, for instance, may be admired greatly by a group of conservative business people, and that idea may constitute a good reason for them to do certain things. But keeping government costs down may be seen as a cruel hoax by welfare recipients or an empty dream by a member of the middle class. Thus, in persuasive settings, good reasons are always *situation-specific.*

Good reasons are also *topic-dependent.* For example, one speaker may urge sending food supplies to a starving country because he or she believes in charitable works. But when speaking to a group of farmers on the topic of inflation, disbursing food supplies via government subsidies may be reasonable because it will be good business for American agriculture! Good reasons, like most things human, are highly dependent upon what individual audiences define as good and reasonable.

For almost any topic and audience, it is a fact of life that the audience will have beliefs that are potentially consistent with the speaker's thesis statement. But they are also likely to have beliefs that run counter to the speaker and his or her purpose, primarily because it is often true that the ideas people hold in the abstract tend to conflict with one another when applied to specific issues. For example, most people believe in the value of defending themselves when attacked. Most people equally believe in the value of peaceful relations. People live quite happily with both values until somebody assaults them, at which point they must decide which value is most important. Beliefs and ideas that are opposed to the thesis statement might be termed *objections.* For instance, if a speaker is asking an audience to support reduced government spending, the audience's values of thriftiness and economy will support such a notion. But the same audience may also value such social services as police, fire protection, military defense, education, and other services subsidized by government budgets. Thus, "good reasons" to believe in a certain way or to do certain things are also a function of the *saliency* of the matter being discussed.

As we move along in this chapter, we will discuss ways in which speakers can cope with the situation—specific, topic-dependent, and saliency-conditioned nature of "good reasons." We shall find that good reasons can be discovered to support most ideas, but they rarely appear to us in a moment of pure inspiration. Good reasons, like good wine or good cheese, are discovered only after much effort has been expended and after some intelligent choices have been made.

Analyzing the Persuasive Situation

In Chapter 4, we spent some time discussing the nature of audience analysis. Here, we would like to (1) broaden our focus a bit by considering the audience in relationship to the actual speaking situation, and (2) present some specific questions you might ask yourself when searching for good reasons. When preparing a persuasive speech, you will find questions like the following quite helpful.

What Impact Will the Audience's Reference Groups Have on the Topic at Hand?

Earlier, we considered the idea that the audiences' reference groups are an important source of the audiences' beliefs, values, and ideas. If they believe in the value of getting a good education, for instance, that value did not just appear in a dream but probably derived from the social groups of which they are a part—their family probably emphasizes education. The persuasive speaker should thus ask him- or herself if identification with a particular reference group means that the audience is likely to have a predictable attitude on the topic at hand, or if the audience's demographic profile will have *systematic* effects on the speaking situation. After all, the public speaker rarely needs to concern himself or herself with the idiosyncratic reactions of individual listeners.

But even if a speaker knows an audience's dominant reference group makeup, those groups will not always be relevant to every topic. For instance, if one is speaking about affirmative action programs, one is safe in assuming that a predominantly black audience from an industrial neighborhood will likely be in favor of such programs, whereas a middle-class white audience may not. But if one is urging public support for the arts, the racial makeup of the audience probably won't have much bearing on the speaker's success. In such a situation, a speaker will have to look to other influences upon the audience—for instance, their educational level. So, let's supplement our earlier discussion of reference groups and demographic clusters by considering some specific sources of influence.

1. *Political groups.* Very often, people believe what they believe because of the political groups to which they belong. Democrats tend to be liberal, in favor of government intervention, and supportive of expansionist programs in foreign policy. Republicans tend to believe just the opposite. Members of the John Birch Society tend to be extremely conservative, very patriotic, and opposed to big government, whereas members of the American Civil Liberties Union tend to favor personal rights and freedoms, and to be tolerant of differences among people. Because such world views will color the reactions of listeners on so many topics, the persuasive speaker should probably make an especially *early* determination of an audience's political leanings.

2. *Racial and ethnic groups.* On issues that involve race (and what issues don't in a heterogeneous country like the contemporary United States?), the racial and ethnic makeup of the audience can indicate what their ideas, values, and beliefs on the topic may be. On the matter of sending economic aid to poorer, developing countries, for instance, Mexican-Americans may be more acquiescent than people from northern European backgrounds. On the issue of controlling drug traffic, the racial makeup of the audience may not matter. As aculturation takes place in a society, these ethnicity-based attitudes tend to change, so be sure that your observations are based on current assumptions and not on outdated stereotypes.

3. *Economic/professional groups.* A matter relevant to many issues is the economic well-being of the audience. Tied to that is the professional status of the audience: Are they executives, white-collar workers, blue-collar, skilled, unskilled? Again, the particular issue being addressed will determine whether or not the audience's economic status is a major source of resistance. If the topic is city subsidies for day-care centers, rich professionals who can afford private care but who pay more taxes will probably be against such government expenditures, while working-class persons who would use such services will likely favor spending public money in these ways. Economic and professional groups can also tell the speaker something about the educational level of the audience. Usually, richer professional peo-

ple are better educated and better informed than are poorer workers. However, whether that makes your job as a speaker easier or harder is, naturally, an uncertain matter—well-informed people are often highly critical, whereas poorly informed people are sometimes harder to motivate.

4. *Geographical groups.* Often, people develop values and ideas because of where they live. Many people voted for Jimmy Carter in 1976 simply because he was from the South, for instance. If a speaker knows that the audience is from a coal-producing state, the speaker knows that they will probably have some strong (and probably well-informed) attitudes on the topic of nuclear energy. In a speech on state support for urban transportation, a speaker may find a primarily suburban audience to be opposed to his or her proposal, whereas a central city audience will be more likely to favor such measures. A speech on the rights of Native Americans will be taken very differently by audiences in Minnesota, where there are many Native Americans, than it will be by audiences in Rhode Island, where there are fewer. An audience in North Dakota is more likely to favor government price supports than is an audience in an industrial state like New Jersey. So, for many topics, the geographical orientation of the audience will be an important clue to some of their thinking.

5. *Religious, age, and gender groups.* These three kinds of groups are probably decreasing in importance as reference groups. However, they may still tell a speaker something about an audience's attitudes on certain topics. Religious differences among members of particular churches seem to be fading in our society; Methodists probably do not hold markedly different values from Presbyterians, for example, on the matter of foreign aid. But conservative Catholics are still strongly opposed to legalized abortion, for instance, while liberal Unitarians favor freedom of choice on such matters. Sometimes, the age of the audience can tell a speaker something about their values; older listeners are less likely to be open to new and untried ideas than are younger audiences. Too, an audience of senior citizens is more likely to favor government medical aid than will the members of a younger audience, who would actually have to pay the additional tax money needed to support such forms of assistance.

Attitudes linked to sex are changing, as sex roles themselves change. Fewer women today are tied to the home, and fewer men work exclusively from 9 to 5 at the office. Thus, men's and women's attitudes are becoming more homogeneous on a great variety of matters. But on issues like rape, abortion, women's rights, and related subjects, an audience of women is still likely to have far different concerns from an audience of men. Thus, simply knowing listeners' general reference group or demographic makeup will do you little good as a persuasive speaker. In addition, *you must consider the matter of topic-dependence, thus transforming audience analysis into situational analysis.* Such a transformation is necessary lest audience analysis become a mere sociological exercise for the persuasive speaker.

What Past Statements Has the Audience Made that Reveal their Notions of Good Reasons?

Often, the audience being addressed will be a group that has taken a public stand on some set of issues in the past. You can look at those past statements to see which ideas, values, and beliefs have been expressed. This source of audience information is obviously useful in a public speaking class because every time people get up to speak, they reveal a portion of their world views. By the time a class has had a round or two of speeches, one should know a good deal about the class's typical modes of thinking. Outside of school, the groups speakers address will have made public statements more often than one might suspect. Labor unions and professional organizations such as the United Auto Workers and the American Medical Association regularly endorse political candidates, pass resolutions, and take stands on issues relevant to their concerns. Social or service organizations such as the Daughters of the American Revolution and the Kiwanis Club usually have statements of principles that their members are expected to support.

Representatives of such groups may also make public statements that reflect their constituents' feelings. For instance, someone who is going to speak to a group of high school teachers should pay attention to what the President of their Teacher's Association said in last week's newspaper. It may well be profitable for a speaker to "research" the audience to see if that audience, or the groups within it, have made explicit statements of their beliefs or have behaved in some way that provides a subtle index of their feelings.

Will Matters of Timing Affect What Listeners Will Define as Good Reasons?

We have already discussed the importance of situational expectation on the attitudes of the audience. If one is urging listeners to make sacrifices for their country, that speech will have very different effects depending on whether it is given immediately before a battle or back home in a V.F.W. hall on the Fourth of July. Because the situations are so different in terms of psychological immediacy, the respective audiences will have different ideas uppermost in their minds. Thus, it becomes important for a speaker to ask what events are transpiring in the surrounding time and place, and how they will affect the audience's resistance to the message. Suppose, for example, that one has decided to speak on the Arab-Israeli conflict in the Middle East. If the Arabs launched a surprise guerilla attack on an Israeli settlement on the day preceding the speech, the audience's normally neutral feelings may be more pro-Israeli at the moment. If you are speaking on the subject of tuition increases, your audience will feel one way early in the term (when fees have just been paid) but may have different attitudes in the middle of the term when the sting of sudden poverty has faded.

At times, the speaking situation carries with it built-in attitudes of what topics can be appropriately addressed. If a union organizer speaks to a group of men in a bar after a day's work in the factory, the audience will undoubtedly expect to hear a straightforward, frank, nuts-and-bolts approach to whatever topic is discussed. When talking to the same group in a church service on Sunday morning, a speaker may be permitted to become more abstract and more moralistic as well. To the best of our knowledge, there are very few universal standards for judging propriety in a persuasive speaking situation. By remembering that there is no such thing as an *inherently* good reason, a speaker will be careful to filter his or her thoughts through situationally sensitive sieves. In persuasion, as in the newspaper business, there is nothing so stale as yesterday's attitudes.

The persuasive speaker deals in a world of probabilities, a world in which biases and prejudices determine much, a world in which facts are neither hard nor cold. Situational analysis helps us cope somewhat with this built-in source of frustrations. Yes, people are contrary animals, and they are not easily predicted. But they *are* somewhat "imprisoned" by their reference groups and demographic heritage, they normally reveal something about themselves when they behave publicly, and they usually are highly responsive to their immediate surroundings. Knowing these things, the speaker has more than an even chance of generating good reasons for the listeners he or she wishes to influence.

Generating Good Reasons

Essentially, situational analysis introduces us to the audience's pool of good reasons. Eventually, you will want to reach into that pool and use some of these good reasons in the service of the new idea you're attempting to support. But first, let's turn back to the new idea itself—the thesis statement. We need to discover, first, what *might* be a good reason or a set of good reasons for accepting this new idea. Since the speaker already has good reasons for accepting the thesis, and since he or she wants the audience to accept the thesis for some of the same reasons, the speaker must discover arguments that can serve as common ground for agreement between him- or herself and the audience.

Finding Common Ground

The speaker should take a good hard look at the thesis statement and ask, What are all the possible good reasons for accepting this idea? Why would a reasonable person want to agree with this thesis statement? Regardless of why *I* believe in the thesis statement, why should *other people* be moved to agree with me?

As we noted earlier, a good reason for accepting a thesis statement is an idea, need, or value that seems to be consistent with that thesis statement. Suppose that one's thesis is that capital punishment should be abolished in the United States. What ideas might be "borrowed" from the audience's pool of good reasons and used on behalf of the capital punishment argument? A concern for the rights of racial minorities might stimulate one to advocate the abolishing of capital punishment because a disproportionate number of minority group members are executed. The Judeo-Christian belief in the value of mercy would also be consistent with such a proposition. A desire to avoid executing someone who might possibly be innocent would also motivate many people to advocate doing away with capital punishment.

As we mentioned in Chapter 9, common ground just doesn't exist. There is no *necessary* relationship between capital punishment and the three good reasons we have just mentioned. It is the persuader who must forge the linkages between these diverse ideas. Thus, when hunting for good reasons, a speaker is wise to generate as many commonly accepted premises as he or she can so that a great number of these linkages will be available for use.

Reckoning with Objections

On almost any topic, almost any audience will also have ideas and beliefs that will be *inconsistent* or even *opposed* to the thesis statement. For instance, many people believe in the simple justice of an eye for an eye. Others believe that even the remotest possibility that dangerous criminals would harm others a second time should be eliminated. As the speaker puts together a set of good reasons supportive of the thesis statement, therefore, he or she should also construct a list of objections

—reasons why a fair person might oppose the thesis statement being presented. On the subject of abolishing capital punishment, a fairly complete list of good reasons might look like the following:

THESIS: CAPITAL PUNISHMENT IN THE UNITED STATES SHOULD BE ABOLISHED

Good Reasons for the Thesis	*Good Reasons Against the Thesis*
1. A concern for racial minority rights	10. A belief in simple justice
2. A desire to avoid killing someone who may be innocent	11. A desire to keep criminals from harming others in the future
3. A belief in the value of mercy	12. A desire to keep rehabilitive costs to government at a minimum
4. A belief in the possibility of rehabilitating criminals	
5. A belief that the Constitution forbids "cruel and unusual punishment"	13. A desire to make criminals suffer for their wrongs
6. A concern for the families of prisoners	14. A belief that execution is more humane than life imprisonment
7. A distaste for the violent and gruesome methods used in execution	15. A desire to deter other criminals from committing similar crimes
8. A belief that criminals should be put to work constructively by serving the state and their victims	16. A belief that victims of crimes should have a chance for revenge through execution
9. A desire to see the criminal punished and a belief that life imprisonment is the harshest punishment	

It is especially important that the persuader be aware of what *might* be argued on each side of the thesis. Most audiences will have conflicting beliefs on most issues a persuader deals with because persuaders always deal in the realm of the probable. It is not unreasonable to believe, for instance, that an audience may be concerned for the families of prisoners (good reason no. 6) *and* want to see future crimes deterred (no. 15). So, persuasive speakers need to be aware of both pros and cons. As we mentioned in Chapter 9, it is sometimes wise for a speaker to mention (and dismiss) the arguments opposed to the thesis so that the listener doesn't spend his or her time discounting what the speaker says *while* the speaker is saying it.

Narrowing the Focus of Appeal

Another job for the speaker is that of focusing the number of good reasons to be used in the speech. Nobody can reasonably cover in a single speech all of the good reasons supportive of a thesis and downplay all the reasons opposed to it. But how can a speaker narrow the range of issues he or she wants to discuss?

One good method is to look for *clusters* of good reasons, reasons that psychologically "go together" and that are consistent with one another logically. The idea that drivers should obey a 55 mile per hour speed limit, for instance, clusters with the idea that people should buy smaller cars in an energy-precious era. Both ideas also cluster with the notion that people should use less energy when heating their homes. These ideas are linked together by the more general desire to avoid having to import expensive foreign oil.

Now, let's consider again the list of good reasons surrounding the issue of capital punishment. Since nobody can cover all of these good reasons in one persuasive message, let's narrow the choices by asking if there are any usable clusters of good reasons. For instance, good reasons 9 and 4 are both good reasons not to execute criminals. But reason 9 is vindictive, whereas reason 4 is more constructive. Since it is unlikely that a single audience will hold both attitudes, a speaker really cannot use both arguments in the same speech. On the other hand, good reasons 1 and 2 *do* seem to cluster because both are concerned with the rights of individuals. Good reasons 5 and 7 cluster together because they center on the violence involved in capital punishment. Good reasons 4, 6, and 8 cluster together because all seek to promote the well-being of society in general, including families and victims of the criminals as well as the criminals themselves. By going through a list of good reasons in this fashion, a speaker begins to develop major themes or arguments that will (1) bring coherence to his or her persuasive case and (2) simplify the scope of ideas the audience will be asked to inspect during the speaking event.

The next step, of course, is to choose among the *clusters* of good reasons. One good way to do this is to inspect what has been learned via situational analysis. For example, when addressing the American Civil Liberties Union, the cluster of good reasons 1 and 2 will be most persuasive because that audience is most concerned with individual rights. When speaking to a group of city or state government officials, on the other hand, the cluster of good reasons 4, 6, and 8 might be chosen because such an audience would be most concerned with the families and victims of criminals who remain under their jurisdiction in society. Pacifists, in contrast, might favor good reasons 5 and 7 because they cluster around a dislike for violence.

No textbook, of course, can provide very much additional help with regard to generating good reasons. When preparing a persuasive message, the very best insurance policy is careful and detailed research in the subject matter of your speech. Library research and other types of fact-gathering will give you a well-rounded perspective on the issue in question. When doing your research, be especially sure to inform yourself about *objections* to the thesis you'll be supporting. The general rule of thumb in persuasive speaking seems to be that the more aware you are of why your proposal *shouldn't* be adopted, the more likely you'll be to get your audience to adopt it.

Testing Good Reasons for Completeness

Some people are born knowing how to put actual arguments together. From the cradle, these lucky individuals know what to say and how to say it when they wish to persuade others. Not everybody has that natural ability, however. Even persons who know the basic principles of persuasive speaking, who have analyzed their audience carefully, and who have collected the appropriate facts and figures still may have trouble putting together all of their information into *particular* arguments. Fortunately (for that perplexed majority of speakers), Professor Stephen Toulmin has constructed a model of argumentation.[2] We present that model here because we feel it will help you to test the goodness of your good reasons *before* you actually present your case to your audience.

The parts of the Toulmin model describe what speakers need to build into an argument for it to be *ideally* persuasive. Speakers can use the model as a checklist to insure they have familiarized themselves with the essential parts of a good argument. Thus, the Toulmin model can help us test the overall completeness of the argument we have generated. In this sense, it is a helpful form of homework.

Major Argumentative Tests

In its complete form, the Toulmin model appears as follows:

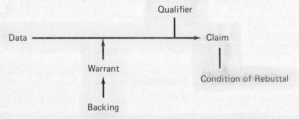

First, to have a good argument, a speaker must argue a clear and definite point. Everyone has suffered through speakers who pile evi-

[2] S. Toulmin, *The Uses of Argument* (Cambridge, Mass.: Cambridge University Press, 1958).

dence on top of evidence, who appeal to every value known to human-kind, but who never quite seem to draw a conclusion. So, a speaker should be sure that the *claim* or conclusion of the argument is clearly formulated in his or her mind and that—at some point in the speech—the listeners are presented with the speaker's basic request of them.

Suppose, for example, that Honduras has had an earthquake and that a speaker wishes to urge that U.S. aid be sent to that country. Naturally, a speaker could compose a speech on this topic by simply generating many different restatements of this claim. Such a strategy seems foolish, however, especially when listeners are likely to resist such a notion. The simple asserting of a claim does not make an argument. A speaker must support the claim with evidence, testimony, examples, facts and figures, and so on. Toulmin calls these items *data*. A speaker claiming that the United States should aid Honduras might support such a claim by dramatizing the extent of the earthquake damage, by showing vivid examples of great devastation, or by presenting the testimony of Honduran leaders that aid is vitally needed to save lives. The argument might then look like this:

> 1. Statistics showing damage ⟶ The United States should
> 2. Examples of devastation   give aid to Honduras.
> 3. Testimony of need from leaders

Data and claims rarely pass for arguments by themselves, however. They need help to make a really persuasive argument. If you stop to think about the relationship between the data and the claim in our Honduras argument, you'll see that the data *by themselves* don't really justify the claim. Suppose, for example, that an audience for some reason hates Honduras and wishes that country ill. For such an audience, the data do not justify the claim. What, then, is missing from our developing argument? A *warrant*, or a statement that allows an arguer to justify a claim given a set of data, is perhaps the essential part of any argument. In ordinary language, a warrant justifies somebody's doing something; a search warrant justifies the police's search of a drug dealer's home, for instance.

A warrant justifies a claim because it appeals to or expresses a value, a rule, or a *set of principles* in which the audience believes. Because this is true, speakers can use situational analysis to discover the "warranting potential" lying within the audience. In the Honduras example, which rules or values justify the claim (send aid) given the available data (great devastation and need)? Humanitarianism, the desire to help others, and respect for the sanctity of life all justify drawing such a claim from that data; if the audience holds any of those values or rules, then appealing to them on such bases should make a persuasive argument if, of course, the speaker can artfully heighten in listeners' minds the continued importance of such values and rules. After all, in the hustle and bustle of daily life, it is often possible to forget, momentarily, exactly what sorts of things are most important to us as listeners.

Persuaders should pay close attention to the warrants they use because different audiences may need to hear different values and rules linked to the data before they can accept a particular claim. An audience of hard-bitten business people, for instance, may not be moved by an argument based on humanitarian values, but a speaker may persuade them to aid Honduras by using warrants such as, "Aiding other countries is good for the national image," or "Aiding other countries keeps out communists." Notice that different warrants can justify the same claim to different audiences. Arguers should, therefore, ask which warrants will be most persuasive for the particular audience they are facing.

Thus, at this point in our "logical homework," the overall argument appears as follows:

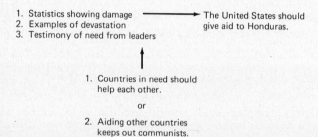

1. Statistics showing damage   → The United States should
2. Examples of devastation   give aid to Honduras.
3. Testimony of need from leaders

↑

1. Countries in need should
   help each other.

or

2. Aiding other countries
   keeps out communists.

Minor Argumentative Tests

Data, claim, and warrant are the major parts of any persuasive argument. Speakers need all three to have a complete argument. But Toulmin calls our attention to three other argumentative structures that might be necessary for inclusion in certain instances. Sometimes, for example, the warrant used in an argument needs support, especially if the audience also holds values or rules opposed to the claim being argued. Speakers can usually provide *backing* to explain why the warrant being used in the argument is a good and reasonable value or rule to follow. A speaker might give backing for the warrant "Aiding other countries keeps out communists" by giving examples of where that value or rule has proven true and reliable in the past. For example:

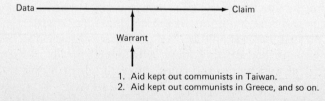

Data ————————————————→ Claim

↑

Warrant

↑

1. Aid kept out communists in Taiwan.
2. Aid kept out communists in Greece, and so on.

The strength with which a speaker wishes to make a claim also must be made explicit on occasion. Over- or underarguing a claim can lead an audience to reject it completely. So, persuaders may need to include in their arguments brief statements—called *qualifiers*—about how strongly the claim is meant to be taken: "*Certainly* the United States should send aid," or "*Maybe* the United States should send aid," or "*Only if it will keep out communists* should the United States send aid."

To every rule there is an exception, some set of conditions under which one would reasonably disobey the rule. We might make it a rule never to kick a dog, but we can surely imagine conditions under which we would break the rule: The dog is rabid and attacking us, the dog is about to run into a busy street, and so on. Sometimes, an audience thinks of certain conditions under which the warrant appealed to, even though generally a good one, should be set aside. These elements of argument are *conditions of rebuttal.*

For instance, it may be true that one country should generally help another needy country. But if Honduras (1) has just become fabulously wealthy from discovery of oil and (2) is notorious for its anti-American violence, those specific conditions may make it difficult to argue for our claim. A speaker will usually not want to raise a condition of rebuttal against his or her own argument! Rather, speakers should be aware that the audience may raise such objections in their own minds. In such circumstances, the persuader should include in his or her argument explanations of why likely conditions of rebuttal are *not valid.* For instance, "It is true that Honduras has found oil, but the earthquake destroyed their oil rigs, so they still need our help." In other words, the condition of rebuttal should be seen as a warning indicator useful for reminding yourself that the audience will fail to "plug in" the necessary warrant in certain cases.

The most useful feature of the Toulmin model, we feel, is that it helps you to sketch out the case you're going to make in broad brush strokes. By examining your essential argument in this fashion, you can then outline your speech and structure your thoughts in ways that will help listeners move easily from the data to the claim. Thus, the Toulmin model can be used as a checklist: Do I have a definite claim, is it supported by data, and is the claim justified by a warrant? Does the warrant need backing or does the claim need a qualifier? Do I need to argue explicitly that no conditions of rebuttal exist that might weaken my warrant? Answers to questions such as these can tell us much about the basic completeness of a persuader's case.

Testing Good Reasons for Suitability

No matter how good an argument may look when sketched out on paper, it takes much more to be truly persuasive. An argument must be complete, but it must also be carefully adjusted to local tastes. To dramatize this point, let us consider the case of a would-be president.

In the 1960 presidential campaign, John F. Kennedy faced a great deal of opposition to his candidacy because he was a member of the Roman Catholic Church. A number of people feared that if he were elected, Kennedy would follow the dictates of the Church rather than the interests of the United States when making decisions. Kennedy decided to address this religious issue by speaking to the Greater Houston Ministerial Association, a group of predominantly Southern Baptist ministers.

We will use Kennedy's speech as a good example of how a persuasive case can be made suitable for particular listeners. We will see that Kennedy analyzed his audience to determine the values and beliefs they held most strongly, used those values and beliefs to support his thesis, and answered objections to his candidacy that the audience harbored.

John F. Kennedy, Address to the Greater Houston Ministerial Association, September 12, 1960.

(1) I am grateful for your generous invitation to state my views. While the so-called religious issue is necessarily and properly the chief topic here tonight, I want to emphasize from the outset that I believe that we have far more critical issues in the 1960 election: the spread of Communist influence, until it now festers only ninety miles off the coast of Florida—the humiliating treatment of our President and Vice President by those who no longer respect our power—the hungry children I saw in West Virginia, the old people who cannot pay their doctor's bills, the families forced to give up their farms—an America with too many slums, with too few schools, and too late to the moon and outer space.

(2) These are the real issues which should decide this campaign. And they are not religious issues—for war and hunger and ignorance and despair know no religious barrier.

(3) But because I am a Catholic and no Catholic has ever been elected President, the real issues in this campaign have been obscured—perhaps deliberately in some quarters less responsible than this. So it is apparently necessary for me to state once again—not what kind of church I believe in, for that should be important only to me, but what kind of America I believe in.

(4) I believe in an America where the separation of church and state is absolute—where no Catholic prelate would tell the President (should he be a Catholic) how to act and no Protestant minister would tell his parishioners for whom to vote—where no church or church school is granted any public funds or political preference—and where no man is denied public office merely because his religion differs from the President who might appoint him or the people who might elect him.

(5) I believe in an America that is neither officially Catholic, Protestant,

nor Jewish—where no public official either requests or accepts instruction on public policy from the Pope, the National Council of Churches or any other ecclesiastical source—where no religious body seeks to impose its will directly or indirectly upon the general populace or the public acts of its officials— and where religious liberty is so indivisible that an act against one church is treated as an act against all.

(6) For while this year it may be a Catholic against whom the finger of suspicion is pointed, in other years it has been, and may someday be again, a Jew—or a Quaker—or a Unitarian—or a Baptist. It was Virginia's harassment of Baptist preachers, for example, that led to Jefferson's statute of religious freedom. Today I may be the victim—but tomorrow it may be you—until the whole fabric of our harmonious society is ripped apart at a time of great national peril.

(7) Finally, I believe in an America where religious intolerance will someday end—where all men and all churches are treated as equal—where every man has the same right to attend or not attend the church of his choice —where there is no Catholic vote, no anti-Catholic vote, no bloc voting of any kind—and where Catholics, Protestants and Jews, both the lay and the pastoral level, will refrain from those attitudes of disdain and division which have so often marred their works in the past, and promote instead the American ideal of brotherhood.

(8) That is the kind of America in which I believe. And it represents the kind of Presidency in which I believe—a great office that must be neither humbled by making it the instrument of any religious group, nor tarnished by arbitrarily withholding it, its occupancy, from the members of any religious group. I believe in a President whose views on religion are his own private affair, neither imposed by him upon the nation nor imposed by the nation upon him as a condition to holding that office.

(9) I would not look with favor upon a President working to subvert the First Amendment's guarantee of religious liberty (nor would our system of checks and balances permit him to do so). And neither do I look with favor upon those who would work to subvert Article VI of the Constitution by requiring a religious test—even by indirection—for if they disagree with that safeguard, they should be openly working to repeal it.

(10) I want a Chief Executive whose public acts are responsible to all and obligated to none—who can attend any ceremony, service or dinner his office may appropriately require him to fulfill—and whose fulfillment of his Presidential office is not limited or conditioned by any religious oath, ritual, or obligation.

(11) This is the kind of America I believe in—and this is the kind of America I fought for in the South Pacific and the kind my brother died for in Europe. No one suggested then that we might have a "divided loyalty," that we did "not believe in liberty," or that we belonged to a disloyal group that threatened the "freedoms for which our forefathers died."

(12) And in fact this is the kind of America for which our forefathers did die when they fled here to escape religious test oaths that denied office to members of less favored churches, when they fought for the Constitution, the Bill of Rights, the Virginia Statute of Religious Freedom—and when they fought at the shrine I visited today—the Alamo. For side by side with Bowie and Crockett died Fuentes and McCafferty and Bailey and Bedillo and Carey—but no one knows whether they were Catholics or not. For there was no religious test there.

(13) I ask you tonight to follow in that tradition, to judge me on the basis of fourteen years in the Congress—and on my declared stands against an ambassador to the Vatican, against unconstitutional aid to parochial schools, and against any boycott of the public schools (which I attended myself)—instead of judging me on the basis of these pamphlets and publications we have all seen using carefully selected quotations out of context from the statements of Catholic Church leaders, usually in other countries, frequently in other centuries, and rarely relevant to any situation here—and always omitting, of course, that statement of the American bishops in 1948 which strongly endorsed church-state separation.

(14) I do not consider these other quotations binding upon my public acts —why should you? But let me say, with respect to other countries, that I am wholly opposed to the state being used by any religious group, Catholic or Protestant, to compel, prohibit or persecute the free exercise of any other religion. And that goes for any persecution at any time, by anyone, in any country.

(15) And I hope that you and I condemn with equal fervor those nations which deny their Presidency to Protestants and those which deny it to Catholics. And rather than cite the misdeeds of those who differ, I would also cite the record of the Catholic Church in such nations as France and Ireland . . . and the independence of such statesmen as De Gaulle and Adenauer.

(16) But let me stress again that these are my views—for contrary to common newspaper usage, I am not the Catholic candidate for President. I am the Democratic Party's candidate for President, who happens also to be a Catholic. I do not speak for my church on public matters—and the church does not speak for me.

(17) Whatever issue may come before me as President, if I should be elected —on birth control, divorce, censorship, gambling, or any other subject—I will make my decision in accordance with these views, in accordance with what my conscience tells me to be in the national interest, and without regard to outside religious pressure or dictate. And no power or threat of punishment could cause me to decide otherwise.

(18) But if the time should ever come—and I do not concede any conflict to be remotely possible—when my office should require me to either violate

my conscience or violate the national interest, then I would resign the office, I hope any other conscientious public servant would do likewise.

(19) But I do not intend to apologize for these views to my critics of either Catholic or Protestant faith, nor do I intend to disavow either my views or my church in order to win this election. If I should lose on the real issues, I shall return to my seat in the Senate, satisfied that I tried my best and was fairly judged.

(20) But if this election is decided on the basis that forty million Americans lost their chance of being President on the day they were baptized, then it is the whole nation that will be the loser in the eyes of Catholics and non-Catholics around the world, in the eyes of history, and in the eyes of our own people.

(21) But if, on the other hand, I should win this election, I shall devote every effort of mind and spirit to fulfilling the oath of the Presidency— practically identical, I might add, with the oath I have taken for fourteen years in the Congress. For, without reservation, I can, and I quote, "Solemnly swear that I will faithfully execute the office of President of the United States and will to the best of my ability preserve, protect, and defend the Constitution, so help me God."[3]

Appealing to Good Reasons

Although we have talked quite a bit about the importance of good reasons, we have not yet discussed how these good reasons can be appealed to in concrete situations. How do speakers actually use such good reasons to prove a point? We conceive of five major ways.

The thesis is consistent with good reasons the audience presently holds. For instance, we might have expected that Kennedy's audience believed in the American ideal of brotherhood. They probably also felt that people should live in peace and harmony with one another. Kennedy's thesis is that religious intolerance toward him should come to an end. In paragraph 7, he shows that this thesis is *consistent* with that "American ideal of brotherhood." Another argument that Kennedy makes is based on his audience's belief in patriotism, that fighting for one's country shows a selfless sort of love. He argues in paragraph 11 that his religion makes him no less patriotic than the next person since *he* fought for his country in the South Pacific, and his brother died on America's behalf in Europe during World War II. Through such techniques, Kennedy proved himself to be a sterling student of the common premise approach we mentioned in Chapter 9.

[3]Reprinted in T. White, *The Making of the President, 1960* (New York: Atheneum, 1961), pp. 427–430.

The thesis meets the audience's unmet needs. Often, people accept new ideas because they sense a serious sort of deprivation in their lives. Kennedy suggests in his speech that voting for him for president, regardless of his religion, will meet certain important, currently unmet needs. He lists some of those needs in the first paragraph: "the spread of Communist influence . . . the hungry children . . . too many slums," and so on. Naturally, it takes some amount of persuasive skill to fully establish that *you*, as speaker, are in the best position to mollify the problems you've pointed to.

The thesis strengthens and secures presently held values and met needs. An audience will often accept new ideas because they strengthen and secure those things that the audience already hold dear. Sometimes, by listening to new ideas we can keep needs that are presently being met from becoming unmet needs in the future. For instance, candidate Kennedy argues in paragraph 6 that the cherished notion of religious freedom might fall apart if his thesis is not accepted: "Today I may be the victim—but tomorrow it may be you." He also appeals to patriotism and to pride in America, arguing that unless his conceptualization of religious tolerance is accepted, "the whole nation . . . will be the loser . . ."

The thesis has real-life consequences for listeners. The methods of supporting ideas that we mentioned in Chapter 6 really have one main function: to show that the speaker's argument makes a difference *here and now*, that it relates to the real world. Perhaps this is why audiences love statistics, if they can understand them. Few things convince people to accept ideas like cold, hard numbers. Thus, as John Kennedy reminds us in paragraph 20, "forty million American Catholics" are not to be trifled with.

Using the testimony of others in support of a thesis also helps to anchor a speaker's remarks in the world of his or her contemporaries, as does the judicious use of concrete examples. Thus, Kennedy refers to the stand taken by "the American bishops in 1948" during his speech and in paragraph 15 praises De Gaulle of France and Adenauer of West Germany as men who were fiercely independent politically, albeit Catholics as well. Kennedy also argues that fighting for one's country is more than adequate proof of loyalty and patriotism. In support of that appeal, Kennedy mentions his own wartime experiences in paragraph 11 and the men who fought and died in the Alamo in paragraph 12. All of these devices help to convince listeners that what the speaker is saying makes a difference.

The thesis adequately answers listeners' objections. Persuaders typically use one of two methods for answering an audience's objections. *Preempting objections* requires a speaker to convince listeners that their reasons for opposing the thesis are actually the best reasons in the world to *support* the thesis. For example, in the capital punishment speech mentioned earlier, an audience may oppose the suggested abolition of capital punishment because of their desire to keep costs to society at a minimum. But the speaker can argue that such sentiments actually favor the thesis. That is, criminals, when kept alive, can be put to work to support themselves, their families, and their victims' families. Thus, economic wisdom actually requires one to be *against* capital punishment.

In John Kennedy's speech, the audience might oppose him because they interpreted statements made by Catholic leaders as suggesting that a Catholic president would be a mere tool of the Vatican. But in paragraph 13, Kennedy argues that if the opinions of Church officials are of any concern to the audience, then the audience should actually *support* him. After all, he reminds his audience, statements that suggest that American Catholic presidents cannot be independent were made in "other countries" and in "other centuries." The most reliable statements, he suggests, were issued by the American bishops in 1948 when they *supported* the separation of church and state in America.

Sometimes, objections cannot be preempted. Instead, they must be answered as they stand. One way to do so is to argue that the objection is *not relevant* to the topic. If an audience favors capital punishment because execution deters future crimes, for example, the speaker can argue that execution has had little deterrent value in the past. Therefore, a concern for future crimes is not relevant to the topic of capital punishment.

A second way to answer an objection is to argue that the objection is *not as strong* as the audience first thought it to be. If the audience favors capital punishment because they wish to keep convicted criminals from harming others, the speaker can present arguments and statistics to show that very few murderers, for instance, murder repeatedly, and that most murderers commit their crimes in moments of blind passion. Therefore, the problem of repeated murders becomes less an issue than the audience first thought.

Finally, the speaker can argue that objections are *outweighed* by other good reasons. Suppose, for example, that an audience endorses capital punishment because of simple justice—an eye for an eye and a tooth for a tooth.

In such circumstances, a speaker can argue that the value of mercy is a value more worthy of cherishing than is that of simple justice. Similarly, when answering the objection that a Catholic president might follow the dictates of religion instead of respond to the requirements of the national interest, Kennedy argues in paragraph 18 that in the event of such a conflict the national interest would have to outweigh religious sentiments, and that any public servant facing such a dilemma would simply have to resign. When preparing a persuasive speech, then, you should remember that *all* arguments have their counterarguments, and that there is no such thing in the probabalistic world of persuasion as incontravertible argument.

The Preparation Format

As a kind of "preflight checklist" for your excursions into persuasion, the preparation format presented below may help you draw together some of the information we've mentioned in the first ten chapters. As we see it, the preparation format constitutes a record of your precommunicative thoughts. We are not suggesting that the format be used while speaking. Rather, our format may be a way of assuring yourself that you have the bases covered *prior* to speaking.

The primary purpose of such a checklist is to help you clarify to yourself what ends you will be seeking in a given persuasive situation as well as what means are available to you to reach these ends. The preparation format can act as a kind of reminder of some of the demands placed upon you by your subject, audience, situation, and even by you yourself.

Perhaps the most basic value of the preparation format is that it helps you get the "stuff" of your message together before you engage in talk, so that while talking, you will be free to adapt to the situational demands that persuasive speaking always entails. The rationale here is not complex. Why not get your communicative homework done before speaking, so that when the heat of interaction hits, you will have one thing less to worry about? Thus, instead of being a way of preparing *a* communication, the format is a means of preparing *for* communication. Table 10–1, therefore, asks some questions you will be wise to answer before speaking.

Suggestions for Speaking

It is a fundamental tenet of persuasion that people do the things they do for good reasons. Sometimes, of course, other persons' "good reasons" may seem foolish or selfish or ill-considered to us. When we make such observations, we are often prompted to launch persuasion ourselves, thus continuing the endless cycle of human influence. Much of life, in such a scheme, is a matter of convincing others that our best reasons are so compelling and of such immediate importance that they should join our cause for good reasons of their own. Thus, although we may fail to use persuasion successfully, it is a fact that we cannot avoid persuasive contacts in toto. As you seek out good reasons in your own persuasive life, you should keep the thoughts listed on page 286 in mind:

Table 10-1   The Preparation Format

Questions	Commentary
1. *Audience* — How much does the audience know about my subject? — How interested in the subject are they at present? — What attitudes of theirs might create resistance in them to my proposal? — Is there any significant common ground now existing between me and them? — How will I demonstrate my commitment to the audience?	Naturally, many of these questions will not be of crucial concern in some situations. If the audience knows very little about the topic, for example, their attitudes and prejudices may not present significant obstacles to a speaker. Still, the answers to these questions could suggest message options to a speaker that he or she may have not considered otherwise.
2. *Speaker* — What does the audience currently think of me in general? — Do they see me as having made any special commitment to this subject and proposal? — To what extent can I rely on my own thoughts and experiences when preparing my message? — Will I have to borrow from other sources in order to establish or reinforce my credibility?	Obviously, self-analysis is very difficult. We never know for sure what others think about us, but we do "make bets" about their perceptions of us each time we engage others in spoken interaction. Thus, the answers to these questions may help you to better lay your bets about your social image and make use of that image in communication.

Table 10-1 (Continued)

Questions	Commentary
3. *Subject* — What constraints are placed upon me by the nature of the topic being discussed? — Does the topic itself prescribe any appeals or strategies that might be used effectively? — Are there certain aspects of this topic that must be discussed above all else? — Are there certain aspects of this topic that should be precluded from discussion?	Some topics seem to have built-in communicative limitations, but only detailed inspection of the topic as it relates to the audience will substantiate this. For example, who could wax eloquently about garbage? Paul Erlich can. In addition, some themes seem to "jump out" of a subject (e.g., who could discuss leukemia without mentioning its effects on children?), but certain aspects of a topic are sometimes best left unmentioned.
4. *Situation* — Are there any existing psychological aspects of the situation that impinge on the audience? — Are there any existing physical aspects of the situation that may affect my communicative strategies? — Will alterations in the physical or psychological setting be required for me to achieve the effect I desire? — Will my own nonverbal behavior be a significant force in this interaction?	This potpourri of factors can have great impact on our interactions. Aspects of time, space, and physiology may advance or retard our persuasive efforts. Oftentimes, simple alterations in a seating arrangement can create a feeling of intimacy. Similarly, visual aids can add much to the clarity and impact of a spoken message.
5. *Projected Response* What specific response would I like the audience to make to me? _____ _____ _____ _____	Naturally, listeners have a way of frustrating your intentions, but if you have some idea of what you would like them to know or feel as a result of your speech, you are a bit ahead of the game. Knowing what response you would like the audience to make will give you some basis for gauging your impact on them.

6. Central Idea

What one central idea would I like them to remember after they have forgotten the details of the message?

_____

_____

_____

_____

Nichols and Stevens have estimated that after a short time, listeners retain no more than 25 percent of what they hear from a speaker.[4] Thus, our assumption here is that if information can be "packaged" by means of one main thought, the postspeech "residue" in a listener's mind will stand a chance of being a fair representation of the speaker's proposal. Listeners will rarely provide such focus themselves; thus a clearly articulated central idea may assist them in putting the pieces of the speech together. Also, a clearly understood central idea will give the speaker a focal point to fall back on when the pressures of give-and-take interaction become pronounced.

7. Subpoints

— What subpoints will be necessary to reinforce the central idea and add clarity and force to the message?

A._____

B._____

C._____

D._____

E._____

— What unique communicative function is being served by each of these subpoints?

The obvious thing to remember about subpoints is that they should not cloud out the central idea. Some listeners are so enamored by details that the speaker must take pains to insure that the subpoints refocus listeners on the essential information he or she would like them to take away from the communication situation. Speculating about the functions of the subpoints will help to refocus you, the speaker, on the essentials of communication (e.g., does the subpoint reinforce your credibility, summarize previous remarks, reorient the listener, add concreteness, demonstrate message or audience commitment, etc?).

[4]R. Nichols and L. Stevens, _Are You Listening?_ (New York: McGraw-Hill, 1957).

Table 10-1 (Continued)

Questions	Commentary
8. *Supporting Material* — What methods of demonstration will be necessary to clarify, vivify, and reinforce the main and subcontentions? — Do I have any reason to believe that these devices will be effective for this particular audience? — How, specifically, will I use such supporting material?	As we saw in Chapter 5, some methods of clarification are better than others for vivifying (e.g., the extended example), while still others are effective in adding a substantial tone (e.g., testimony) to a speaker's remarks. One basic tenet that must be remembered in regard to supporting materials is that such materials must not be stressed to the extent that listeners fail to focus on the central idea being argued for.
9. *Structure* — Is there any specific plan to the ordering of the message components? — Have I chosen my opening and closing remarks for the best persuasive reasons? — Am I ready to reorient and summarize when the necessity arises?	Most research in message structuring tells us that the sequence of our verbalizations can have dramatic consequences on listeners' reactions. Randomly structured speech elements tend to foster confusion. Since listeners themselves will structure message stimuli in some fashion (a fashion not always favorable to the speaker's purposes), it behooves the speaker to assist listeners in structuring materials in ways that will continually refocus them on the residual message the speaker wishes to impart.
10. *Language* — Should any connotative or denotative problems arise in regard to the types of terms I plan to use? — Are there any terms I plan to use that need to be defined in order to prevent confusion from arising? — Are there any verbal images available for use that will add depth or clarity to my remarks?	Since listeners often respond quickly to certain words (e.g., the words *term paper* often provokes instantaneous negative reactions in students), the speaker is advised to think ahead of time which terms might be troublesome to listeners. Similarly, a clear, concise piece of verbal imagery can often provide linguistic economy and obviate the necessity of having to go into great detail on peripheral issues.

11. *Attention*
— What specific factors of attention are necessary to employ in order to channel listeners' perceptions?
— How, specifically, will I make use of these attention factors?
— Do I have any reason to believe that these factors will serve to focus attention on the central idea or subpoints?
— Will I have any trouble in sustaining attention for the duration of the speech?

Attention is easy to get but often difficult to maintain. Also, a listener's attention has a tendency to scatter, and thus the speaker must constantly be on guard that his or her factors of attention (e.g., humor) are serving to "constrict" the attentive powers of listeners so that they are forced back, again and again, to give the speaker and proposal due consideration.

12. *Motivation*
— How will I demonstrate an awareness of and tolerance for the listeners' value systems?
— What needs and desires of the audience's can be tapped in order to win their adherence to my proposal?
— How, specifically, will I attempt to motivate them to move to the position I am advocating?
— How will I overcome possible apathy or hostility to me or my proposal?
— How will I demonstrate that my message is worth listening to?

Listeners often do not possess an inherent motivation to listen. Before listeners will open their minds to a new body of information or attitudes, they must be satisfied that their lives can be materially improved by the speaker's assertions. Above all, a speaker must demonstrate to listeners that the "gift" of their attention and adherence will be rewarded with important and interesting discourse, and, ideally, with substantive gain.

1. In persuasion, try to give listeners the feeling that the proposal you are advocating is a natural extension of directions in which they are already tending.

2. Because people agree more readily about abstract matters than about concrete matters, be especially choosy about the specific examples you use *early* in your speech.

3. Even though all of us identify with certain reference groups, few of us like to admit such "dependence"; therefore, don't make careless attributions about your audience in their presence.

4. Don't be glib when presenting large-scale statistical information; always try to show the "local consequences" of such data.

5. While it is good to have at hand a number of different reasons to support your thesis, using too many of them will cause your audience to be suspicious of your selectivity.

6. Never underestimate candor; looking at your audience directly and admitting that you disagree with them on some issue can be a prudent course of action.

7. When speaking to a hostile audience, never save your proposal until the conclusion lest you be viewed as a coward.

8. Don't underestimate the power of careful phrasing since language has great power to color ideas; sometimes, the elimination of bothersome bits of jargon or hackneyed expressions can open up listeners' minds.

9. When dealing with a hostile audience, don't allow your voice to become shrill, even though your frustration at their resistance will push you in that direction.

10. Don't just scan our preparation format; *use it.*

UNIT IV

Special Challenges in Public Communication

CHAPTER 11

The Reinforcing Speech

Be seated.

I want you to remember that no bastard ever won a war by dying for his country.

He won it by making the other poor dumb bastard die for his country.

Men, all this stuff you've heard about America not wanting to fight, wanting to stay out of the war, is a lot of horse dung.

Americans traditionally love to fight.

All real Americans love the sting of battle.

When you were kids, you all admired the champion marble shooter, the fastest runner, the big league ball player, the toughest boxer.

Americans love the winner and will not tolerate a loser.

Americans play to win all the time.

(I wouldn't give a hoot in hell for a man who lost and laughed.)

That's why Americans have never lost and will never lose a war.

Because the very thought of losing is hateful to Americans.

Now, an army is a team.

It lives, eats, sleeps, fights as a team.

This individuality stuff is a bunch of crap.

The bilious bastards who wrote that stuff about individuality for the *Saturday Evening Post* don't know anything more about real battle than they do about fornicating!

Now, we have the finest food and equipment, the best spirit, and the best men in the world.

You know, my God, I actually pity those poor bastards we're going up against.

My God, I do.

We're not just going to shoot the bastards.

We're going to cut out their living guts and use them to grease the treads of our tanks!

We're going to murder those lousy Hun bastards by the bushel!

Now,

Some of you boys are wondering whether or not you'll chicken out under fire.

Don't worry about it.

I can assure you that you will all do your duty.

The Nazis are the enemy!

Wade into them!

Spill their blood!

Shoot them in the belly!

When you put your hand into a bunch of goo that a moment before was your best friend's face, you'll know what to do.

Now, there's another thing I want you to remember.

I don't want to get any messages saying that, "We are holding our position."

We're not holding anything.

Let the Hun do that.

We are advancing constantly and we're not interested in holding on anything except the enemy.

We're going to hold onto him by the nose and we're going to kick him in the ass!

We're going to kick the hell out of him all the time and we're going to go through him like crap through a goose!

Now, there's one thing that you men will be able to say when you get back home.

And you may thank God for it.

Thirty years from now when you're sitting around your fireside with your grandson on your knee, and he asks you, "What did you do in the great World War II?", you won't have to say, "Well, I shoveled shit in Louisiana."

All right, now, you sons of bitches; you know how I feel.

Go on.

I will be proud to lead you wonderful guys into battle anytime, anywhere.

That's all.[1]

[1]From the 20th Century-Fox release, *Patton*. Reprinted by permission.

This is Hollywood's version of General George S. ("Blood and Guts") Patton's speech to his men prior to the launching of an Allied attack in World War II. Patton's task was not that of reducing the complexity of ideas for his men, nor did he face collective hostility. Rather, his communicative job was that of heightening the emotions and feelings needed by his troops to reach their military objective.

This chapter deals with communication needed to keep men marching, churchgoers praying, and footballers charging. Such speaking events, of course, span a wide range of emotional intensity—from very strong emotion (Patton's speech or Rockne's "Get One for the Gipper" oration) to rather mild feelings (a speech of welcome to first-year students on campus). The sort of talk we will focus upon in this chapter constitutes some of our most ordinary experiences with public communication. We hear pep talks from teachers just before they give us exams, from parents prior to their sending us off to City U., and from preachers before they allow us to say "I do." All this chatter is designed not to inculcate new beliefs in us but to remind us to keep the faith.

Thus, in this chapter we will examine how a public speaker can keep his or her audience tending in the same direction. Even when we believe in something a good deal, we oftentimes let those commitments slide or forget just how much our beliefs mean to us. The busy world of everyday life sometimes blinds us to truths we have seen with great clarity at other times.

As we consider the various techniques useful for reinforcing ideas within listeners, you may want to return from time to time to Patton's

speech (if you can stomach it) to see how he attempted to overcome the fears and anxieties that threatened to undermine his troops' motivation, how he reinforced his audience's desire to do battle for Old Glory. Should you choose to reread the speech, you will find Patton relating past experiences that his men remembered fondly, the forces of evil that they denounced, the goals to which they aspired, and the obligations that they imposed upon themselves when they chose to wear a uniform and carry a weapon. After considering such sobering realities, you may want to scout around in locker rooms on Sunday afternoons to see if Patton talk is still alive.

Creating Group Concern

Religious services, fund-raising dinners, professional conventions, keynote addresses, and sales promotion meetings are all examples of speech used to sustain *group* concern. Such speeches are necessary because we humans are a forgetful lot. Sometimes, the speeches are local in origin, modest in scope, and limited in effect, but sometimes, they draw international attention.

For example, one of the most important steps in building the Western bloc as a political and economic force was John F. Kennedy's tour of Europe in 1963. The high point of his highly successful trip came in West Berlin, where he was given a veritable hero's reception. Almost two-thirds of the population of West Berlin poured into the streets, throwing flowers, waving flags, and cheering. After visiting the Berlin Wall and city hall (where he signed the Golden Book), Kennedy mounted the platform erected on the steps of the city hall and gave his "Ich Bin Ein Berliner" speech. Schlesinger reports that "the crowd shook itself and rose and roared like an animal," and Kennedy remarked, following the speech, that if he had said, "March to the wall —tear it down," the crowd would have done so.[2] There seems to be little question that Kennedy successfully cut across gaps of culture and geography to bring together rather diverse peoples. It is said that when Kennedy proclaimed, "I, too, am a Berliner!" there were few dry eyes in the audience—a rather remarkable set of circumstances, given the fragile American-German bonds that are said to have existed prior to Kennedy's speech.

To get some idea of the strategies available to the public speaker for reinforcing and inspiring listeners, let us consider General Edwin Walker, a one-time major general in the armed forces, a sometimes

[2]A. Schlesinger, *A Thousand Days* (Cambridge, Mass.: Riverside Press, 1965), pp. 884–885.

candidate for governor of Texas, and a perennial John Bircher. On a rather blustery evening in February of 1962, General Walker addressed an overflowing crowd of fellow conservatives in Chicago's McCormick Auditorium. Because he was addressing a similarly committed group of individuals, he proceeded in the following way:

Yesterday I was a soldier—a Major General in your Armed Forces. Today I am a Civilian. My aim and purpose has not changed. This is to keep the American eagle flying, and not to see it caged or become a "dead duck." My cause is national survival. . . .

Thirty years of military strategy and tactics have convinced me that we are not in "dire peril," but that the course of our national leadership has involved deception and misrepresentation of the American people. I would not degrade or limit the issue by unnecessarily criticizing individuals. Individuals as such, including card-carrying Communists, are not my basic concern. But I must criticize, and I give no quarter to, the total leadership responsible for our national peril from the date we recognized the Soviet Union 28 years ago. . . .

The American people are awakening. Who would have dreamed a year ago that we would be here tonight? When President Kennedy warned us of dire peril, he perhaps did not expect this response. He failed to realize the people of this Republic have been educated by the Tehran New Deal and the Camp David Coexistence Crusade. The United States has committed many national follies under the leadership of two decades of Potomac Pretenders, all in the name of One World. But the people of the United States are not going to commit national suicide by releasing their army from its responsibility when they are facing dire peril—even though they are being called superpatriots.

We have a duty to perform, and that is to restore and preserve the Constitution. We must release the Supreme Court and the State Department from the bonds of subversion and captivity. The Congress and the Military must be prevented from being captured by the enemy. Arouse your indignation and let it continue righteously until victory is achieved. Through faith in our Divine Savior, and loyalty to our beloved country, we shall meet the forces of darkness and destruction with light and truth that shatter their evil power to bits.

Put on the whole armor of God, so that you can speak boldly.
The order is: Attack on all fronts!
Your greatest weapon is the truth.
Man your weapon and speak boldly.[3]

[3] E. A. Walker, *Walker Speaks Unmuzzled* (Dallas: American Eagle Publishing Co., 1962), pp. 47–48, 64–65.

Although it would be interesting to concentrate on the political and psychological dimensions of Walker's remarks, we shall refrain from doing so. Rather, let us consider these excerpts from Walker's speech as an example of in-group talk used to intensify common motivations. While Walker's words alone cannot reveal all of the techniques found in speeches used to create concern, they do show common strategies used in such circumstances, some of which are as follows:

1. *Contrasting emotions.* One characteristic immediately evident in virtually all speeches seeking to revitalize commitments to values is a balancing of emotional opposites. We might call such an approach the "carrot and the club" strategy. Any number of persons have identified the strategy, but Samuel Johnson stated it succinctly when he once said that the two greatest movers of the human mind are the desire of good and the fear of evil. Stated another way (as it is applied to motivation), it involves urging an audience to accept our remarks because they will provide them with a tasty treat *and* prevent them from getting bashed over the head!

   Using both the carrot and the club in the same speech is rather like a "double whammy." This strategy is readily apparent in the Patton speech presented at the beginning of the chapter. Notice how the emotions of shame and pride, fear and security, and affection and hate are used by Patton to create a powerful emotional impact. Notice also how fellow militarist Walker contrasts God and communism, individuality and subjugation, and strength and defenselessness.

2. *Visualizing through imagery.* If you are astute, you will notice eagles, dead ducks, and monsters trotting through Walker's speech. While Freud might have a field day with such metaphors, this sort of imagery is most necessary when relatively abstract goals and values must be reinforced through speech. Such aspects of language give life to otherwise dormant values; they enliven otherwise trite expressions of ends and means. Notice how Patton adapts his unquestionably earthy images to the dreary, groveling life of the combat soldier. Such "mind-pictures" are rich in their connotative trappings and serve to put new life into favored, but sometimes remote, goals and values.

3. *Simplifying the group's values and goals.* More important than contrasting "enlivened" images is the uncomplicated expression of the group's aspirations. This simplification procedure is, perhaps, the essence of communication designed to heighten and

sustain people's motivations. The speaker becomes the representative of the audience. They want or need certain values and goals stated and restated, and the speaker is their agent designated to do the job. The successful inspirational speaker articulates feelings that individual members are unable to express themselves and does so in the manner deemed appropriate by that audience.

Moreover, the expression of such values and goals must be simple and straightforward. Whether they be Patton's troops or Walker's right-wingers, listeners usually demand that easily understood forces of good and evil be contrasted, that *an* answer to their problems be put forth, and that *one* overriding goal be offered by the speaker. Should a speaker in such circumstances become too complicated in the discussion, or should he or she confuse the issue with a complex statement of goals, the very motivational core of the audience might be undermined.

4. *Monitoring nonverbal elements.* At the risk of seeming obvious, it is especially important for the "inspiring" speaker to modulate carefully the nonverbal factors that affect an audience's perceptions. In the movie *Patton,* it was probably a bit more than the usual Hollywood schtick that determined that Patton should give his speech while standing before an American flag that measured some 20 feet by 30 feet. Similarly, the flower strewing that surrounded Kennedy in Berlin did much to increase the emotional impact of his address.

Equally, speakers who presume to articulate commonly accepted values and goals must do so with vigor and force, in the absence of tension and uncertainty. Nonverbal communication is important in any speaking situation, but it is crucially important in the inspirational speaking situation. It is imperative in such instances that the speaker say what the audience needs to have said and say it well. It is also important for his or her nonverbal behavior to show that his or her feelings and emotions are congruent with those of the audience. In such settings, the audience and the speaker are a team. They have the same goal for the occasion. They have the same feelings. The speaker's mood must be their mood. Wisely chosen gestures and vocal quality help generate such feelings.

5. *Encouraging audience participation.* Comedian Flip Wilson (among others) demonstrates that some fundamentalist congregations are often inhabited by an "Amen Charley," a character whose self-imposed job it is to assert, from time to time, "Amen, Reverend, Amen." When persons gather to share their common aspi-

rations and allegiances, they usually do so with a good deal of powerful emotion welling up within them. Thus, it is not unreasonable for them to wish to be a part of the action, to give voice to their approval of the speaker addressing them. Cheering, clapping, or more demonstrative signs of approval are often part and parcel of speeches designed to intensify goals and values. As we saw in Chapter 4, intra-audience responses can do much to further the cause of the speaker, and thus the speaker is often wise to permit and sometimes to encourage such reinforcings of his or her reinforcing.

So far in this chapter, we have painted a rather rosy picture of how public communication is used to reinforce and to sustain the motivations of human listeners. We have talked a bit about speakers who found themselves in very favorable circumstances as they went about their business of intensifying the solidarity of the group to which they spoke or of revivifying that group's common goals and values. Our speakers were met with flowers, amens, and thunderous applause.

In the next section, we will darken the picture a bit. We will consider why our speakers spoke in the first place—they had competition. Walker, Patton, and Kennedy all apparently perceived that some problem existed that threatened to pull their listeners away from the straight and narrow. General Walker, for example, knew that motivation for conservative ideals is not a constant thing; he also knew that for every self-respecting John Birch spokesperson in the world, there is a liberal advocating what Walker considered to be a form of socialism. General Walker further knew that his remarks would form only a portion of the blanket of communication with which his listeners would be enveloped.

Factors Affecting Motivation

Consider the college freshman from a solid midwestern heritage and religious background, a young man from an environment of varsity sports, church suppers, and traditional American values. After one semester, he returns home to visit and proceeds to horrify his parents with his vehement denunciation of the Administration's economic and nuclear policies as well as his outspoken contempt for the religious and philosophical values inculcated in him from childhood. In the eyes of his parents, he has become a cynical, obstinate know-it-all who has all too easily forsaken everything ever taught him. His parents are confused and upset. They blame themselves for the change in their son. What they cannot understand is that very special communicative techniques are required if listeners are to resist the influence of unseemly persuaders. Whereas "good" attitudes and values can be strengthened in a listener, it is simultaneously necessary to help a listener resist "bad" attitudes and values. That is, speech can act as an inhibitor of change, as a kind of serum designed to protect the mind from unsavory parasites.

In this section, then, we will consider how one's resistance to persuasion can be increased. We will do so by examining the psychological factors that motivate us to believe as we do. Although there are many personality factors that cause us to withstand persuasion, we will identify only three here. These three—self-esteem, hostility, and anxiety— are selected because they have been researched rather thoroughly. Such studies indicate that when a listener possesses a good opinion of himself or herself or when the listener is distraught in some fashion, he or she will be likely to resist the influence of others in rather wholesale fashion.

Self-Esteem

Persons of high self-esteem are, other things being equal, better able to resist persuasion than are persons who think ill of themselves. Apparently, the strength of one's ego is related to one's ability to defend against "attack" and to withstand persuasive attempts by others. Scholars have discovered that providing a person with a "success experience" prior to a persuasive attempt makes that person quite resistant to change.[4] In contrast, we are especially likely to respond favorably to the will of others when we feel discouraged. It is for these reasons that cult figures like Charles Manson and Jim Jones had special attraction for society's "unsuccessful" persons.

On the basis of such findings, a public speaker is well advised in reminding his or her audience initially of how wise they are to hold their current beliefs, while simultaneously pointing out the many rewards their present beliefs have provided for them in the past. Obviously, such *vicarious* success experiences will not be as potent resistance-inducers as would immediate, more tangible rewards.

Other research has discovered that these success-experience approaches are especially bolstering to people low in self-esteem.[5] Consider, for example, a speaker who is addressing new members of Alcoholics Anonymous and exhorting them to refrain from drinking. Having only recently had their consciousness raised, such listeners are

[4]K. G. Stukat, *Suggestibility: A Factorial and Experimental Study* (Stockholm: Almquist, 1958).
[5]D. M. Gelfand, "The Influence of Self-Esteem on the Rate of Verbal Conditioning and Social Matching Behavior," *Journal of Abnormal and Social Psychology*, 65:259–265 (1962).

probably still wallowing in depression and self-hatred. A speaker who adopts a Pollyanna approach in such a set of circumstances is obviously unwise. Rather, many trained professionals who deal with alcoholics extensively begin their remarks with the straightforward statement that "we are alcoholics and always will be." Such speakers are quick to assert, however, that their listeners have already turned the corner by deciding to forsake further imbibing (Success Experience 1) and have demonstrated that commitment by joining with other alcoholics in a remarkably successful organization (Success Experience 2).

Drug rehabilitation centers operate in much the same way. However, one danger is that such an approach may actually backfire on the persuader because it gives the listener a false sense of security in his or her new, still-fragile attitudes. Thus, the no-nonsense approaches used by drug rehabilitators indicate that self-esteem and "success" must be built into their clients, but not at the expense of providing the former addicts with still more rationalizations for renewing their self-destruction.

Hostility

A second factor related to one's general ability to resist persuasion is aggressiveness or hostility. Research indicates that aggressive people are particularly likely to resist the influence of others.[6] That is, if a speaker can cause an audience to feel angry (perhaps by showing them how "their" values have been trampled upon), they will be especially apt to cling to their basic values with special tenacity.

Thus, Patton chose wisely when detailing what his men should be prepared to do when meeting the German armies in battle. Assuming that Patton's troops were aggressive, that Patton's speech gave them ample opportunity to direct their frustrations toward others, and that the general's listeners were receptive to his colorful appeals to their basic, motivating drives, then such hearers would undoubtedly resist any *Saturday Evening Post* "nonsense" about individuality and would also turn a deaf ear on the preachments of those who urged human kindness in the battlefield situation. Interestingly, some commentators are now suggesting that it was the very lack of such aggressiveness on the part of some GIs in Vietnam that rendered them particularly susceptible to the persuasion of the Peace Movement in the late 1960s.

Passive and contented people, it seems, are the ideal candidates for persuasion in the eyes of most speakers. Thus, political candidates

[6]W. Weiss and B. Fine, "The Effect of Induced Aggressiveness on Opinion Change," *Journal of Abnormal and Social Psychology*, 52:109–114 (1956).

rarely attempt to convert highly polarized (often aggressive) voters, concentrating instead on middle-of-the-roaders.

Anxiety

Research in persuasion has discovered the interesting fact that very anxious people are sometimes quite suggestible.[7] That is, when people become concerned or afraid, they seem to seek out whatever persuasive messages that will provide them with some sort of assurance. Thus, the speaker who wishes to *maintain* motivation should always be certain to rebuild the attractiveness of the audience's current values. "Hell's fire and brimstone" sermons may be theatrically appealing, but if they succeed only in frightening churchgoers, they may have a decided boomerang effect on listeners' attitudes.

Such thinking may help to explain why some college freshmen become "subverted" by the so-called negative influences on campus. Bereft of the sustaining influence of parents and well-established reference groups back home, he or she must now find new and local forms of social support. The life of the college freshman being what it is, the intense pressures of study and peer group begin to take their toll. It is difficult to make friends. The grades come harder than they did in high school. Few people make the college varsity. All of this creates a relatively high amount of anxiety, which makes the student less responsive to the influence of parents back home and more susceptible to the whims of all the other searching individuals on campus.

In fact, there is every reason to suspect that the new student's self-esteem is lowered by the buffetings he or she must take during those first few lonely days on campus, and that this makes the student aggressive to the folks back home who allowed him or her to get into such a mess. Since he or she would thus combine all of the traits of the prototype nonresistor to persuasion, it is little wonder that the new student becomes an attitudinal weathervane until he or she is able to sort things out.

This phenomenon is not a figment of our imagination. Attitudinal surveys constantly show that college students undergo a 25 percent attitudinal swing during their four years, with seniors being much more liberal when they graduate than they were as freshmen.[8] Presumably, such changes occur, in part, because the reinforcing speeches of parents

---

[7]J. Nunnally and H. Bobren, "Variables Influencing the Willingness to Receive Communications on Mental Health," *Journal of Personality*, 27:38–46 (1959).

[8]A. W. Astin, *Four Critical Years: Effects of College on Beliefs, Attitudes, and Knowledge* (San Francisco: Jossey Bass, 1978).

are no longer available. Unless it is fed on a rather constant basis, motivation becomes undernourished and, ultimately, susceptible to attitudinal disease. In the following sections, we will discuss the "serums" available to repel this tendency to change our minds.

Commitment and Anchoring Strategies

If we start with the assumption that most of us like to be consistent in our beliefs, we are afforded a unique view of the forces that affect suggestibility. That is, many of us seek to keep our attitudes in line with one another (e.g., if I liked Richard Nixon, I should have liked the principle of executive privilege). Similarly, we seem to prefer that our attitudes and behaviors coincide (e.g., I liked Richard Nixon and I voted for him). Called by various names (cognitive consistency, balance, the principle of congruity), this concept of attitudinal "sameness" does much to determine how, and to what extent, we will maintain our present beliefs and, consequently, what new beliefs we will consider adopting. In other words, we structure our beliefs, and it is not until these "structures" are upset in some fashion that we will be tempted to alter our beliefs. Remembering this assumption of cognitive consistency, then, let us look at a few of the conditions under which we will resist persuasion.

Commitment

The intensity of a belief, or the extent to which we are committed to it, is an important factor in determining one's resistance to persuasion. The more committed we are to a belief, the more we are willing to do on its behalf; consequently, the more difficult it is for an outsider to change that belief. It seems to follow, therefore, that we will hold fast to a belief if we are required to demonstrate our commitment to it. Three common approaches are available to speakers when attempting to build audience commitment. They include:

1. *Continually remind listeners of their beliefs.* Since we believe in so many things, our attention is often diverted from specific attitudes we supposedly hold. In one sense, at least, the weekly sermon is designed to remind us of (and hence to reinforce) our beliefs about good and evil. In safety campaigns, in heart-fund appeals, and the like, we see the use of symbols and slogans designed to call to mind, easily and quickly, beliefs and values that demand continued reinforcement lest they become dormant.

2. *Encourage the audience to make positive statements about the belief or even to verbalize the belief itself.* One research summary indicates that writing positive statements about a belief even in a relatively private setting has the result of deepening one's commitment to the belief.[9] Similarly, *publicly* verbalizing the belief has been found to be superior to private opinion-stating. After all, we know that people often try to avoid committing themselves to ideas they really seem to hold because, if they do so, they are stuck with the belief (or so run many native psychologies). We know also that it requires some loss of face, some inconsistency and admission of error, to later reverse ourselves on a belief we have admitted in public to holding.

This technique of strengthening commitment is widely used in public speech settings, rather notably, for example, by Weight Watchers. At a typical meeting of the organization, members of the group are encouraged, one by one, to sing their praises (if they have dutifully fasted) or to heap abuse upon themselves (if they have not lost weight). Besides reinforcing the value of a slim figure in the mind of the individual in question and making him or her resistant to the pleadings of Ronald McDonald, such verbal commitment also does much to inculcate similar feelings in the other members of the audience.

3. *Encourage the audience to take some public, nonverbal action that irreversibly links them to the belief.* Such overt action is the nearest thing we have to a 100-percent guarantee that the belief will be unshakable. Chevrolet salespeople try to get you to take a test drive. Catholic priests encourage the renewal of marriage vows. Solicitors for charity encourage us to sign pledge cards. Cheerleaders demand that their audience sing the old fight song and give the old school sign. All of these techniques take advantage of our desire to be consistent in thought and deed. Thus, as a speaker, any overt commitment you can get from your audience (no matter how minor) is a great advantage attitudinally as well.

Anchoring

A second technique for keeping beliefs in place can be called anchoring. If a specific attitude is tied to other salient beliefs a person holds, that belief will be more resistant to change than if it were not so anchored. If a cluster of beliefs is closely interrelated, then all members

[9] W. McGuire, "The Nature of Attitudes and Attitude Change," in *The Handbook of Social Psychology*, vol. 3, eds. G. Lindsey and E. Aronson (Reading, Mass.: Addison-Wesley, 1969).

of the cluster may help to sustain any one of these that happens to come under attack. However, anchoring may become a two-edged sword, working either for strengthening beliefs or against strengthening beliefs. Tying beliefs together may mean that if a persuasive campaign can be generated that is strong enough to cause the one belief under attack to fall, then all the other beliefs tied to it may also fall—the straw that breaks the back of the attitudinal camel.

Consider the average pre-Watergate Republican. His or her beliefs were "clustered" tightly: Richard Nixon = law and order = rejection of immorality = ethical conduct in government = good conservative principles, and so on. As the facts concerning Watergate slowly were made known, the attitudes and values that anchored "Richard Nixon" in the belief system of such an individual came under significant bombardment. High ranking administration people had deceived the public. Cabinet officers came under indictment. Nixon himself became more reclusive and defensive than usual. As the various pieces and parts of the "Richard Nixon" cluster of beliefs were torn asunder, for many people the target belief (Nixon) also began to crumble. Some persons were able to resist such cave-ins. But others gave up the ghost entirely and rejected all of the beliefs in the cluster in question (e.g., why believe in political morality and ethical conduct? Nixon's like all the rest of the politicians—just a crook).

Thus, the anchoring process is a two-humped camel. It makes each individual belief quite resistant to change; but if an attack is strong enough to cause one belief to fall, then all beliefs in that cluster are apt to fall under certain conditions.

McGuire has identified four of the most effective anchoring techniques, techniques that you might find of practical use.[10] They include:

1. *Link the target belief to other, related beliefs.* Researchers asked people in experiments to study several beliefs and then to estimate the extent to which each belief was consistent with all others. The relationships among the beliefs were identified, and the subjects were then shown specifically how very great the inconsistency would be if they would change a single belief in the cluster. Being the consistency-seeking humans they were, such an anchoring strategy made the beliefs quite resistant to change for the subjects involved.

   The rationale behind such an anchoring strategy may help to explain why Nixon, during the Watergate investigation, attempted to protect all of his flanks—guarding tapes, defending

[10]Ibid.

former associates, refusing subpoenas—lest one chink in the armor cause the whole suit to disintegrate.

2. *Link the target belief to a highly important value.* It is often helpful to build such a "bridge" immediately before your listeners will hear the other side of the story. Keeping an audience focused upon *values* builds the importance of your case. Reminding a person of his or her long-term goals and of their importance to him or her increases the resistance to attack of individual beliefs.

   Thus, during Watergate, we found Nixon continually urging that the people in the country forget the incident and turn their attention to more important goals such as world peace. Similarly, he argued from time to time that the values of executive privilege and separation of powers were being undermined by the Senate's excessive scrutiny of the whole affair.

3. *Link the target belief to a highly credible individual or group.* This piece of advice springs directly from our remarks in Chapter 8. Listeners prefer to have consistency between what they believe and what the persons they respect believe. Using "high status" sources in defense of our position as a speaker oftentimes causes listeners to pay special attention to the ideas we are espousing. This is probably what Richard Nixon had in mind when he brought in independent prosecutors like Elliott Richardson and Archibald Cox to clean house and to lend their prestige to the Nixon administration in those first few post-Watergate days.

4. *Characterize those who attack the target belief as improperly motivated.* Another method of anchoring is also related to the issue of credibility. Numerous researchers have discovered that the attractiveness of a persuasive proposal can be diminished if the person backing such a proposal can be shown to be untrustworthy or otherwise corrupted. Thus, when trying to hold onto his following, Nixon (through intermediaries) cast aspersions on the integrity and motivations of the Senate investigators. Because they wished to believe only the issues backed by reputable sources, many Republicans bought into Nixon's reasoning—thus avoiding attitudinal inconsistency.

Naturally, anchoring strategies and commitment strategies are not techniques guaranteed to produce the precise effect we are seeking as speakers. But these approaches can be highly effective if we are thoughtful enough in applying them. Creativity and perseverence will be demanded of us when using such techniques because nothing insults an audience as much as a speaker who *self-consciously* attempts to be clever.

Inoculating Strategies

Return with us, if you will, for one final look at the plight of the college freshman. As we pointed out, many college undergrads undergo great psychological upheaval during that first painful year. Academic and psychiatric counselors are deluged with countless new students who are suddenly barraged with new and strange persuasive messages that push them all over the psychological countryside. And parents often receive the brunt of such sortings-out. In this section, we would like to discuss one of the reasons that may account for the Jekyll-and-Hyde turnabout our aforementioned student effected during his freshman year.

Social psychologist William J. McGuire has been interested in what he has called the immunization or inoculation approach to sustaining beliefs. In a number of studies, McGuire validated a metaphorical explanation of the college freshman phenomenon that runs something like this: Beliefs are susceptible to disease (i.e., persuasion) if they are not immunized (usually through communicative contacts) in some fashion prior to the infestation of (persuasive) germs which intend to feed upon those beliefs.[11]

While argument by analogy is not the strongest mode of proof, McGuire's conceptualization makes sense. For example, while still at home, our college freshman knew little of drugs, alcohol, atheism, and sexual expression. Obviously, the parents were not inclined to mention such subjects to him. Thus, neither forearmed nor forewarned, he arrived on campus—ripe for the social "ills" he would face at a liberal school and with no attitudinal "antibodies" with which to ward them off.

If we follow through with McGuire's analogy, the parents could have attempted to immunize him against such "sickness." By discussing frankly and openly alternative life-styles prior to his arrival on campus, the parents could have hedged their bets a bit more insightfully than they did with their see-no-evil-hear-no-evil approach. That is, by having been given a weak dose of the disease he was about to encounter, he could have generated his own psychological defense system against untoward persuasive messages. Naturally, as in medical treatments, this inoculation should be weak enough so as not to overcome the person but strong enough to encourage him to discover *why* he believed what he believed before he entered a "hostile" environment.

He then could have been guided through a particular way of experiencing the expected persuasive message before it was actually pre-

[11]W. McGuire, "The Effectiveness of Supportive and Refutational Defenses in Immunizing and Restoring Belief Against Persuasion," *Sociometry*, 26:189–197 (1961).

sented to him. The message of liberalism, when it did come, would not have caught him off guard, and the pattern of thinking suggested by his collegiate peers would not have been the only pattern available to him. Rather, he would have had available an alternative route, over which his mind had traveled already.

There are at least three ways of inoculating a person against subsequent persuasive attempts: first, warning of future attack; second, providing counterarguments against the assertions he or she will receive in the real attack; and third, identifying weaknesses in the arguments he or she will receive in the real attack. When attempting such inoculation, it is wise both to strengthen the "good" beliefs (via commitment and anchoring) and to prepare the patient for the onset of the "bad" attitudes. A combination of strengthening and reinforcing existing beliefs (taking a vitamin pill) and giving the person a weakened form of the persuasion (the immunization shot) results in optimal resistance. Let us now consider the three inoculation strategies briefly:

1. *Forewarning strategy.* One of the most efficient strategies is that of previewing the coming attack. The mere warning of future attack has been found to decrease later suggestibility. Apparently, a child who is reared into adulthood in a shielded and protected environment may not be able to maintain his or her beliefs, values, and behaviors as well as can a person who has been exposed to other ideologies, philosophies, values, and lifestyles when growing up. A person could be shielded so well from other points of view that although his or her beliefs are constantly reinforced as to their goodness and rightness, he or she would be highly susceptible to persuasive influences once outside that sheltered environment.

2. *Creation of counterarguments.* A second strategy is to present to the listener a weakened form of the expected persuasion so that counterarguments can be created to refute the impending assertions. Two types of procedures (passive or active) may be used. One procedure is simply to furnish the "patient" with possible counterarguments, or, at least, to provide him or her with a maximum amount of information. This technique treats the listener somewhat passively but helps to build immediate resistance to persuasion. It has been found, however, that this type of inoculation decays over time and that "booster shots" are required before each persuasive attack.

   The second technique requires the person to construct his or her own counterarguments. With this procedure, the person becomes active; no information or ready-made counterarguments are given to him or her. Rather, the person receives the weakened dose of the expected attack and is left to create his or her own counterarguments. Such a procedure is recommended for long-range resistance to persuasion. It requires some time for such a type of inoculation to "take," but it does not subsequently decay as does the former type of resistance. In fact, this type of active protection tends to become stronger over time.

3. *Identification of weaknesses.* A third inoculation strategy is that of identifying weaknesses in the anticipated arguments so that one can refute them rather than simply offering counterclaims. As with the creation of counterarguments, if the person actively discovers the weaknesses and creates the refutational stance, the inoculation will be more effective than if the refutations are handed to him or her ready-made.

Inoculating strategies are especially helpful to the public speaker. A speaker can "rehearse" for listeners the arguments for and against his or her position. By explaining to listeners the inadequacies of the opposition's case, the speaker can generate an image of knowledgeability *and* fair-mindedness. Beliefs, it seems, simply won't "stay still." Much public speaking, as we have seen in this chapter, is designed to keep our beliefs "settled down." Much of life, in turn, is a constant struggle between persuasion and counterpersuasion. We trust that the techniques covered in this chapter will assist you greatly in this struggle.

Practical Approaches to Reinforcement

Throughout this chapter, we have presented a number of possible techniques for use in inspiring listeners, for insuring that they remain committed to their current commitments. Each of these techniques might well be used when speaking to reinforce. For example, let us suppose that you are a campaign manager scheduled to address a group of precinct workers three weeks prior to the election that will decide your (and their) political candidate's future. This is usually a critical time in a political campaign. The initial flush of excitement has long since passed, drained by months and months of thankless work such as stuffing envelopes, ringing doorbells, and so on. Furthermore, the end is not yet in sight. If your candidate is ahead in the polls, you have a tendency to skip the remaining hard work and begin to coast; if your candidate is steadily losing the voters' confidence, you are tempted to throw up your hands and save yourself additional labor. This is precisely the time, therefore, that a speech to reinforce is mandated. In Table 11-1 we suggest some practical ways for assembling such a speech.

Suggestions for Speaking

The reinforcing speech is a particularly demanding sort of communication. It requires special skills and a special tolerance for frustration as well. When dealing with hostile listeners, after all, we normally can see the objections raised against us and thus prepare ourselves for a challenging speaking experience. But when an audience already agrees with us but doesn't do much about their beliefs, care and patience are demanded of us. In many ways, people are lazy and would rather not *test* their beliefs unless forced to do so. Salespersons, preachers, teachers, and lawyers, and other workaday public speakers are well aware of these tendencies but must attempt to build motivation in their audiences nonetheless. Thus, while life is a struggle, communicative life is a *constant* struggle. Listeners' commitments slip when the going gets rough, their efforts flag when obstacles are presented, and, at times, they even become confused about what they believe. The following suggestions for speaking may help you, as a speaker, cope with such tendencies:

1. Frequently, *one* carefully detailed and well-embellished example will have more motivating power than a host of sophisticated arguments.

Table 11-1 Strategies for Reinforcement: An Example

General Strategy	Specific Technique	Example
Create group concern.	Contrast emotional opposites.	"So here it is. Three weeks before the election and our choice is still the same: two years of progress with Sampson or another endless term with the Turkey-of-the-Year."
	Stimulate verbal images.	"Just think about what this city will look like if we get another blizzard like last year and still have the same folks in city hall running the clean-up operation."
	Employ nonverbal images.	"Take a good look at that campaign button on your lapel. If we want that man in the mayor's office rather than on your lapel, we'd better get working."
	Encourage audience participation.	"John, how many doorbells do you think you could ring by ten o'clock tomorrow morning? Fifty? How about trying one hundred?"

Table 11-1 (Continued)

General Strategy	Specific Technique	Example
Stimulate motivational resources.	Applaud listeners' self-esteem.	"You know, there's a good reason that every one of you was chosen for this campaign. Each of you is a thorough professional."
	Channel listeners' hostility.	"Sure your feet hurt. Sure you're tired of shaking hands. Well, I can tell you one thing: If our opponent is elected, you'll have plenty of time to rest."
	Demonstrate dangers of noncommitment.	"Maybe you can sleep tonight knowing that our opponent is one step closer to the mayor's office. But not me. I'd like to see the swimming pools open this summer."
Build commitment to existing beliefs.	Recall listeners' basic attitudes.	"Let's not forget why we all started on this campaign in the first place. Our opponent is the toady of the builders in this town and doesn't give a hoot about the environment."
	Encourage verbalization of beliefs.	"How many of you people still feel as I do about Roger Sampson? What? I can't hear you."

Encourage behavioral commitment.	"Look, I've got a sign-up sheet here for anybody who's willing to work another three hours in Precinct 7 on Saturday. How about putting your pen where your mouth is?"
Anchor beliefs to stable sources.	
Link proposal to related values.	"We all knew when we started this campaign that it wouldn't be easy. Well, you all made your promises to fight 'til the end. I expect those promises are still good, aren't they?"
Link proposal to related beliefs.	"Sure Roger Sampson's not perfect. But he voted in the city council to decriminalize pot, didn't he?"
Link proposal to credible sources.	"Hey, folks, Paul just told me that the governor has endorsed Sampson. Let's hear it for the gov!"
Characterize motives of those who disagree with the proposal.	"Now I don't necessarily believe this, but some people have told me that our opponent has been financing payoffs to some of our campaign workers to get them to slow down. Any truth to that rumor?"

Table 11-1   (Continued)

General Strategy	Specific Technique	Example
Inoculate listeners against change.	Warn audience about alternative viewpoints.	"No doubt about it. The temptation to slack off is a real one. You'll wake up in the morning and say, 'I can't take another day of this.' Well, I say you can."
	Suggest useful counterarguments.	"I don't care what the press is saying about our standing in the polls. Don't forget that those are the same folks who predicted that the bond referendum would go against us. Some crystal ball, huh?"
	Identify basic weakness of alternative case.	"When it comes right down to it, you people will have to decide how hard you're going to work. As for me, I couldn't stand to live in this town with a fascist for a mayor. That's why I'm going to break my back for our next mayor, Roger Sampson!"

2. Motivation is contagious; up to a point, the more rapid your speech and the more animated your delivery, the more likely the audience will warm to your cause.

3. Calling on a friendly face in the audience to support your assertions is often helpful for generating a sense of common orientation with your listeners.

4. Pay attention to pronouns; references to what "we" believe or how a matter affects "us" may slowly build bridges between you and your listeners.

5. Imaginary dialogue is often an effective technique for dramatizing opposing viewpoints and for getting listeners to see the basic clash of ideas.

6. Although moderation is normally in order, sometimes the use of an *excessive* number of examples can be impressive, especially if each of them tells the same story.

7. In a classroom speaking situation, be careful not to overdo your emotional state; credibility can be lost if you are too worked up and, hence, not competent or trustworthy.

8. A public speaker must be an optimist; listeners often give scant attention to what they really believe, and that is to the speaker's advantage.

9. Don't taunt an audience by accusing them of attitudinal inconsistency; it is your job as a speaker to give listeners a *convenient* way of accepting your viewpoint.

10. Never be discouraged by the immediate feedback you receive since persuasion often takes time to "unfold"; your speaking efforts may have long-term effects on your audience.

CHAPTER 12

The Occasional Speech

It is a pleasure and a privilege to be here with you today. These great annual meetings are always an inspiration to me, and doubly so today. But we're in the midst of trying times. So you'll pardon me if I cast aside the glib reverberations of glittering generalities and the soothing syrup of sugar-coated platitudes and put it to you the only way I can, straight English.

We're losing the battle!

From every corner the people are being weaned away from the doctrine of the Founding Fathers. They are being detoured from the high-speed highways of progress by the utopian highwaymen.

Now let me say that I do not wish to turn the clock back. None of us do. All forward-looking businessmen see themselves as partners on a team in which the worker is a full-fledged member. I regard our employees as our greatest business asset, and I am sure, mindful as I am of the towering potentials of purposeful energy in this group of clear-sighted leaders, that, in the final analysis, it is the rock foundation of your policies, too.

But the team can't put the ball across for a first down just by pushing it. The guards and the tackles can't do their job if the quarterback doesn't let them in on the play. And we, the quarterbacks, are muffing the ball.

How are we to go over for a touchdown? My friends, this is the 64-dollar question. I don't know the answers. I am just a plain-spoken businessman. I am not a soothsayer. I have no secret crystal ball. But I do know one thing: before we round the curve into the homestretch we have a job to do. It will not be easy. I offer no panaceas or nostrums. Instead I would like to suggest that the real key to our problem lies in the application of the three Es. What are the three Es? Enterprise! Endeavor! Effort!

Much has been done already. But let's not fool ourselves: the surface has hardly been scratched. The program is still in its infancy. So let me give it to you straight from the shoulder. The full implication, gentlemen, depends on us.

We have the know-how.

With sights set high, let's go over the top![1]

Over the top, indeed! If you are having trouble sorting out the meaning, let alone the impact, of this rhetorical foolishness, you have read carefully! It really is just a "nonspeech," a put-on that was concocted by a humorist in order to dramatize the usual fare served up at the annual business meeting of Anycompany, Inc. But it

[1]"The Language of Business," *Fortune,* November 1950, p. 114. Reprinted by permission of *Fortune* magazine.

makes a delightful point about public speaking: Speeches come in all shapes, sizes, and types. Often they don't neatly fit into informative, persuasive, or reinforcing niches. Like our example above, some speeches are ceremonial, designed to celebrate some occasion such as a sales convention or a national holiday. Some speeches serve special purposes—impromptu participation in public meetings, lively entertainment after a church dinner or club event, or fulfillment of such social obligations as introducing or welcoming dignitaries. In short, the types of public speeches are myriad.

In this chapter, we would like to focus on four of the most common types of special speeches and thereby put into practice what has been learned in earlier chapters of this book. In a sense, these addresses given on special occasions are some of the most ordinary speeches a public communicator can make. The four speeches we will focus upon are the impromptu speech, the ceremonial speech, the entertaining speech, and the speech of recognition.

A Model of Occasional Speaking

Before considering the four specific occasional types of speeches, let us consider a model that may assist you in thinking about the possibilities inherent in such speeches. Although the model in Figure 12-1 mentions only four special speeches, it does highlight some of the basic sociopsychological forces operating in many communicative settings. These forces combine in unique ways and present interesting challenges to the public speaker. Thus, when preparing a speech for a special occasion, it helps to think about two kinds of issues: What sort of impact do I want to have on my listeners—short-term or long-term? Will I be facing formal or informal constraints when talking to my audience?

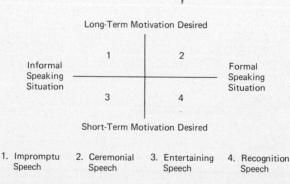

Figure 12-1 A Model for Occasional Speaking

Short- or Long-Term Motivation

Sometimes, speakers wish to have an immediate impact on their hearers. Effectiveness of the moment becomes of prime importance. For instance, when telling a joke to a friend, you hardly expect your companion to continue laughing into the next millenium; you only wish to prompt him or her to enjoy themselves for a moment or two. So it is with some speeches; what the audience does *now* becomes important. The speech is actually designed to be forgotten because it plays second fiddle to some other social event (e.g., another speech).

On the other hand, some speakers wish to leave a lasting impression on their listeners, to insure that sustained motivation is unleashed by their words. The outraged speech at the city council meeting or the eulogy delivered on behalf of a departed leader are meant to operate as "tiny time pills," slowly but steadily increasing their potency as the days pass.

Formal or Informal Situations

When speaking about the formality of a speaking situation, we are considering how specific, rigorous, and traditional the audiences' *expectations* are for the speaker they will hear and the speech the speaker will deliver. If you are invited to a party and are told to dress formally, you know that you are expected to wear very specific attire, usually a tuxedo or a long evening gown. Your options for response are limited. On the other hand, an invitation to come dressed as you are means that the host or hostess has no specific expectations for your behavior and that you are allowed to dress as you please. The specificity of the social invitation will no doubt affect how you feel about yourself in such situations and what pleasure you will derive from the social event you attend.

So it is with public speeches. Sometimes, the topic a speaker addresses, the way the speaker presents himself or herself, and the kinds of things that can appropriately be said are highly conventional and restricted; the audience expects a particular style of speaking, and the speaker is made to comply in minute detail. At other times, the speaker is given wider latitude by custom and by the audience to cover the issues and to use the style of presentation that he or she chooses. Listeners' expectations are less clear to them, their standards for communicative appropriateness less commonly shared among them, and, therefore, a speaker's guidelines for success become more intuitive and idiosyncratic.

Between formal and informal situations and long- and short-term motivation, four general types of speeches lie. Each impromptu, ceremonial, entertaining, and recognition speech combines a number of unique rhetorical features and thereby "binds" a speaker in special ways. Moreover, each type of speech creates a different motivational atmosphere and allows certain kinds of linkages to develop between speakers and hearers. Let us examine each of these four basic types of occasional speeches to consider the strategies available for meeting such communicative demands satisfactorily.

Impromptu Speaking

An impromptu speech is one in which a speaker is called upon to speak brilliantly and movingly without much prior warning. Doesn't sound difficult at all, does it? People are asked to give impromptu speeches rather frequently in daily affairs (more often, we are sure, than some would prefer). But since impromptu speeches are common, let us see how they can be created and delivered with grace, style, and confidence.

The most typical setting for an impromptu speech is a group situation in which a speaker is asked to make a response to the remarks of another. Impromptu speeches thus tend to chain together, creating a matrix of communication in which speakers respond to and extend the ideas offered by other group members. Situations calling for impromptu speeches are town meetings or political rallies, gatherings of fraternal or civic organizations, or business meetings in which some economic proposal or corporate plan of action is debated.

Because listeners do not expect a great deal of preparation on the parts of speakers in such settings, and because the topics dealt with in an impromptu speech are typically varied, the speaking situation is a highly informal one. But impromptu speakers nevertheless wish to

leave a lasting impression on their audience. An impromptu speech in a business meeting, for instance, will be a success to the extent that it has a long-term effect on company policy or upon the speaker's status in the organization. Because impromptu speeches are given on the spur of the moment, and because they must get to the heart of the matter with dispatch, the key to a good impromptu speech is *clarity*. Rather than try to crowd ten weighty ideas into a hastily prepared speech that few will understand, speakers are better advised to enunciate one clear idea that will motivate the audience long after the speech is delivered. What, then, might be some keys to delivering a clear and motivating impromptu speech?

Preparation

Although it may sound contradictory, the best impromptu speeches are those for which one has prepared! But how, you might rightfully ask, can you prepare for a speech that you didn't know you would have to give until the moment arrived? Listed below are some suggestions for reaching this worthy, if seemingly improbable, goal:

1. *Speak often.* The more practice people get in speaking, the better able they will be to speak when asked to do so. Experience adds to both poise and confidence, and to intelligibility as well.

2. *Listen carefully to what is being said in situations that have previously fostered impromptu speaking.* As we pointed out above, most impromptu speeches are given in group situations involving a number of other people discussing, briefly, important issues. The success of your speech will depend on how well it clearly

relates to what has been said by others. The lasting impression you make will be the wrong one if your speech is merely repetitious of others' remarks.

3. *Take notes on what is being said.* Such a practice helps speakers to listen carefully. More important, the notes can be in the form of an impromptu speech that one may give if asked to speak at that very moment. Taking notes can be a way of anticipating what you would say *if* you spoke next; you would thus be able to rise up instantly and to speak fluently with the brief outline of a speech (your notes) already before you.

4. *Understand why you are speaking at that moment and select a single argument to make.* Be clear in your own mind how your speech fits in with what has been said up to that point. If someone is responding to a direct question, the person should be sure that he or she understands the question asked. Select a single idea because it will be clearer and more motivating to enforce one telling point than to wander among a dozen half-formed and poorly organized notions.

5. *Fight terror.* Stage fright can be especially acute during impromptu speeches, but you can beat it. Take a few deep, slow breaths as you rise. Keep your hands free of pencils or other objects so that you may gesture naturally. If necessary, step to a place near your seat where you can face the greatest number of people possible. Use the notes you have been jotting down, but place them on a chair or table in front of you, if possible, so that you will maximize your eye contact with your listeners.

Organization

Now that you are prepared (intellectually and emotionally) to speak, the only thing left to do is to give a crystal-clear speech. The key to a clear impromptu speech is to put a single idea into a clear pattern of organization. We would like to suggest a number of patterns of organization uniquely suited to impromptu speaking. Ideally, speakers should internalize these patterns so that as they rise to speak, they can easily choose a pattern from their rhetorical war chest and fire away. Until one becomes familiar with these patterns, though, it may be a good idea to keep a list of them at hand. Your authors are indebted to Bryant and Wallace for these suggestions.[2]

[2]D. C. Bryant and K. R. Wallace, *Oral Communication: A Short Course in Public Speaking*, 4th ed. (Englewood Cliffs, N.J.: Prentice-Hall, 1976), p. 186.

To illustrate the usefulness of these patterns of organization, let us suppose that you are attending a town meeting devoted to discussing whether or not to raise the property tax rate in support of local schools. We will use that as our rhetorical example and also give some sample cues that one may use for putting these organizational plans into action. As with most impromptu speeches, we will assume that the resulting speeches will be fairly brief (i.e., 2–3 minutes). Table 12-1 contains our suggestions for getting such an impromptu show on the road.

You may notice that none of these patterns of organization possesses the introduction or conclusion normally found in more fully developed speeches. For such a short speech, there is little need for such elaboration. Get up, make a clear point, and sit down. Clarity, brevity, and good organization are the keys to effective impromptu speaking. And let us not underestimate the impact that a single impromptu speech can have. History is filled with stories of persons who have been suddenly "discovered" or whose careers have suddenly taken off because of their well-chosen and strikingly judicious impromptu remarks. By thinking carefully during public discussions and thereby readying yourself for impromptu remarks, you, too, can make a bit of history!

Ceremonial Speaking

Like the impromptu speech, the ceremonial speech tries to motivate the audience in a deep-seated and lasting way. Unlike the impromptu speech, ceremonial speaking takes place in situations marked by formality. We are all familiar with ceremonial speeches, even though most of us live fairly informal lives. Speeches designed to recognize such holidays as the Fourth of July or Labor Day, funeral eulogies, presidential inaugural addresses, and commencement speeches all exemplify ceremonial events.

What makes such speeches formal? The answer to that question will also reveal the most distinctive characteristic of ceremonial speaking. Ceremonial speeches are designed to punctuate some pivotal occasion: Someone is born or has died, a young person is welcomed into adulthood, a nation or society passes some milestone or builds a great building or monument. Public ceremonies or rituals celebrate and emphasize these important occasions in the life of a person or a society and typically do so in formal, standardized ways. There are precious few "legitimate" ways to be inaugurated into political office, to get married, or to mourn the dead.

Some of our best remembered speeches are of this type. If someone were to ask you to name a famous oration, what speech would you

Table 12-1 Organizational Patterns for Impromptu Speaking

Organizational Patterns for Responding to Other Speakers	Sample Use
1. Review what has been said.	"Now a number of people tonight have told us how much they are spending in taxes. Mr. Smith told us that he's taxed more than he can bear. Ms. Jones claims that . . ."
React to your summary.	"But I don't feel that anybody is so burdened by taxes that he or she is going cold or hungry. . . ."
Defend your reaction.	"In fact, a report in this evening's newspaper shows that this county has the lowest rate . . ."
2. Offer an example or illustration.	"You know, this reminds me of what happened to my Aunt Sally when they cut property taxes in California. . . ."
And draw a principle from the illustration.	"But Aunt Sally always said that she would have preferred slightly higher taxes that would have produced better schools. There's a lesson here. . . ."
3. Explain that an issue has been overlooked.	"Nobody here tonight has talked about what effect a property tax cut would have on income tax. . . ."
Explain the consequences of overlooking that issue.	"It looks to me as if any cut in property tax would automatically be eaten up by higher income taxes, and therefore . . ."
4. Disagree with someone's particular argument.	"Now, Ms. Johnson said a little earlier that we don't really need a new gym at the high school. I'm afraid I have to disagree. . . ."
Support your position.	"A recent survey shows that of all the athletic programs in the state, ours is the only one . . ."

5. Disagree with the way the whole problem has been viewed	"We've been speaking as if an increase in property taxes was automatically a burden. That's not so. . . ."
a. because the problem isn't as bad as it seems, *or*	"I've been doing some calculations, and the proposed increase only comes to about . . ."
b. because the proposed solution is either undesirable or not the best one available.	"Avoiding a property tax increase is not the way to relieve most of the tax burden. Wouldn't a better route be to . . ."
6. The reasoning in a particular speaker's argument is faulty, because of	"Mr. Anderson argued forcefully against taxes that would not benefit the elderly with no children. But I think his argument is off-base because . . ."
a. insufficient or untrustworthy fact.	"The study he cited is long out of date. . . ."
b. inadequate or irrelevant expert testimony.	"Although the economist Mr. Anderson refers to is quite expert, she was talking about sales taxes, which are not relevant. . . ."
c. faulty analogy.	"Our situation is not, as Mr. Anderson claims, similar to that of Middletown. Their population distribution is far more . . ."
d. faulty cause-effect analysis.	"High taxes are not the cause of poverty among the elderly. Instead, fixed incomes . . ."
e. inconsistency.	"Earlier, Mr. Anderson supported higher taxes for a senior center. But that is inconsistent with his argument against the elderly paying taxes for schools because . . ."

Table 12-1 (Continued)

Organizational Patterns for Responding to Other Speakers	Sample Use

Organizational Patterns for Initiating a Discussion	

7. Describe a problem.	"I think we all know the terrible state our schools are in. Owing to low funds, . . ."
Give the history of the problem.	"We've come to this sorry pass because for years we've had no tax increase . . ."
Offer a brief solution.	"The best way out of this mess is to support the proposed tax increase. . . ."

| 8. Describe a goal. | "I think all of us here want to have quality schools. By a quality school, I mean . . ." |
| Describe barriers to meeting the goal. | "But we can't have the highest quality schools for one simple reason. The taxes needed to finance schools . . ." |

9. Announce a principle or value.	"Let me say this quite simply: No community can be better than the quality of its schools. . . ."
Give some examples.	"For instance, if young people are not educated well, they can't get good jobs, and the economic base of the town declines. . . ."
Apply the principle.	"Tonight we're faced with the choice of whether to have high quality schools or not by raising taxes. . . ."

name? Probably, it would be Lincoln's "Gettysburg Address." It is not surprising that such speeches are remembered so clearly since they deal with our feelings, emotions, and our strongest values. They hit us where we live. Moreover, in such situations the speaker becomes the personification of the audience. The speaker is their representative, their mouthpiece. He or she is "expressing" for them. The speaker is not teacher or advocate, but simply conducts or presides over the speaking situation. Such speeches help us rededicate ourselves to our beliefs. They give us a shot in the attitudinal arm so as to ward off unsavory, intruding beliefs. They rebuild our spirits, refocus our motivations, and help us to recoup our emotional losses.

Functions of Ceremonial Speaking

A ceremonial speech is a speech keyed to the moment, to an immediate sense of why people have gathered together. The focus of a ceremonial speech is therefore always on the occasion itself. But good ceremonial speakers do not content themselves to drone on about the occasion alone; the dullest commemorative speeches are those that discuss the Fourth of July and nothing else. Instead, enterprising speakers explain the *extended significance* of the occasion; they celebrate or interpret the occasion as it relates to groups of people, to individuals, or to principles and ideals.

The occasion and social groups. Often, the meaning of a great occasion is best seen by examining the ways in which it affects or relates to groups of people: nations, religious assemblages, political parties, families, clubs, and so on. When an elderly relative rises at a family reunion to say a few words about the occasion, for example, he or she will usually talk about how the annual gathering has served to reaffirm and strengthen family ties. At other times, a speaker will relate the occasion to a group of people in order to inspire them in the face of adversity. For instance, early in World War II, the British people faced a turning point. The British army had suffered a painful defeat at Dunkirk. The loss in lives and equipment was heavy, and the nation was overrun with fear and despair. Hope, loyalty, and perseverance needed to be identified, expressed, and renewed. The occasion called for a ceremony that would mark the defeat at Dunkirk, which would explain its significance to the British people but which would inspire and uplift them as well. Prime Minister Winston Churchill responded to all of these duties admirably on June 4, 1940, when he said,

> *We shall go on to the end, we shall fight in France, we shall fight on the seas and oceans, we shall fight with growing confidence and growing strength in the air, we shall defend our Island, whatever the cost may be, we shall fight*

*on the beaches, we shall fight on the landing grounds, we shall fight in the
fields, and in the streets, we shall fight in the hills; we shall never surrender.
. . .*[3]

On other occasions, a speaker may use ceremonial speaking to pro-
pose certain goals for the group he or she represents or to suggest a
means of assessing the group's goals and directions in life. On December
10, 1950, William Faulkner accepted the Nobel Prize for Literature. He
used that occasion to address the members of his literary profession and
persons everywhere who were interested in the role that writers should
play when confronting social problems. Notice in the following excerpt
how Faulkner turned the occasion into a chance to go beyond the
trappings of ceremony to urge his fellow authors to write of "courage
and honor and hope and pride" and to devote their craftsmanship to
recognizing that "man will not merely endure: he will prevail."

> *I feel that this award was not made to me as a man, but to my work—a
> life's work in the agony and sweat of the human spirit, not for glory and
> least of all for profit, but to create out of the materials of the human spirit
> something which did not exist before. So this award is only mine in trust.
> It will not be difficult to find a dedication for the money part of it commen-
> surate with the purpose and significance of its origin. But I would like to
> do the same with the acclaim too, by using this moment as a pinnacle from
> which I might be listened to by the young men and women already dedicated
> to the same anguish and travail, among whom is already that one who will
> someday stand here where I am standing.*
>
> *Our tragedy today is a general and universal physical fear so long sus-
> tained by now that we can even bear it. There are no longer problems of the
> spirit. There is only the question: when will I be blown up? Because of this,
> the young man or woman writing today has forgotten the problems of the
> human heart in conflict with itself which alone can make good writing
> because only that is worth writing about, worth the agony and the sweat.*
>
> *He must learn them again. He must teach himself that the basest of all
> things is to be afraid; and, teaching himself that, forget it forever, leaving
> no room in his workshop for anything but the old verities and truths of the
> heart, the old universal truths lacking which any story is ephemeral and
> doomed—love and honor and pity and pride and compassion and sacrifice.
> Until he does so, he labors under a curse. He writes not of love but of lust,
> of defeats in which nobody loses anything of value, of victories without hope,
> and, worst of all, without pity or compassion. His griefs grieve on no
> universal bones, leaving no scars. He writes not of the heart but of the
> glands.*

[3]From W. Churchill, *Blood, Sweat and Tears* (New York: Putnam, 1941), p. 297.

Until he relearns these things, he will write as though he stood among and watched the end of man. I decline to accept the end of man. It is easy enough to say that man is immortal simply because he will endure; that when the last ding dong of doom has clanged and faded from the last worthless rock hanging tideless in the last red and dying evening, that even then there will still be one more sound: that of his puny inexhaustible voice, still talking. I refuse to accept this. I believe that man will not merely endure: he will prevail.[4]

Another way in which speakers might use ceremonial occasions would be to urge a group to rally around a cause, an issue, or a leader. When candidates for the U.S. presidency accept their party's nomination, they often use their moment of glory to unify the group around themselves and their common cause. In accepting the 1980 nomination for president, Ronald Reagan operated in precisely this way by describing the Republicans before him as "a party united, with positive programs for solving the nation's problems." Later in his speech, he appealed not only to Republicans but to all Americans to find common meaning in his and his party's principles:

Tonight, let us dedicate ourselves to renewing the American compact. I ask you not simply to "trust me," but to trust your values—our values—and to hold me responsible for living up to them. I ask you to trust that American spirit which knows no ethnic, religious, social, political, regional or economic boundaries; the spirit that burned with zeal in the hearts of millions of immigrants from every corner of the earth who came here in search of freedom.[5]

The occasion and particular individuals. Often, a speaker will use ceremonial surroundings to talk about a person, his or her life, accomplishments, good works, or general importance. Such ceremonial speeches might, for example, occur at a christening, a wedding, a funeral, or a Bar Mitvah or Bat Mitzvah (occasions upon which a young person is welcomed into adulthood).

Some of the most stirring ceremonial speeches are funeral eulogies, speeches during which a person's death is used to recall the full dimension of that person and what that life has meant to his or her contemporaries. On January 30, 1948, Jawaharlal Nehru spoke to the Indian people by radio to mourn the death of their great patriot and spiritual leader, Mahatma Gandhi. Nehru used the occasion to "resurrect" Gandhi by dramatizing what he had meant to the Indian nation:

[4]W. Faulkner, "Nobel Prize Speech," in *A Treasury of the World's Great Speeches*, ed. H. Peterson (New York: Simon and Schuster, 1965), pp. 814–815.
[5]"Acceptance Address," *Vital Speeches of the Day*, 46 (August 15, 1980), p. 646.

Friends and comrades, the light has gone out of our lives and there is darkness everywhere. I do not know what to tell you and how to say it. Our beloved leader, Bapu as we called him, the father of the nation, is no more. Perhaps I am wrong to say that. Nevertheless, we will not see him again as we have seen him for these many years. We will not run to him for advice and seek solace from him, and that is a terrible blow, not to me only, but to millions and millions in this country, and it is difficult to soften the blow by any other advice that I or anyone else can give you. The light has gone out, I said, and yet I was wrong. For the light that shone in this country was no ordinary light. The light that has illumined this country for these many years will illumine this country for many more years, and a thousand years later that light will still be seen in this country and the world will see it and it will give solace to innumerable hearts. [6]

In more recent years, the death of Winston Churchill was used as an occasion to celebrate that man's life, work, and genius. A fine example of relating the occasion to a specific person was provided by the late Adlai E. Stevenson, a man who was particularly sensitive to the demands of public ritual and who also had a brilliant command of the English language. In a speech given at the National Cathedral in Washington, D. C., on the occasion of Winston Churchill's death, Stevenson began by acknowledging his ritualistic duties.

Today we meet in sadness to mourn one of the world's greatest citizens. Sir Winston Churchill is dead. The voice that led nations, raised armies, inspired victories and blew fresh courage into the hearts of men is silenced. We shall hear no longer the remembered eloquence and wit, the old courage and defiance, the robust serenity of indomitable faith. Our world is thus poorer, our political dialogue is diminished and the sources of public inspiration run more thinly for all of us. There is a lonesome place against the sky. So, we are right to mourn. . . . [7]

He concludes the eulogy by reaffirming his listeners' values and the ultimate significance of Churchill's life:

In the last analysis, all the zest and life and confidence of this incomparable man sprang, I believe, not only from the rich endowment of his nature, but also from a profound and simple faith in God. In the prime of his powers, confronted with the apocalyptic risks of annihilation, he said serenely: "I do not believe that God has despaired his children." And in old age, as the honors and excitements faded, his resignation had a touching simplicity: "Only faith," he said, "in a life after death, in a brighter world where dear ones

[6]"Gandi Eulogy," in Peterson, op. cit., p. 810.
[7]"Churchill Eulogy," *Washington Post*, January 29, 1965, p. A45.

will meet again—only that and the measured tramp of time can give consolation."

The great aristocrat, the beloved leader, the profound historian, the gifted painter, the superb politician, the lord of language, the orator, the wit—yes, and the dedicated bricklayer—behind all of them was the man of simple faith, steadfast in defeat, generous in victory, resigned in age, trusting in a loving providence and committing his achievements and his triumphs to a higher power.

Like the patriarchs of old, he waited on God's judgment and it could be said of him—as of the immortals that went before him—that God magnified him in the fear of his enemies and with his words he made prodigies to cease. He glorified him in the sight of kings and gave him commandments in the sight of his people. He showed him his Glory and sanctified him in his faith.
. . .[8]

When we look at ceremonial speeches like Stevenson's, we cannot help but be impressed by his pronounced ability to make a man's passing appear much more than physiological stoppage and the subsequent opening of a grave. In Stevenson's hands, Churchill lives again. Indeed, Churchill perhaps lives in this speech in a grander and more exalted way than he did when his biological apparatus was still functioning. That a speaker like Stevenson can use the miracle of public communication to raise Churchill from the dead so that he may be viewed once again, and lovingly, is a Lazarus-like event indeed.

The occasion and principle. Finally, ceremonial speakers often use the speaking occasion to talk about the great values held in common by members of a society. All of us have experienced such speakers. We need only remember how our parents used the occasion of our being licensed to drive as a chance to declaim upon the principles of responsibility, safe driving, and basic Americanism!

Perhaps the most famous ceremonial address of this type was Abraham Lincoln's "Gettysburg Address." Lincoln spoke at the dedication of the Gettysburg battlefield, not merely to honor the dead, but to relate that occasion to the great democratic principle that was endangered at the time: "that government of the people, by the people, for the people, shall not perish from the earth." The introduction to Lincoln's address has now passed into the annals of great American literature, but we tend to forget that his goals in the speech were pragmatic, not aesthetic, and that he was, in a sense, exploiting the immediate occasion in order to further a greater communicative good:

[8]Ibid.

Fourscore and seven years ago, our fathers brought forth upon this continent a new nation, conceived in liberty, and dedicated to the proposition that all men are created equal. Now we are engaged in a great civil war, testing whether that nation, or any nation so conceived and so dedicated, can long endure. We are met on a great battlefield of that war. We are met to dedicate a portion of it as the final resting place of those who here gave their lives that that nation might live. It is altogether fitting and proper that we should do this. But in a larger sense we cannot dedicate—we cannot consecrate— we cannot hallow this ground. The brave men, living and dead, who struggled here, have consecrated it far above our poor power to add or detract. The world will little note, nor long remember, what we say here, but it can never forget what they did here. It is for us, the living, rather to be dedicated here to the unfinished work that they have thus far so nobly advanced. It is rather for us to be here dedicated to the great task remaining before us, that from these honored dead we take increased devotion to that cause for which they here gave the last full measure of devotion; that we here highly resolve that these dead shall not have died in vain; that this nation, under God, shall have a new birth of freedom, and that government of the people, by the people, for the people, shall not perish from the earth.[9]

In thus going beyond the practical factors prompting his speech, Lincoln demonstrates the wide range of rhetorical opportunities available in ceremonial situations. Such situations often permit a speaker to cast new sentiments into old formulas, thus causing listeners to rise above their immediate circumstances. Lincoln, in short, found principle amidst chaos.

Audience Expectations for Ceremonies

As we have said previously, the formality native to ceremonial speeches derives from the specific expectations listeners have for what should happen during such exchanges. There are, of course, many different kinds of ceremonial speeches, each of which has particular expectations tied to them. Rather than review these myriad types, we urge the speaker to consider three broad sets of expectations:

Personal presentation: Audiences expect that speakers will present themselves in particular ways for particular occasions. Clothing, mannerisms, and personal demeanor can all contribute to an appropriate sense of the occasion. Conservative clothing and a serious expression are often appropriate, and delivery is often energetic, but not gauche.

[9]A. Lincoln, "Gettysburg Address," in Peterson, op. cit., p. 522.

Language style: Ceremonial speaking usually calls for an elevated style of language, as opposed to a conversational or everyday style. Metaphors and other stylistic devices can be more elaborate in such surroundings. Abstract terms are often employed to convey the far-reaching principles that ceremony celebrates. Dignity and decorum should permeate one's words during most ceremonial occasions.

Tone: Through language choice, through the topics or issues discussed, and through the moods or emotions a speech arouses, a tone is established by the speaker for the speech and ceremony. The tone might be one of joy and love at family reunions, sadness and loss at funerals, inspiration and conviction at political rallies. Audiences naturally expect tones to be consistent with the values they have gathered to celebrate.

Good ceremonial speaking can sometimes approach an art form. It is among the most difficult types of speaking one can attempt, primarily because the emotional surroundings are so delicate and listeners' needs so specific. It is probably no accident that the speeches excerpted in this discussion of ceremonial speaking were delivered by the great personages of our age—the Churchills, Stevensons and others. A society's leaders are, quite naturally, expected to be able to express hard-to-express thoughts and to find an appropriate message even during times of privation and travail.

But this is not to say that a nation's leaders alone carry the ceremonial burden. Each of us who has long-standing community ties and who has the capacity to feel strong emotion should be expected to lend our voice to the individuals, groups, and principles that we find important. Until birth, growth, triumph, and death disappear, none of us can escape the impulse to participate in ceremony.

Speaking to Entertain

While impromptu and ceremonial speaking try to establish long-term motivation within their listeners, speeches to entertain are meant to excite an audience only momentarily. They seek merely to divert an audience's attention from the cares of the moment and do not presume to create long-term attitudinal changes within their hearers.

Entertaining speeches can be some of the most unusual, distracting and, well, entertaining types of speeches for special occasions. They are usually delivered within highly informal circumstances. Since informal situations place relatively few specific constraints on what a speaker may say or do, speeches to entertain can occur anywhere from the local pool hall to the halls of Congress, and they can be effective in all such circumstances as long as the audience relaxes its expectations for appropriate speech and gives the speaker a free reign to operate creatively.

Functions of Entertaining Speeches

Entertaining speeches are special in a couple of ways. First, they can occur in a variety of situations: after dinner speeches, "roasts," awards banquets, social or club meetings, family gatherings. Second, they sometimes act as preludes to other sorts of more serious or somber events and thereby serve to warm up an audience and to insure that they are emotionally ready to handle the subsequent activity.

In fact, as an introduction to their more serious efforts, some speakers give what amounts to an entertaining minispeech that goes beyond a mere introduction and has a substance of its own. We shall examine some instances of such humorous preludes later.

As with ceremonial speeches, entertaining speeches serve specific communicative functions. The best entertaining speeches are not only entertaining, just as the best ceremonial speeches do not merely address the immediate occasion. Instead, a good entertaining speech uses a humorous and lighthearted style to create social cohesion, to teach some lesson of merit, or to defeat an adversary or a loathsome idea.

Creating social cohesion. This function of entertaining speeches is the closest to pure enjoyment. Here, the speaker wants the audience to laugh but also wants them *to laugh together.* In such circumstances, the audience should feel not only momentarily diverted but closer to each other because of having shared a pleasurable experience. Such speeches, in effect, serve as a large-scale in-joke for their listeners.

President John Kennedy was a skilled entertainer as well a gifted political speaker. He once addressed an AFL-CIO convention with then-Secretary of Labor, Arthur Goldberg, appearing on the platform with him. Kennedy used his sharp wit not just to get the audience to laugh but to break the ice and to create social cohesion within his audience as well:

> I am delighted to be here with you and with the Secretary of Labor, Arthur Goldberg. I was up in New York, stressing physical fitness, and in line with that, Arthur went over with a group to Switzerland to climb some of the mountains there. They got up about five and he was in bed. He got up to join them later and when they all came back at four o'clock in the afternoon he didn't come back with them. So they sent out search parties and there was not a sign that afternoon and night. The next day, the Red Cross went out

and around, calling "Goldberg, Goldberg, it's the Red Cross!" Then his voice came down from the mountain, "I gave at the office!"[10]

Teaching a lesson. Entertaining speeches can often be used for a more serious purpose—to teach a practical lesson or to elucidate a principle for the audience. Such entertainment is common; the fairy tales we heard as children charmed us, but they also sought to dramatize some moral lesson about life's truths. Religious leaders frequently combine serious messages with light entertainment; rock bands-for-Jesus, lively gospel choirs, and sermons replete with topical humor are some familiar examples of how serious preachment and lightheartedness can be combined. Notice, for example, how an entertaining speech by Douglas Martin uses humor to make a rather serious point about optimism:

> *Somebody else pointed out the differences between an optimist and a pessimist this way: An optimist looks at an oyster and expects a pearl; a pessimist looks at an oyster and expects ptomaine poisoning. Even if the pessimist is right, which I doubt, he probably won't enjoy himself either before or after he proves it. But the optimist is happy because he always is expecting pearls.* [11]

Often, audiences will accept a lesson or principle more easily if it is presented in such a humorous way because the humor used makes it appear that listeners will have to give up only a portion, a small portion, of their current attitudes and values.

In another example, Anson Mount, the Manager of Public Affairs for *Playboy* magazine, participated in a debate before a Southern Baptist Convention in 1970. Although his speech was not primarily entertaining, several portions of it tried to make a serious point in a humorous way. Notice how his lesson about human presumptuousness is disguised in an off-handed anecdote:

> *For the first few years of* Playboy's *existence, churchmen did a pretty good job of ignoring us. No leading church spokesman took notice of our presence and we were rarely if ever damned from the pulpit—at least we didn't hear about it. The only exceptions to this general rule were the occasional irate letters that came in from fundamentalist preachers. One or two of these letters would arrive each month, and occasionally one of them would find its way into our letters to the editor column. Most of these rustic epistles were remarkably alike. Aside from expressing indignation and predicting eternal*

---

[10]Quoted in R. G. King, *Forms of Public Address* (Indianapolis, Ind: Bobbs-Merrill, 1969), p. 116.

[11]For a more complete version of D. Martin's speech, see D. Ehninger et al., *Principles and Types of Speech Communication*, 8th ed. (Glenview, Ill.: Scott-Foresman and Company, 1978), p. 124.

torment for our souls, virtually all of our irate clerical correspondents took pains to explain the accidental circumstances under which they just happened to have come across a copy of Playboy.[12]

Defeating an adversary or idea. Humor is often the best weapon for dispatching even the most vicious and foolish of doctrines. When we say that an idea will be "laughed out of court," we are saying that it will be *substantially* rejected by public opinion. Part of Winston Churchill's formidable verbal arsenal during World War II was his ability to use humor to combat Nazism. An opponent or an ideology that is treated with seriousness by a speaker is often treated seriously by an audience as well. But an idea that has been "laughed out of court" often dies an ignominious death indeed.

In many ways, the nineteenth century was more extravagant in its tastes for humor than we are today. Then, when a speaker decided to destroy an opponent through humor, he or she went directly for the jugular. For example, in January of 1871, the U.S. House of Representatives was considering a bill that would finance construction of a railroad stretching through the wilderness of Wisconsin, along the St. Croix River, and terminating in what was then the small, dirty mining town of Duluth, Minnesota. J. Proctor Knott of Kentucky saw this bill as an attempt to spend government money to finance a private railroad, and he opposed such a notion forcefully. Furthermore, he saw no practical value at all in connecting Duluth to the rest of the civilized United States. He rose in the House on January 27, 1871, to deliver an entertaining but devastating speech opposed to the bill, a speech that included this satiric depiction of Duluth:

In fact, sir, I was overwhelmed with the conviction that Duluth not only existed somewhere, but that, wherever it was, it was a great and glorious place. I was convinced that the greatest calamity that ever befell the benighted nations of the ancient world was in their having passed away without a knowledge of the actual existence of Duluth; that their faded Atlantis, never seen save by the hallowed vision of inspired poesy, was, in fact, but another name for Duluth; that the golden orchard of the Hesperides was but a poetical synonym for the beer gardens in the vicinity of Duluth. I was certain that Herodotus had died a miserable death, because in all his travels and with all his geographical research he had never heard of Duluth. . . . Yet, sir, had it not been for this map, kindly furnished me by the legislature of Minnesota, I might have gone down to my obscure and humble grave in an agony of despair, because I could nowhere find Duluth. Had such

[12]A. Mount, "Speech at Baptist Convention," in W. Linkugel et al., *Contemporary American Speeches* (Dubuque, Iowa: Kendall-Hunt, 1978), p. 183.

been my melancholy fate, I have no doubt that with the last feeble pulsation of my breaking heart, with the last faint exhalation of my fleeting breath, I should have whispered: "Where is Duluth?"[13]

You can imagine how telling such an attack must have been. Even the supporters of the railroad allowed Knott to speak beyond his allotted time and the bill was defeated soundly.

General Principles of Entertaining Speaking

Deciding which general goal of entertaining speaking is being sought is half the battle because that gives a needed sense of direction to the speech and prohibits it from developing into a stand-up comedy routine. After all, unlike a professional entertainer, an entertaining *speaker* always has a pragmatic job to do—to awaken concern, to point up human foibles, to give the audience a respite from worry. Thus, unlike the professional entertainer, the public speaker who uses humor liberally is well advised to follow certain general guidelines when speaking. Some of these include the following:

Be appropriate and tasteful. This really should not need emphasizing, but after hearing so many after-dinner boors, we feel compelled to make the point. What is tasteful and appropriate is, of course, determined by the audience and the context. One may say things to lumberjacks around a Canadian campfire that one cannot say to the Lowells and the Cabots in a Boston supper club. To be effective, consider carefully your listeners' standards of right and wrong.

Serve some function beyond humor. If you only want to do a Johnny Carson imitation, go on the stage. The best entertaining speeches entertain, but they don't *just* entertain. They carry out one of the three important functions mentioned above and do so, ideally, without their audiences being aware of their artistry.

Maintain your own dignity. Everybody loves a clown, but sometimes for the wrong reasons. It is possible to entertain but at the same time keep your poise and dignity about you. Adlai Stevenson and John F. Kennedy are wondrous examples of such a feat. Laughter is not as important as the more lasting impression that *you* as a person might leave. Remember that entertaining speeches rarely establish long-term motivation; when they do, it is sometimes motivation of an unflattering sort for a speaker who has stooped too low in pursuing a few ephemeral chuckles.

[13]J. P. Knott, "Speech in the House of Representatives," in Peterson, op. cit., pp. 610–611.

Good entertaining speeches amuse the audience but perform a useful and more substantial function as well. Entertainment, therefore, should not be looked upon as a time to relax your standards of public communication. The art of making a worthwhile point through humor requires as much skill, practice, and grace as any occasional speech.

Speaking in Recognition

Speeches of recognition seek short-term motivation in formal situations and tend to be rather common in our everyday lives. Their most distinctive characteristic is that *they relate people to one another* so that they may interact further. Such speeches of personal recognition might involve welcoming a visitor to a country, company, school, or city; introducing a speaker or a panel of speakers at a public meeting; or announcing the appearance of a celebrity at a pep rally or a political gathering. In the business, religious, political, and social arenas of our lives, we are constantly welcoming and introducing people; thus, the speech of recognition is a practically important one and one of the most humanizing in addition.

The speech of recognition is self-effacing. Its purpose is to bring on or "set up" a person more important than its creator (or, at least, more important at the moment). Therefore, the speech of recognition seeks short-term motivation; it consumes itself. But the rules surrounding introductions are somewhat formalized in this culture, especially when those introductions are made in highly public settings. Thus, the speaker whose job it is to introduce or recognize another oftentimes cannot rely on the inspiration of the moment for guidance, nor can he or she normally afford to be overly flippant. Listeners' expectations are rather demanding when it comes to speeches of recognition.

Functions of Speaking in Recognition

Although there are a great variety of recognition speeches, we think that they might best be thought of as lying on a continuum based on how familiar the audience for the speech is with the person or persons being introduced. At one end of the continuum is the speech that introduces to an audience somebody that they know well (e.g., the introduction of a coach at a school pep rally). The other end of the continuum involves discourse designed to bring together strangers (e.g., the introduction of an outside consultant at a business meeting or convention).

The function performed by the speech of recognition will vary depending on where the rhetorical situation falls on such a continuum. When the audience knows well the person being introduced, the speech will serve a largely inspirational function for the audience, strengthening their existing bonds with the person and preparing them to welcome him or her with feeling and gusto. Otherwise, the speech will serve more of an informative function, providing background information about the person that the audience will need to understand and accept if they are to respond appreciatively to the person being introduced. Thus, an important first step for the speaker who does the introducing is to reckon carefully with the prior relationship enjoyed by the main speaker and his or her listeners.

We would like to present two brief developmental patterns for a speech of recognition, one pattern for each end of our continuum. As the speaking situations you face move toward the middle, you might well combine features from each suggested pattern. As with impromptu speaking, the patterns suggested here are brief and lack some of the characteristics (such as overviews, summaries, etc.) possessed by more fully developed speeches, a feature that becomes necessary for the speech of recognition lest it take too much of the audience's time or draw undue attention to itself. Also, because we are sometimes asked to introduce or welcome people on short notice, the speech of recognition often has the "telegraphic" qualities possessed by some impromptu speeches. Thus, we feel that mastery of a few brief patterns will allow the speaker to give an adequate speech of recognition on short notice. Table 12-2 presents our suggestions for developing such a speech.

Suggestions for Recognition Speeches

Most speeches of recognition will combine aspects of the two patterns given above because they will fall toward the middle of the continuum. In closing, we would like to offer a few general suggestions for dealing with the opportunities for recognition that may come your way:

1. *Humor varies inversely with formality.* Although humor is certainly not a necessary part of recognition speeches, it often serves well the need to introduce or welcome people because it creates feelings of warmth. Usually, the better an audience knows the main speaker, the more humor is allowed the introducer.

2. *Be brief.* The job of a recognition speech is to make further interaction between people possible. Make your point and then get out of the way.

3. *Don't upstage.* Remember, the speech of recognition is only a means to an end. It should be neat and efficient, and should not call attention to itself.

Table 12-2 Organizational Patterns for Recognition Speeches

Speaking Pattern	Sample Use
1. *Introducing a person with whom the audience is familiar. (Inspirational)*	
Acknowledge the occasion or reason for gathering.	"Students of Quacker High School! As we all know, tomorrow our Fighting Mallards take on Johnson High in the season opener. And tonight we're going to show our team and coach that we're behind them 100 percent. . . ."
Discuss what the person or persons to be introduced mean to the audience.	"I know that, like me, you are all proud to be a Fighting Mallard! This team stands for what's best about our school. Their dedication and hard work. . . ."
Add any new information that will update the audience.	"What some of you may not know is that tonight for the first time our team will appear in their new uniforms, donated by the . . ."
Finally, recognize and introduce.	"So here they are, Coach Anderson and our team. . . ."
2. *Introducing a person with whom the audience is unfamiliar. (Informative)*	
Briefly acknowledge the occasion or reason for gathering.	"Ladies and Gentlemen, welcome to the thirty-second annual convention of the National Marketing Congress. We are gathered here in beautiful Birmingham to renew old acquaintances, review new ideas . . ."

Give basic biographical information by way of a first introduction.	"Our speaker tonight is Professor Jane Sampson of Minnesota Polytechnic Institute. . . ."
Give more detailed biographical information, which may include	
a. relevant education.	"Professor Sampson took her degree in marketing from U.S.C., where she studied under . . ."
b. career.	"Our speaker's first position upon completing her education was in the Federal Commerce Commission. After four years in Washington, she was asked to join the faculty at Dartmouth, where she . . ."
c. personal background.	"Professor Sampson currently resides in St. Paul with her husband and two children. Her interests beyond her work include . . ."
If necessary, explain what the person will do or say today.	"Professor Sampson will be talking to us tonight about her work in . . ."
Go into further detail about the relevance of the person to this particular audience.	"These are issues that our own committee on professional responsibility took up just this afternoon. . . ."
Finally, recognize and introduce.	"My friends, I give you Professor Jane Sampson."

Suggestions for Speaking

While the informative and persuasive speeches place great demands upon our intellectual capacities, the occasional speech tests our emotional mettle. In the impromptu situation, we must fight our own senses of inadequacy as we try to be fluent and coherent on short notice. Our nervousness in ceremonial situations is a natural outgrowth of its rule-bound formalisms, while the need to enlighten and entertain an audience simultaneously can be nerve-racking indeed. The speech of recognition, too, can generate feelings of inadequacy in us as we try to do justice to the importance of the occasion. Yet in many senses, these occasional speeches point up in dramatic ways the pleasures of human speech mentioned in the very first chapter of this book. The occasional speech, after all, has been with us for some time in human history and has proven to be the source of much comfort, satisfaction, and delight for those who hear it. This most humanizing of speeches attends listeners during periods of heightened emotion, and the truly accomplished speaker can handle such situations with grace and aplomb. For those of you who still feel a bit graceless about such speaking opportunities, we offer you the following suggestions for speaking:

1. Be conventional. Don't depart too far from traditional expectations since history tends to be a rather fine teacher where human emotions are concerned.

2. Be unconventional. On the other hand, don't stick so closely to formula that you miss opportunities for human contact; while we do not normally guffaw at funerals, gentle humor can make for a meaningful eulogy, which is, after all, a celebration of a life.

3. Speak as a team player. Know when to subordinate yourself to the occasion, the main speaker, or the function at hand.

4. Be prepared to extemporize. Having general knowledge of the functions and organizational patterns native to the occasional speech will help you to deal professionally, yet flexibly, with changing circumstances.

5. Learn to appreciate pomp and ritual. Even though we live in a most informal age, gaucherie is almost never in step; by looking behind the "rules" surrounding special occasions, you will often find a just and humane reason for their existence.

6. Don't become pompous and ritualistic. Because speech is so intensely personal, never attempt to follow rhetorical rules that

make no sense to you or that will make your remarks sound alien and, hence, alienating.

7. Just because it can be said doesn't mean that you're the one to say it. And just because you're the one to say it doesn't mean that it needs to be said again.

8. Be of good cheer. Special occasions are normally times for fostering positive feelings; even when disagreeing with someone or something, one need not be disagreeable.

9. Don't become typecast. Try not to be too extreme when speaking on special occasions because the audience may wrongfully infer that you have no "range" as a human being, that you are excessively one-dimensional.

10. Brevity is almost always a virtue. Enough said.

AUTHOR INDEX

SUBJECT INDEX

83 84 85 9 8 7 6 5 4 3 2 1